TREATING WOMEN MOLESTED IN CHILDHOOD

THE JOSSEY-BASS LIBRARY OF CURRENT CLINICAL TECHNIQUE

IRVIN D. YALOM, GENERAL EDITOR

NOW AVAILABLE

Treating Alcoholism
Stephanie Brown, Editor

Treating Schizophrenia
Sophia Vinogradov, Editor

Treating Women Molested in Childhood
Catherine Classen, Editor

FORTHCOMING

Treating Depression
Ira D. Glick, Editor

Treating Eating Disorders
Joellen Werne, Editor

Treating Dissociative Identity Disorders
James L. Spira, Editor

Treating Adolescents
Hans Steiner, Editor

Treating the Elderly
Javaid I. Sheikh, Editor

Treating Posttraumatic Stress Disorder
Charles R. Marmar, Editor

Treating Anxiety Disorders
Walton T. Roth, Editor

Treating Couples
Hilda Kessler, Editor

Treating Difficult Personality Disorders
Michael Rosenbluth, Editor

TREATING WOMEN
MOLESTED IN CHILDHOOD

A VOLUME IN THE JOSSEY-BASS
LIBRARY OF CURRENT CLINICAL TECHNIQUE

Catherine Classen, EDITOR
Irvin D. Yalom, GENERAL EDITOR

Jossey-Bass Publishers • San Francisco

Substantial discounts on bulk quantities of Jossey-Bass books are available to corporations, professional associations, and other organizations. For details and discount information, contact the special sales department at Jossey-Bass Inc., Publishers. (415)433-1740; Fax (800)605-2665.

For sales outside the United States, please contact your local Paramount Publishing International Office.

 Manufactured in the United States of America on Lyons Falls Pathfinder Tradebook. This paper is acid-free and 100 percent totally chlorine-free.

Library of Congress Cataloging-in-Publication Data

Treating women molested in childhood/Catherine Classen, editor.
     p.   cm.—(A volume in the Jossey-Bass library of current clinical technique)
    Includes bibliographical references and index.
    ISBN 0-7879-0078-8
    1. Adult child sexual abuse victims—Rehabilitation. 2. Psychotherapy.
I. Classen, Catherine, 1955–. II. Series: Jossey-Bass library of current clinical technique.
RC569. 5. A28T74 1995
616.85'83690651—dc20
                                94-39886
                                    CIP

FIRST EDITION
HB Printing 10 9 8 7 6 5 4 3 2 1   *Code 9536*

CONTENTS

To my mother
for always believing in me

FOREWORD

At a recent meeting of clinical practitioners, a senior practitioner declared that more change had occurred in his practice of psychotherapy in the past year than in the twenty preceding years. Nodding assent, the others all agreed.

And was that a good thing for their practice? A resounding "No!" Again, unanimous concurrence—too much interference from managed care; too much bureaucracy; too much paper work; too many limits set on fees, length, and format of therapy; too much competition from new psychotherapy professions.

Were these changes a good or a bad thing for the general public? Less unanimity on this question. Some pointed to recent positive developments. Psychotherapy was becoming more mainstream, more available, and more acceptable to larger segments of the American public. It was being subjected to closer scrutiny and accountability—uncomfortable for the practitioner but, if done properly, of potential benefit to the quality and efficiency of behavioral health care delivery.

But without dissent this discussion group agreed—and every aggregate of therapists would concur—that astounding changes are looming for our profession: changes in the reasons that clients request therapy; changes in the perception and practice of mental health care; changes in therapeutic theory and technique; and changes in the training, certification, and supervision of professional therapists.

From the perspective of the clientele, several important currents are apparent. A major development is the de-stigmatization of psychotherapy. No longer is psychotherapy invariably a hush-hush affair, laced with shame and conducted in offices with separate entrance and exit doors to prevent the uncomfortable possibility of clients meeting one another.

Today such shame and secrecy have been exploded. Television talk shows—Oprah, Geraldo, Donahue—have normalized psychopathology and psychotherapy by presenting a continuous public parade of dysfunctional human situations: hardly a day passes without television fare of confessions and audience interactions with deadbeat fathers, sex addicts, adult children of alcoholics, battering husbands and abused wives, drug dealers and substance abusers, food bingers and purgers, thieving children, abusing parents, victimized children suing parents.

The implications of such de-stigmatization have not been lost on professionals who no longer concentrate their efforts on the increasingly elusive analytically suitable neurotic patient. Clinics everywhere are dealing with a far broader spectrum of problem areas and must be prepared to offer help to substance abusers and their families, to patients with a wide variety of eating disorders, adult survivors of incest, victims and perpetrators of domestic abuse. No longer do trauma victims or substance abusers furtively seek counseling. Public awareness of the noxious long-term effect of trauma has been so sensitized that there is an increasing call for public counseling facilities and a growing demand for adequate counseling provisions in health care plans.

The mental health profession is changing as well. No longer is there such automatic adoration of lengthy "depth" psychotherapy where "deep" or "profound" is equated with a focus on the earliest years of the patient's life. The contemporary field is more pluralistic: many diverse approaches have proven therapeutically effective, and the therapist of today is more apt to tailor the therapy to fit the particular clinical needs of each patient.

In past years there was an unproductive emphasis on territoriality and on the maintaining of hierarchy and status—with the more prestigious professions like psychiatry and doctoral-level psychology expending considerable energy toward excluding master's level therapists. But those battles belong more to the psychotherapists of yesterday; today there is a significant shift toward a more collaborative interdisciplinary climate.

Managed care and cost containment is driving some of these changes. The role of the psychiatrist has been particularly affected as cost efficiency has decreed that psychiatrists will less frequently deliver psychotherapy personally but, instead, limit their activities to supervision and to psychopharmacological treatment.

In its efforts to contain costs, managed care has asked therapists to deliver a briefer, focused therapy. But gradually managed care is realizing that the bulk of mental health treatment cost is consumed by inpatient care and that outpatient treatment, even long-term therapy, is not only salubrious for the patient but far less costly. Another looming change is that the field is turning more frequently toward the group therapies. How much longer can we ignore the many comparative research studies demonstrating that the group therapy format is equally or more effective than higher cost individual therapies?

Some of these cost-driven edicts may prove to be good for the patients; but many of the changes that issue from medical model mimicry—for example, efforts at extreme brevity and overly precise treatment plans and goals that are inappropriate to the therapy endeavor and provide only the illusion of efficiency—can hamper the therapeutic work. Consequently, it is of paramount importance that therapists gain control of their field and that managed care administrators not be permitted to dictate how psychotherapy or, for that matter, any other form of health care be conducted. That is one of the goals of this series of texts: to provide mental health professionals with such a deep grounding in theory and such a clear vision of effective therapeutic technique that they will be empowered to fight confidently for the highest standards of patient care.

The Jossey-Bass Library of Current Clinical Technique is directed and dedicated to the frontline therapist—to master's and doctoral-level clinicians who personally provide the great bulk of mental health care. The purpose of this entire series is to offer state-of-the-art instruction in treatment techniques for the most commonly encountered clinical conditions. Each volume offers a focused theoretical background as a foundation for practice and then dedicates itself to the practical task of what to do for the patient—how to assess, diagnose, and treat.

I have selected volume editors who are either nationally recognized experts or are rising young stars. In either case, they possess a comprehensive view of their specialty field and have selected leading therapists of a variety of persuasions to describe their therapeutic approaches.

Although all the contributors have incorporated the most recent and relevant clinical research in their chapters, the emphasis in these volumes is the practical technique of therapy. We shall offer specific therapeutic guidelines, and augment concrete suggestions with the liberal use of clinical vignettes and detailed case histories. Our intention is not to impress or to awe the reader, and not to add footnotes to arcane academic debates. Instead, each chapter is designed to communicate guidelines of immediate pragmatic value to the practicing clinician. In fact, the general editor, the volume editors, and the chapter contributors have all accepted our assignments for that very reason: a rare opportunity to make a significant, immediate, and concrete contribution to the lives of our patients.

February 1995   Irvin D. Yalom, M.D.
                               Professor Emeritus of Psychiatry
                               Stanford University

INTRODUCTION

Catherine Classen

Nearly one hundred years ago, Freud courageously pronounced his theory regarding the cause of hysteria among women—"at the bottom of every case of hysteria there are one or more occurrences of premature sexual experience." But this was ultimately too threatening a position for Freud to hold. Shortly after his landmark publication, Freud abandoned the theory because of its implications: hysteria was so rampant in the population that he simply could not believe there was that much sexual violation of children.

One hundred years later, it's clear that as a society we continue to find the notion of childhood sexual abuse deeply disturbing. It is not simply that we grapple with how to solve the problem of child sexual abuse but, like Freud, we have difficulty believing that it is so widespread. Recent research shows that the prevalence of childhood sexual abuse among females ranges from 27 percent to 51 percent when sexual abuse is narrowly defined and involves an older perpetrator, and from 31 percent to 67 percent if abuse involving noncontact is included. Even if we were to accept the lowest estimate of 27 percent, this is a shocking statistic.

Society's reluctance to accept the truth of this sad state of affairs is best exemplified by the False Memory Syndrome Foundation, a parents' group formed on behalf of parents who claim to have been falsely accused by their adult children of sexually abusing them during childhood. The aim of this foundation is to combat the "cultural hysteria" that they believe has developed because of psychotherapy gone awry. The False Memory Syndrome Foundation would have us believe that many, if not most, adult children who claim to have uncovered repressed memories of childhood molestation actually had the memories implanted by their psychotherapists.

Certainly it would be foolish to deny that some accusations are false or that there are therapists who have implanted memories of abuse in their clients. Both situations are to be deplored. On the other hand, there is plenty of anecdotal clinical evidence suggesting that victims of trauma do indeed repress some or all of their traumatic experiences. There is also recent empirical evidence showing that of 129 women with documented histories of childhood sexual abuse, 38 percent did not recall the abuse seventeen years later. Clearly, this is a situation without easy answers.

In recent months, the media have provided extensive coverage of legal trials involving victims' recovered memories of childhood sexual abuse. Increasingly, psychotherapists are the targets of these lawsuits. One of the more publicized cases occurred in California where a father sued his daughter's psychotherapists for malpractice; he claimed that they had implanted false memories in his daughter, leading to the breakdown of his family. He won the suit.

Realizing that the current social climate exists despite what we know about the prevalence of childhood sexual abuse, it is essential for us as psychotherapists to educate ourselves about the long-term psychological consequences of sexual abuse, to learn how to conduct assessments of sexual abuse, and to know how to provide the best psychological treatment. We must learn not only how to recognize the possible signs of sexual abuse but also how to probe without suggesting that the person has been abused. And we must be able to recognize the special treatment needs and issues that arise when we work with survivors.

The aim of this book is to educate the novice therapist as well as to deepen the understanding of the more seasoned clinician. We have chosen to focus on women because they are the majority of victims of sexual abuse; however, this decision is in no way intended to minimize the trauma inflicted upon or the consequent needs of male survivors. In working with any survivors of sexual abuse, there are several issues that you should be aware of. I have described a number of these in the following section.

FACTORS THAT INFLUENCE THE VICTIM'S RESPONSE

In exploring the likely impact of sexual abuse on the adult survivor, it is important that you not consider the contributing factors in isolation. None of these alone is sufficient to predict the likely effect of the abuse; rather, they should be considered together. Although the factors described here are not exhaustive, they are important and will provide some of the context you'll need to understand your client's response to the abuse.

Severity of the Abuse

Severity is often the first factor we consider when judging the likely impact of the abuse on the survivor. This refers to the nature, duration, and frequency of the abuse, and whether force was used.

In relation to the nature of the abuse, the more invasive the sexual contact, the more traumatizing the experience is likely to be. Thus, penetration—whether it be oral, anal, or vaginal—is likely to be more traumatizing than fondling. Even so, it is important not to minimize the effect of the abuse when it is "less severe"; it can still have a devastating effect on your client.

The duration and frequency of abuse has been shown, although not conclusively, to be related to severity of symptoms, suggesting that there may be other factors to take into account. In general, studies have found that greater frequency and longer duration of sexual contact is associated with greater trauma. This is not true in all cases, however, as some studies have shown just the reverse.

Most research has found that children who had sexual contact forced on them were more traumatized than children who participated without the use of overt force although this too is an area of some controversy. It is important to distinguish here between coercion and the use of force. Every child who is sexually victimized has been subjected to coercion. It might not take the form of physical force but instead could be a subtle pressure such as the promise of affection; this tactic is especially effective with a child who is otherwise deprived of love and nurturing. Many survivors suffer from confusion, guilt, and shame because they were not physically forced to participate. The deleterious effect of these feelings should not be underestimated.

When physical force is applied by the perpetrator to ensure his sexual gratification, it's not unusual to find physical abuse occurring along with the sexual abuse. Often the physical abuse is so severe that its effect outweighs that of the sexual abuse. In such a case, the sexual molestation may be delayed as a focus of therapy while the clinician helps the client work through the effects of the physical violence.

Characteristics of the Victim

The age of the client at the time of the abuse is important. Although little research has directly examined the influence of the victim's age at the time of the abuse on subsequent symptomatology, the research and clinical work in child development is suggestive of the symptomatology to expect.

Infancy and Toddlerhood. Sexual abuse during infancy appears to be relatively infrequent, but if it does occur the infant will be affected by the physical trauma of the experience. The trauma will jeopardize the infant's basic trust, physical integrity, and sense of having control over external events. At this age, the infant will not have any awareness of the inappropriateness of what is occurring.

Research in the area of childhood amnesia suggests that the earliest childhood memories do not occur before the age of three or four. Therefore, if the abuse occurred only during infancy, the survivor is not likely to have memories of the abuse. What is less clear is whether it is possible for the survivor to have "body memories" of the abuse—that is, a physical feeling or sensation that corresponds to the abuse experience in infancy. Because we don't know whether body memories from infancy are possible, it seems that we should not discount this possibility. In order to presume that a given body memory relates to sexual abuse, however, it would be important that the victim have a specific memory of abuse or some corroborating evidence. In the absence of other evidence, we can never be certain of what experience the body memory relates to.

Toddlers are already beginning to show an awareness of social situations. Research suggests that they experience distress when social conventions are transgressed and that they have an awareness of when they have misbehaved. At this age, however, they have little awareness of impropriety. Nevertheless, they are making significant advances in the development of a sense of self and sensitivity to social interactions. Consequently, sexual violation at this time is likely to result in both physical and emotional trauma, even though the child is still too young to have specific memories.

Preschoolers. From the age of about two to five, the child is working to integrate a sense of herself as an active agent in the world with the restrictions imposed on her by the outside world. The preschooler is also beginning to learn skills for coping with distress. However, in situations when the preschooler lacks strategies for coping, denial or dissociation are common. This appears to be an age when the child's dissociative capacity rapidly increases. Consequently, during the abuse the child may use denial or dissocation as a way to protect herself from the experience.

These defense strategies are highly effective, and therefore the victim may continue to use them throughout her life as a way of coping with the pain surrounding the abuse. Until she enters therapy, she may not even know that she habitually dissociates.

There has been some controversy about whether sexual abuse at this stage (or earlier) is more or less traumatic than sexual abuse at a later stage. Some have argued that the child is protected from feelings of guilt. Others claim that molestation at this age has a profoundly negative effect on ego development. Research appears to support the latter, although it is still open to debate.

Elementary School Years. From about the age of six to adolescence, the child's cognitive capacities increase along with her social competence. She is now able to reflect on herself as an object and can consider others' perspectives. She has also developed the capacity for guilt based on a moral sense of right and wrong. The child has abandoned the use of denial and dissociation as defenses and has begun to rely instead on defenses such as rationalization and blaming others. The formation of social relationships has become important as she learns that she can share enjoyable activities with friends and rely on them for social support. Consequently, their evaluation of her is important.

Sexual abuse during this period is much more common. At this age molestation will result in feelings of shame, guilt, and confusion, a combination likely to make the child feel insecure and thereby hinder the development of interpersonal relations. The developmental task of integrating positive and negative aspects of self will be seriously challenged, particularly because of the intense emotions that the abuse elicits.

While ordinarily children will develop new defense mechanisms, children who have been abused will continue to rely heavily on denial and dissociation as a way to protect themselves. Memory of the abuse can then become unavailable for integration.

Adolescence. Sexual abuse during adolescence occurs at a time in life when the child is struggling with issues of identity and sexuality. The adolescent has developed the ability for abstract thinking, which enables her to reflect on her inner experience and the thoughts and feelings of others. Molestation at this time in her life will also lead to confusion, shame, and guilt, having an adverse effect on her developing self-identity. Her exploration of relationships with the opposite sex will be negatively affected and may lead to her exhibiting fear and avoidance or, conversely, to sexual acting out.

Rather than using more mature coping strategies of reflection, reasoning, and planning to manage uncomfortable feelings, the sexually abused adolescent may act impulsively and engage in self-destructive behavior such as substance abuse, running away, or promiscuity. For many survivors, the abuse begins in childhood and continues into adolescence. These victims are likely to be worse off than those whose abuse began in adolescence.

❧

In working with survivors of child sexual abuse, it is important to consider the developmental stage at which the abuse occurred, along with the duration of the abuse. Research on the relationship of the child's age at the time of the abuse and later symptomatology has not yet provided clear answers but it has shown that the onset of abuse at an early age is related to amnesia in adult survivors and late presentation for therapy. Even though we have little direct empirical data to inform us, it is reasonable to assume that sexual abuse will interfere with the victim's normal development.

The age of onset and the developmental stages during which the abuse occurs are likely to have a significant effect on the person's later symptomatology. Understanding the developmental task that the child is engaged in at the time of the abuse and how the abuse thwarts the resolution of that stage will also help to define the issues the survivor needs to resolve in therapy. It is possible that her coping strategy has been arrested at the developmental stage at which the abuse began. Thus, a developmental model can give us some clues as to the nature of the injury and provide a useful framework from which to work.

Characteristics of the Perpetrator

The relationship of the child to the perpetrator is also important. The psychological consequences are generally thought to be far worse for the survivor if the perpetrator is her father or stepfather. Unfortunately, except for uncle-niece incest, it appears that abuse by a father or stepfather is more prevalent than molestation by other relatives, acquaintances, or strangers. It also appears that stepfathers are more likely to abuse than natural fathers. The research suggests that beyond the father figure, it does not make a difference if the perpetrator is a family member or someone outside the family: in either case, the trauma will be less severe for the victim.

Being abused by a father is a betrayal of the father's role as protector and provider; it places the child in the position of being the father's lover, thereby replacing the mother. It is a violation of a major taboo in our society. Typically, such fathers fall into one of two categories: they are either passive and ineffectual or dominant and controlling. In both situations, the child often feels entrapped in the family.

Sibling incest is another relatively common phenomenon. These experiences can be mutual and exploratory or they can be abusive. In understanding the significance of the experience it's necessary to consider the ages of the siblings and their age difference, the quality of their relationship, how the sexual behavior was initiated, the motivation underlying the activity, and the nature of the sexual behavior.

It appears that the emotional closeness of the victim to the perpetrator is an important variable. Consequently, abuse by a stranger will not be as detrimental as abuse by someone the child knows and trusts.

Context of the Abuse

When working with a survivor of sexual abuse, you must consider the context in which the abuse occurred. What was the family environment like? Was it chaotic and unpredictable or was it "normal" in appearance? In chaotic families, children often are forced to raise themselves and consequently are vulnerable to abuse both inside and outside the home. Abuse in these households is more likely to come to light and to result in legal action than in a family that appears typical. When the abuse occurs in a "normal" family, it is usually invisible to outsiders. Although the family may appear to be like most others, there is often pathology beneath the surface. Typically the parents are unable to nurture one another emotionally or sexually, leading to estrangement over time and the eventual reliance by them on the children to meet their needs.

When the perpetrator is the father, the role of the mother is critical. Was the mother available to the child, either physically or emotionally? Was she aware of the abuse? If so, did she collude with the perpetrator? Did she try to protect the child? The research shows clearly that a lack of support from the mother is related to increased symptoms in the survivor.

Often the child does not tell anyone what is happening; just as often, she may not be believed or supported when she does tell, leaving her on her own to find a way to stop the abuse. Frequently the child is unable to do this until she is older, understands the potential consequences of the abuse (for example, pregnancy), and is less emotionally and physically dependent. The cost of exposing the perpetrator may be estrangement from the family.

The context in which the abuse occurs can influence its psychological aftermath. It is important to keep contextual issues in mind when helping a survivor work through the emotional ramifications.

The Psychological Consequences of Childhood Sexual Abuse

Adult survivors can exhibit a variety of symptoms because of childhood sexual abuse. These include a broad range of emotional reactions, low self-esteem, relationship problems, sexual difficulties, and somatic complaints.

Emotional Problems

Sexual abuse survivors can suffer from feelings of guilt, shame, confusion, anxiety, sadness, depression, and rage. Not all these feelings will necessarily be felt by all survivors or experienced at the same time. The emotional response may reflect aspects of the abuse or where the survivor is in the process of recovery.

The survivor may experience guilt if she feels that she received something positive or pleasurable from the experience. This may also be her reaction if she felt she was taking the place of her mother, or that she let the abuse go on for too long. Along with the guilt, there is often shame—shame about having received some gratification, about allowing the abuse to continue, or about having people know what happened to her. Often if the child was very young and particularly if she received mixed messages, her response may be confusion. She may also be confused if she experienced conflicting feelings, such as pleasure and pain.

Low Self-Esteem and Identity Problems

Low self-esteem is a common response in women who have been sexually abused in childhood. The survivor may believe she was abused because there was something inherently wrong with her and therefore she deserved it. Or she may feel that because of the abuse she is now bad or worthless. She may feel hopeless about ever putting the abuse behind her.

The use of dissociation as a way to protect herself during the course of the abuse can result in the development of unintegrated aspects of self. Consequently, disruptions in identity frequently result from childhood abuse. The most extreme example of this is dissociative identity disorder. A borderline personality disorder can also result from damage to the self structure.

Relationship Problems

Having been betrayed and traumatized, the survivor may have difficulty forming close and trusting relationships. After being betrayed by someone she trusted and on whom she was dependent for love and protection, she may be unable to trust anyone or form an intimate relationship. Instead, she may become withdrawn, using whatever strategy she can to protect herself and to keep people at a distance. Thus, it is not uncommon to find sexual abuse victims with eating disorders, dissociative disorders, substance abuse disorders, affective disorders, anxiety disorders, or some type of character dysfunction.

Sexual Problems

If the survivor is able to form an intimate relationship, she may have sexual problems, which can take the form of approach or avoidance—compulsive sexual acting out or a sexual dysfunction. She may become promiscuous out of a need to feel in control sexually, or she may believe that sex is the only thing of value she has to offer. The sexual dysfunction may involve difficulty in becoming aroused, in having her arousal dependent on being in control, or in her inability to have an orgasm or to experience pleasure in an orgasm.

The range of possible symptoms for a victim of childhood sexual abuse is broad. Unfortunately, there is a popular misconception that there is a psychological profile that readily identifies a victim. While it is true that sometimes the therapist can "know" that a client is a victim before the client herself knows this, we would do well to let the client discover it for herself. This guards against our misdiagnosing someone, and it recognizes that the client is a better judge of the right time for her to "know" about the abuse. This does not mean that as therapists we should avoid issues we believe are related to the hypothesized abuse, but we must be careful that we do not lead the client to "discover" what is not true or to learn the truth before she is ready.

REPRESSED MEMORIES

The issue of repressed versus false memories has created tremendous controversy and heartache for survivors, their families, and the clinicians who work with them. Virtually any experienced clinician would testify to the existence of repressed memories and would not be surprised to find this phenomenon among survivors of childhood sexual abuse, particularly those who were abused at a young age. At the same time, an individual who is deeply troubled for other reasons may come to the false belief that her problems stem from childhood sexual abuse.

How is a therapist to deal with this uncertainty? Surely we cannot claim to be omniscient. We don't want to introduce problems into a client's life or the lives of others, but we also cannot refuse to believe a woman who has finally reached a point in her life where she is able to face her abuse. Ultimately, we have a responsibility to honor our client's "knowing" and to be judicious in how we work.

A MODEL FOR RECOVERY

Psychiatrist Judith Herman provides a useful model for understanding what is involved in recovering from childhood sexual abuse. According to Herman, recovery occurs in three stages: (1) establishing a sense of safety, (2) remembering and mourning the trauma, and finally (3) reconnecting with oneself and with others. As Herman cautions, these "stages" should be used as guideposts, not as absolutes. A survivor may not necessarily progress through these in a linear fashion. Instead, these issues may need to be revisited again and again, with progress having more the shape of a helix than of a straight line.

Safety

When a survivor first begins to deal with her abuse or simply begins to explore a new aspect of the abuse experience, it's important that she feel a sense of safety both within herself and in her environment. Physical safety always takes precedence. For instance, if your client is engaging in some self-destructive behavior such as abusing drugs or alcohol, or if she is suffering posttraumatic symptoms such as hyperarousal, these issues must be dealt with first.

In a therapeutic relationship, the therapist must also create a safe environment within which the survivor can work along with establishing the survivor's physical safety. You must help your client feel a sense of control over her participation in the therapy as well as protected and supported as she struggles to explore the effects of her abuse.

Remembering and Mourning

Experiencing a sense of safety, the survivor can begin to explore the abuse experience at a pace she determines and in which she feels comfortable. This involves remembering all aspects of what happened to her including the abuse events, the context of the abuse, and how it has affected her. Having examined the abuse and its consequences, the survivor must grieve what she has lost. This may include a lessening of her ability to become attached to others or the realization that she had no control over her physical being during the abuse. It may be the recognition of the childhood she didn't have. Mourning these losses is essential for her to move forward and put the abuse behind her.

Reconnecting

In the final stage of recovery, the survivor integrates the abuse into her life history, thereby freeing herself to reclaim her life and her future. By recognizing what she has lost, what enabled her to survive, and how the abuse has shaped her, she can begin to reconnect with herself. This phase involves recognizing the impact of the abuse in her life and the meaning she gave to it. Understanding how the abuse affected her internally, she can make the decision to redefine it and give it new meaning. By so doing she will achieve a renewed sense of self and reconnection with others and the world.

Herman's stages of recovery model can be useful as you work with victims of sexual abuse. You will find that it enhances your understanding of both the broad course of treatment and the individual therapy session. The utility of this model should also be apparent as you read the various chapters in this book.

OVERVIEW OF THE CONTENTS

This volume, intended for psychotherapists, is an introduction to the issues and treatment methods for working with women who were molested in childhood. The various chapters were written by clinicians who have extensive experience with victims of childhood sexual abuse. The insights they provide should prove invaluable for both the novice and seasoned clinician. The authors have drawn on clinical examples throughout for illustration. In the case studies, all names have been changed and any identifying information has been removed.

Christine Courtois brings her considerable clinical expertise to the assessment and diagnosis of women who were molested in childhood. On this important topic, Courtois discusses the fine line the therapist walks when assessing for childhood sexual abuse. She provides clear guidelines for conducting assessments of childhood molestation without suggesting or assuming. This is an especially critical topic given the current social climate, and Courtois provides sound advice on how to approach it.

Joan Turkus provides an invaluable discussion of how to respond to the survivor who is in crisis. Here we see that establishing safety and stabilization is of foremost concern. Turkus takes a problem-solving approach that addresses both the symptoms and the level of impairment of the client; she provides a range of possible interventions. Along with guidelines for the therapeutic response to crisis, she will also help you to plan ahead so your resources will be in place before the crises arise.

The chapter on individual psychotherapy is based on the model used at the Cambridge Hospital Victims of Violence Program in Boston, a program founded by Mary Harvey and Judith Herman. Harvey and Patricia Harney have written a thoughtful piece on their ecological model and stages-by-dimensions framework for treating adult survivors. Using four clinical cases, they show why it is important to consider the characteristics of the victim, the nature of the event, and environmental factors in order to understand the individual's unique adaptation to childhood sexual abuse. They describe their multidimensional treatment goals and ways to work toward attaining these goals in each of the three stages of recovery. They offer a clinically rich presentation of the complex issues involved in working with survivors of childhood sexual abuse.

Brian Abbott applies his considerable experience in treating victims of childhood sexual abuse to the subject of group psychotherapy for adult survivors. Based on the Giarretto Institute's Child Sexual Abuse Treatment Program, Abbott presents a thorough and clear description of how to form and conduct survivor groups. He offers guidelines for screening and forming a group, methods and issues pertinent to beginning a group, techniques for working with symptoms as well as the variety of reactions that can emerge as members react to one another's stories, techniques for working with transference, and a discussion of issues involved in termination. This chapter is full of ideas and specific intervention strategies for leading survivor groups.

Couples therapy, where one of the partners has experienced childhood sexual abuse, is described in a chapter by Victoria Follette and Jacqueline Pistorello. The authors describe ways in which the survivor's history can affect each partner and their relationship and how to work with that material in couples therapy. Given the intimate and interpersonal nature of molestation, couples therapy can be an especially powerful form of treatment.

The use of hypnosis with this population is a controversial issue. Two experts in hypnosis, Jose Maldonado and David Spiegel, have applied their expertise to the subject of hypnosis in the treatment of sexual abuse survivors. They describe the natural hypnotic-like capacities of many childhood victims, how that functions as a protective device during the time of the abuse but later in life becomes a problem, and finally how that natural capacity can be used in therapy in a constructive and healing manner. They also discuss therapeutic precautions and the potential legal implications in using hypnosis. This is crucial reading for anyone considering the use of hypnosis in treating survivors.

A discussion of transference and countertransference is provided by Diana Elliott and John Briere. This is a particularly important topic given the profound injury that has been inflicted on victims of childhood sexual abuse and the intense feelings it can elicit in both the survivor and therapist. Elliott and Briere describe four abuse-related transferential responses that are typical of survivors of molestation, but they also caution us of the need to acknowledge contemporaneous or reality-based responses of the survivor. Guidelines in working with this material are provided. The important topic of countertransference is given equal and careful coverage.

This chapter is essential reading, particularly for the novice therapist with little experience in treating sexual abuse survivors.

A PERSONAL NOTE

I come to this book as a clinician, a researcher, and a survivor. My experience in each of these roles adds to the sense of responsibility I feel toward those who have suffered the fear, confusion, shame, and guilt that comes from having been sexually abused as a child. Although most of us would like to believe that the sexual exploitation of children is a rarity, it is not. As psychotherapists, we have a profound responsibility to our clients—a responsibility to believe in them, to help them find and explore the truth and, most important, to guide them in finding a way to live with that truth. As the material in this volume attests, fulfilling these responsibilities is a difficult endeavor. My hope is that this book provides you with the tools you need to do this work.

I would like to thank the many individuals who have contributed to the development of this volume. First, of course, are the chapter authors. Bringing together and reviewing their material has been an enriching experience for me. I am grateful to Irv Yalom, with whom I co-led a sexual abuse group and who gave me the opportunity to edit this book. He, David Spiegel, and Cheryl Koopman, have been my collaborators on a project to evaluate alternative group approaches for treating adult survivors. Our work together has been endlessly rewarding.

I would like to thank the women survivors who have entrusted their stories to us. I have also benefited from the contributions to this ongoing work of Barbara Ballinger, Julia Zarcone, Cheryl Gore-Felton, Lynn Henderson, Chip Harkness, Manuela Kogan, Sophia Abramson, Janine Giese-Davis, Karyn Angell, Janet Spraggins, Colleen Slattery, Ami Atkinson, Bita Nouriani, Lisa Butler, Deborah Rose, Lou Moffat, and Tom Miller. It has been both a pleasure and a great help to work with Alan Rinzler, editor at Jossey-Bass. Finally, thanks to my husband, Bill McGirr, for his multifaceted support.

NOTES

P. xiii, *"at the bottom . . . premature sexual experience"*: Freud, S. (1962). The aetiology of hysteria. In J. Strachey (Ed. and Trans.), *The standard edition of the complete psychological works of Sigmund Freud* (Vol. 3, p. 203). London: Hogarth Press.

P. xiii, *Recent research . . . noncontact is included:* Pope, H. G., & Hudson, J. I. (1992). Is childhood sexual abuse a risk factor for bulimia nervosa? *American Journal of Psychiatry*, 149(4), 455–463.

P. xiv, *there is plenty of clinical evidence . . . repress some or all of their traumatic experiences:* Singler, J. L. Repression and dissociation. Chicago: University Press of Chicago; Herman, J. L., & Schatzow, E. (1987). Recovery and verification of memories of childhood sexual trauma. *Psychoanalytic Psychology*, 4(1), 1–14; Terr, L. (1988). What happens to early memories of trauma? A study of twenty children under age five at the time of documented traumatic events. *Journal of the American Academy of Child and Adolescent Psychiatry*, 27, 96–104.

P. xiv, *There is also recent empirical evidence . . . seventeen years later:* Williams, L. M. (1993, October). *Recall of childhood trauma: A prospective study of women's memories of child sexual abuse.* Paper presented at the Annual Meeting of the American Society of Criminology, Phoenix, AZ.

P. xiv, *We have chosen to focus on women because they are the majority of victims of sexual abuse:* Courtois, C. A. (1988). *Healing the incest wound.* New York: Norton.

P. xv, *the more invasive the sexual contact, the more traumatizing the experience is likely to be:* Kendall-Tackett, K. A., Williams, L. M., & Finkelhor, D. (1993). Impact of sexual abuse on children: A review and synthesis of recent empirical studies. *Psychological Bulletin*, 113(1), 164–180; Schetky, D. (1990). A review of the literature on the long-term effects of childhood sexual abuse. In R. P. Kluft (Ed.), Incest-related syndromes of adult psychopathology. Washington, DC: American Psychiatric Press.

P. xv, *The duration and frequency has been shown . . . to be related to severity of symptoms:* Kendall-Tackett, K. A., Williams, L. M., & Finkelhor, D. (1993). Impact of sexual abuse on children: A review and synthesis of recent empirical studies. *Psychological Bulletin*, 113(1), 164–180.

P. xv, *some studies have shown just the reverse:* Courtois, C. A. (1979). Characteristics of a volunteer sample of adult women who experienced incest in childhood and adolescence. *Dissertation Abstracts International*, 40A, November–December, 1979, 3194-A.

P. xv, *although this too is an area with some controversy:* Kendall-Tackett, K. A., Williams, L. M., & Finkelhor, D. (1993). Impact of sexual abuse on children: A review and synthesis of recent empirical studies. *Psychological Bulletin*, 113(1), 164–180.

P. xvi, *the research and clinical work in child development is suggestive of the symptoma-tology to expect:* Cole, P. M., & Putnam, F. W. (1992). Effect of incest on self and social functioning: A developmental psychopathology perspective. *Journal of Consulting and Clinical Psychology, 60*(2), 174–184.

P. xvi, *Research . . . before the age of three or four:* Howe, M. L., & Courage, M. L. (1993). On resolving the enigma of infantile amnesia. *Psychological Bulletin, 113*, 305–326; Kihlstrom, J. F., & Harackiewizc, J. (1982). The earliest recollection: A new survey. *Journal of Personality, 50*, 134–148; Pillemer, D. B., & While, S. H. (1989). Childhood events recalled by children and adults. In *Advances in child development and behavior* (Vol. 21). San Diego, CA: Academic Press.

P. xvii, *experience distress when social conventions are transgressed:* Kagan, J. (1981). *The second year: The emergence of self-awareness.* Cambridge, MA: Harvard University Press.

P. xvii, *awareness of when they have misbehaved:* Dunn, J. (1988). *The beginnings of social understanding.* London: Basil Blackwell; Stipek, D. J., Gralinski, J. H., & Koop, C. M. (1991). Self-concept development in the toddler years. *Developmental Psychology, 26*, 972–977.

P. xvii, *This appears to be an age when the child's dissociative capacity rapidly increases:* Gardner, G. G., & Olness, K. (1981). *Hypnosis and hypnotherapy with children.* New York: Grune & Stratton.

P. xvii, *Research appears to support the latter:* Cole, P. M., & Putnam, F. W. (1992). Effect of incest on self and social functioning: A developmental psychopathology perspective. *Journal of Consulting and Clinical Psychology, 60*(2), 174–184.

P. xvii, *From about the age of six . . . along with her social competence:* Cole, P. M., & Putnam, F. W. (1992). Effect of incest on self and social functioning: A developmental psychopathology perspective. *Journal of Consulting and Clinical Psychology, 60*(2), 174–184.

P. xix, *the onset of abuse at an early age is related to amnesia in adult survivors:* Briere, J., & Conte, J. (1993). Self-reported amnesia for abuse in adults molested as children. *Journal of Traumatic Stress, 6*(1), 21–31.

P. xix, *late presentation for therapy:* Kendall-Tackett, K. A., Williams, L. M., & Finkelhor, D. (1993). Impact of sexual abuse on children: A review and synthesis of recent empirical studies. *Psychological Bulletin, 113*(1), 164–180.

P. xix, *The psychological consequences are generally thought to be far worse for the survivor if the perpetrator is her father or stepfather:* Herman, J., Russell, D., & Trocki, K. (1986). Long-term effects of incestuous abuse in childhood. *American Journal of Psychiatry, 143*(10), 1293–1296.

P. xix, *Unfortunately, except for . . . acquaintances, or strangers:* Russell, D.E.H. (1983). The incidence and prevalence of intrafamilial and extrafamilial sexual abuse of female children. *Child Abuse & Neglect, 7*, 133–146.

P. xix, *The research suggests . . . or someone outside the family:* Schetky, D. (1990). A review of the literature on the long-term effects of childhood sexual abuse. In R. P. Kluft (Ed.), *Incest-related syndromes of adult psychopathology.* Washington, DC: American Psychiatric Press.

P. xix, *Typically, such fathers . . . dominant and controlling:* Courtois, C. A. (1988). *Healing the incest wound: Adult survivors in therapy.* New York: Norton.

P. xx, *Sibling incest is another common occurrence:* Finkelhor, D. (1979). *Sexually victimized children.* New York: Free Press.

P. xx, *abuse by a stranger will not be as detrimental as abuse by someone the child knows and trusts:* Kendall-Tackett, K. A., Williams, L. M., & Finkelhor, D. (1993). Impact of sexual abuse on children: A review and synthesis of recent empirical studies. *Psychological Bulletin, 113*(1), 164–180.

P. xx, *you must consider the context in which the abuse occurred:* Courtois, C. A. (1988). *Healing the incest wound: Adult survivors in therapy.* New York: Norton.

P. xx, *a lack of support from the mother is related to increased symptoms in the survivor:* Kendall-Tackett, K. A., Williams, L. M., & Finkelhor, D. (1993). Impact of sexual abuse on children: A review and synthesis of recent empirical studies. *Psychological Bulletin, 113*(1), 164–180.

P. xxi, *Often the child . . . not believed or supported:* Cahil, C., Llewelyn, S. P., & Pearson, C. (1991). Long-term effects of sexual abuse which occurred in childhood: A review. *British Journal of Clinical Psychology, 30,* 117–130.

P. xxi, *These include a range . . . and somatic complaints:* Cahil, C., Llewelyn, S. P., & Pearson, C. (1991). Long-term effects of sexual abuse which occurred in childhood: A review. *British Journal of Clinical Psychology, 30,* 117–130; Courtois, C. A. (1988). *Healing the incest wound: Adult survivors in therapy.* New York: Norton.

P. xxii, *disruptions in identity frequently result from childhood abuse:* McCann, I. L., & Pearlman, L. A. (1990). *Psychological trauma and the adult survivor: Theory, therapy, and transformation.* New York: Brunner/Mazel.

P. xxii, *dissociative identity disorder:* American Psychiatric Association. (1994). *Diagnostic and Statistical Manual of Mental Disorders.* (4th ed.) Washington, DC: American Psychiatric Press.

P. xxii, *Thus, it is not uncommon . . . type of character dysfunction:* Saporta, J. A., & Case, J. (1993). The role of medications in treating adult survivors of childhood trauma. In P. L. Paddison (Ed.), *Treatment of adult survivors of incest.* Washington, DC: American Psychiatric Press.

P. xxiii, *The sexual dysfunction . . . pleasure in an orgasm:* McGuire, L. S., & Wagner, N. N. (1989). Sexual dysfunction among women who were molested as children: One response pattern and suggestion for treatment. *Journal of Sex and Marital Therapy, 4,* 11–15.

P. xxiii, *The issue of repressed versus false memories has created tremendous controversy:* Loftus, E. F. (1993). The reality of repressed memories. *American Psychologist, 48*(5), 518–537.

P. xxiv, *A Model for Recovery*: Herman, J. L. (1992). *Trauma and recovery*. New York: Basic Books.

TREATING WOMEN
MOLESTED IN CHILDHOOD

I

ASSESSMENT AND DIAGNOSIS

Christine A. Courtois

Since the mid-1970s, a shockingly high incidence of child sexual abuse both within and outside the family context has been documented. Before that time, sexual abuse was thought to be rare and to occur very infrequently; as recently as the 1980s, incest was believed to occur with a frequency of one case per million population per year. Current estimates, in contrast, place the likely prevalence at 20 percent to 30 percent of women and 10 percent to 15 percent of men in the general population. The prevalence of all forms of child sexual abuse (especially incest) has long been obscured by the taboo that has surrounded it, a taboo that is now recognized as applying to its disclosure and discussion rather than its occurrence.

The recognition of the prevalence of sexual abuse has led to the investigation of its aftermath, both immediate and long term. At present, all forms of child sexual abuse are considered risk factors for a host of initial and long-term psychological, social, and physical effects. Sexual abuse is identified as a major public health problem with numerous deleterious personal and societal consequences.

The history of treatment for sexual abuse has paralleled recognition of its prevalence and potential for damage. Until recently, reports of current or past child sexual abuse were treated with skepticism and frank disbelief by many mental health professionals. These responses derived, in part, from Freud's abandonment of his seduction or trauma theory. The seduction theory had originally claimed that there were probably incestuous abuse experiences in the backgrounds of his hysterical female patients; Freud rejected this in favor of the oedipal theory, which held that abuse reports involved fantasy or wishes on the part of the child rather than real abuse. As a result, innumerable women and men who sought therapy for the effects of abuse or who disclosed abuse had their experiences denied or minimized and, in many cases, never received the help they sought to deal with these incidents and their associated aftereffects. Such professional denial added another burden to those abused individuals already weighted down by the secrecy and lack of awareness surrounding the occurrence of abuse.

Resources for the assessment and treatment of child victims and adults molested as children have become available to practicing clinicians only during the last decade. These treatment formulations were developed by researcher-clinicians who reviewed and integrated literature from the past as well as the newly available research data on aftereffects. The various treatment approaches and recommendations enjoy a fair degree of consistency, providing some face validity and cross-validation in the absence of outcome data. To date, treatment and technique outcome data and process research are not readily available; they are urgently needed to test the efficacy of this quite new treatment field.

The treatment literature recently developed in this area has tended to identify child sexual abuse as potentially traumatic both as a source of stress and in terms of its initial and long-term effects, which may meet the diagnostic criteria for posttraumatic stress disorder (acute, chronic, and/or delayed). Child sexual abuse, however, has particular characteristics by which it differs from other traumatic stressors:

- It is human-induced and premeditated, often perpetrated by someone whom the child is both attached to and dependent on (especially when the abuser is a close relative).

- Often it entraps the victim because of the length of time it continues—an average duration of four years—and because of its repetitive, intensifying, and increasingly invasive sexual activity.

- Frequently it is in the context of other forms of abuse such as physical mistreatment or neglect.

- It is misrepresented to the child who is enjoined or threatened to keep it secret.

- It is usually chronic if strong protective measures or intervention are not available.

- When the victim is an immature and developing child (as opposed to an adult or even an adolescent whose personality is relatively consolidated), the abuse has the potential to impact seriously and even derail the child's personal and social development.

Adults sexually abused as children frequently describe themselves as having "holes in their sense of self and holes in their development," phrases that eloquently and succinctly describe findings in the research on aftereffects. Researchers and clinicians alike have come to the realization that the aftereffects, like the stressor, are complicated by the childhood occurrence. Additionally, dissociation, a common psychological function that operates as a defense mechanism in traumatic circumstances, has been increasingly identified as an especially likely response in children, who dissociate more readily than adults.

Dissociation involves an alteration in consciousness concerning personal identity, memory, and ongoing awareness. It is inherently logical as a defense against ongoing traumatic intrusion and may account for some of the subjectively perceived "holes in experience" described above. The result is a complex, dissociative form of posttraumatic stress disorder including disturbance in personality development and functioning as well as more classic posttraumatic and associated symptoms (discussed in more detail later in this chapter). The newly available treatment resources emphasize the necessity of treating the client's symptoms (general Axis I as well as specific posttraumatic effects) and developmental issues and deficits (usually identified on Axis II of the current diagnostic formulation).

Resources for the assessment and treatment of adults molested as children have only recently become available to practicing therapists. Clinical interest and application follow two decades of research documenting the widespread prevalence of child sexual abuse and its impact. In particular, studies of abused and nonabused individuals have found correlations between an abuse history and a number of initial and long-term aftereffects. When a specific inquiry is made, a high percentage of clients in inpatient (50 percent to 70 percent) and outpatient (40 percent to 50 percent) settings have reported sexual abuse in childhood. These and related findings have led to the belief among many mental health professionals that sexual abuse constitutes a significant mental health risk throughout the life span and that many abuse-related effects require therapeutic intervention for resolution.

Direct inquiry about a history of sexual abuse is a radical departure from the traditional therapeutic stance based on psychoanalytic theory. Since the early 1900s when Freud repudiated his then-radical seduction theory (stressing the reality of incestuous abuse in the histories of his hysterical female patients) in favor of his oedipal theory (stressing abuse reports as fabrications or frustrated wishes on the part of the patient), innumerable women (and men) who sought therapy for the effects of sexual abuse or who disclosed experience of abuse had their experiences denied or minimized. In many cases, therapists never followed up on these disclosures or never asked the clients directly about the abuse; consequently, the victims did not receive the help they sought to resolve abuse experiences and their associated aftereffects.

Good practice now recommends that therapists routinely ask about sexual abuse experiences as part of their overall clinical assessment since many adults molested as children do not disclose (or in some cases remember) the abuse unless specifically asked. Even with direct inquiry, some adults remain silent for a variety of reasons including the following:

- The amount of time that has passed
- Extreme shame and stigmatization

- Fear and terror

- Protection, loyalty, and attachment to the perpetrator or other family members, especially when the abuse is incestuous

- Previous negative experiences when they tried to disclose; threats of retaliation for disclosure

- Fear of ridicule or abandonment by someone of significance, including the therapist

In the last decade, disclosure has been assisted by a virtual flood of media attention on the topic of sexual abuse, most of which was, until recently, sympathetic to the adult reporting experiences of abuse. The simultaneous publication of numerous self-help books and the development of a number of support and therapeutic programs have also served to assist personal identification and disclosure. Molestation ceased being a taboo subject never to be acknowledged publicly; in contrast, it has been discussed extensively, even to the point of sensationalism and trivialization.

In this changing social climate, many individuals have reported retrieving memories of abuse (both within and outside therapy) that they previously did not remember and which were unavailable to them. Therapists have noted a similar occurrence in their clinical work: some clients who began therapy with no memory (complete amnesia) of such events later developed recall while others had partial memory that was obscured by a mixture of delayed recall, delayed disclosure, or delayed recognition. Many therapists have concluded that partial or complete amnesia and delayed and fragmented disclosure are the norm for some adult survivors. Sexual abuse is considered a major stressor for a young child; the potential for traumatization increases as the occurrences of the abuse continue. Amnesia and disturbances of memory are normal responses to traumatization, especially in situations like incestuous sexual abuse, which are typically entrapping, repetitive, physically intrusive, and involve inner conflict caused by sexual interaction with and betrayal by a significant caretaker in the context of the broader family loyalty structure.

As increasing numbers of women and men have identified sexual abuse in their histories and particularly as some have confronted abusers and family members or sought retrospective legal redress for damages, a countermovement challenging the reality of delayed or repressed memories has developed. A number of prominent experts on human memory have not only criticized the concept of delayed memory as inconsistent with what is currently known from laboratory studies, but they have also challenged the concept of traumatic amnesia and delayed recall. Furthermore and of most relevance to the topic of this chapter, these critics have charged that therapists have suggested or implanted false memories of abuse in susceptible clients through sloppy or improper assessment and inquiry techniques.

Some of the criticism is legitimate, given that the field of sexual abuse treatment is relatively new. Some, however, appears to be in the interest of denial both for personal reasons—since several of the most vocal critics have themselves been accused of incest by their adult children—and for political reasons to suppress the newfound recognition of the pervasiveness of sexual abuse.

Psychiatrist Judith Herman, in her 1992 book *Trauma and Recovery*, anticipated a reaction of just this sort. She discussed the "dialectic" of the typical personal response to traumatization as alternating between acknowledgment and avoidance or suppression. She extrapolated the same dialectic to society at large and traced incest and child sexual abuse through cyclical periods of acknowledgment and disavowal. Today's countermovement should be seen, at least in part, from the perspective of the normal dialectic of trauma.

A new dimension has recently emerged that greatly complicates matters for practicing therapists: the media are giving extensive attention to the claims that therapists are suggesting false memories of abuse to their clients for their own monetary benefit and are further encouraging confrontations and lawsuits against family members based on these false memories. As a result, critics say, innocent people are being falsely accused of the most heinous of crimes and families are being destroyed wholesale. On the basis of this media coverage, much of which presents the critics' position almost exclusively, reports of past abuse are now treated with a skepticism not evident two or three years ago. Therapeutic practice is under fire. Therapists are being sued by former clients and their families, charged with suggesting or implanting false memories of abuse through the unsubstantiated theory of repressed memory.

Undoubtedly, therapists are being scapegoated in part for their role as the "messenger" in naming the reality and "bad news" of incest and sexual abuse in society. These abuses flourish in secrecy and silence, not in the public eye. Yet some of the current criticisms—when taken out of the political sphere—are not without merit and can be useful in the improvement of clinical technique. The treatment of sexual abuse is a new field and does not yet have strong empirical validation for its techniques or efficacy. The professional training of the majority of therapists (except perhaps the most recent graduates or those whose training included Veterans Administration placements) has not included trauma and victimization since trauma has historically been a blind spot in all behavioral sciences curricula.

Working therapists faced with increasing reports of sexual abuse among their clients have had to make do with on-the-job training supplemented with specialized continuing education courses and whatever supervision and consultation they could find. Traumatized clients are notoriously difficult to treat and make heavy demands on the therapist; the untrained, unprepared therapist is therefore doubly challenged.

Complicating the matter further, much professional clinical education includes scant mention of human memory processes and even less information about trauma and memory. Thus the practicing therapist has another information vacuum in trying to deal with reports of absent or delayed memory for childhood abuse.

The goal of this chapter is to offer working clinicians some guidance and structure about the complex issues of assessment for sexual abuse. The author's position is that some criticisms about the treatment of formerly molested adults are valid and should be heeded; some, however, are politically motivated with the aim of returning to the suppression of any information about sexual abuse.

Consequently, the ethical practicing therapist walks a fine line when assessing for a history of sexual abuse or other childhood trauma, especially in the absence of specific disclosure by the client. The therapist can behave irresponsibly by either overemphasizing or by neglecting the significance of past experiences of molestation and trauma and must therefore be careful not to be overly suggestive on one hand or overly suppressive on the other.

Many issues and symptoms to be described below raise the therapist's "index of suspicion" of an abuse history when a client does not know about or disclose such a history. The therapist must be careful, however, not to assume sexual abuse as the only possible explanation of the client's difficulties and must use inquiry techniques that are neutral and nonsuggestive. Together, therapist and client work toward helping the client arrive at an understanding and explanation of her personal history while simultaneously developing symptom management and resolution.

ABUSE RECALL AND DISCLOSURE ISSUES

The following four scenarios illustrate the most common treatment presentations facing therapists. They are included here as the backdrop against which assessment issues are discussed and diagnostic guidelines are formulated.

Scenario 1

The client presents for therapy with relatively continuous memory of having been sexually abused as a child. In some cases, this memory has been previously disclosed and in other cases it has not. Some outside corroboration is available in support of the memory. The client has a variety of symptoms for which she is seeking therapy, many of which have been correlated in the research literature with a history of childhood trauma/sexual abuse. Previous treatment has not included any focus on the abuse history.

In the author's experience, this scenario is the most common and is of the least interest and emphasis in this chapter. The therapist works with the memory presented, being careful not to use techniques that would cause a false expansion or elaboration. Nevertheless, the therapist also understands that the treatment context may allow enough safety and validation for other, possibly more difficult memories and details to emerge.

Scenario 2

The client presents with some of the major symptoms associated in the literature with an abuse history and has partial or vague memory that "something" happened to her as a child. Her symptoms have exacerbated in the recent past because of triggering events in her current life; yet she has little or no understanding of any connection between her past and her current symptoms. This scenario fits the "disguised presentation" suggested by clinician-researcher Denise Gelinas.

Scenario 3

The client presents with some of the major symptoms of abuse history reported in the literature and has no recall and pervasive amnesia for sexual abuse in her past. She may, however, remember other types of abuse such as physical abuse and neglect or parental alcoholism. This scenario also fits Gelinas's "disguised presentation" model.

Scenario 4

The client presents requesting that the therapist help her uncover what she knows to be her "repressed memories" of abuse. She does have some of the symptoms associated in the literature with an abuse history but has no memory for such events. She believes they "must have happened" and are the *only* explanation for her symptoms. She may or may not have memory of other forms of abuse in her childhood.

In my experience, this is the least likely of the four scenarios to be a true case of sexual abuse and the least likely to occur, although it is being presented with more and more frequency. It too fits the "disguised presentation" model, yet calls for great clinical acumen in assessment. This is the most likely scenario in which an abuse history is lacking. "No history of abuse" or "uncertain history of abuse" must be included as rule-outs in the therapist's assessment.

The belief that abuse must have happened may lead to a premature and often inaccurate conclusion on the part of the client that the only likely explanation for her symptoms is abuse that she has repressed. The client prematurely rejects the possibility of other options and might be naive or under some social influence that suggests that she must have repressed her memories. How does this client know she has repressed memories?

As illustrated in these scenarios, partial or total loss of memory of sexual abuse in childhood and delayed or conflicted disclosure are routinely observed in clinical practice. Therapist-researchers have long sought to make sense of these clinical phenomena. They have posited a number of reasons for clients' lack of memory, even in cases of multiple episodes of abuse, and have found a posttraumatic model supplemented by developmental theory to be most explanatory.

Sexual abuse, especially incest, is a form of interpersonal victimization that is intensely shameful and generates much conflict for the victim. It has many traumagenic characteristics. Usually it puts the victim at great odds with other family members and involves betrayal in relationships that are supposed to be safe and nurturing. A child's experience of sexual abuse is buttressed by silence, denial, and threats on the part of the perpetrator to ensure secrecy. Very often the perpetrator is simultaneously a figure of significant attachment and someone for whom the child may have great love (and hence great feelings of ambivalence).

This type of sexual abuse often occurs in the context of other family dysfunction that renders the child vulnerable and may make intervention very difficult if not impossible. Studies have documented that it is repetitive over time: the average duration of incest is four years. It escalates over time: as more intrusive and invasive sexual acts occur, the child is often groomed to respond sexually, then is blamed for enjoying the acts, leaving her with great guilt and shame. Incest may begin when the child is quite young: the average age of onset is currently thought to be about age seven. It may involve physical violence but more often is psychologically or verbally coercive, and is psychologically as well as physically entrapping for a child unable to live or function independently.

Until the last decade or so, the prevailing social context did not encourage discussion of sexual abuse, particularly incest. As recently as the 1980s, incest was believed to occur in one per million population per year, a far cry from the actual prevalence estimate of 20 percent to 30 percent of girls and 10 percent to 20 percent of all boys. Social acknowledgment or validation was therefore lacking and is believed to be another reason that today's adult clients "forgot," suppressed their knowledge of, or did not disclose personal experiences of abuse. Perhaps today's children, living in a different social climate, will be able to be more open.

In studying traumatized children, researchers have found that they often cope by developing acute posttraumatic reactions and symptoms that usually resolve with time, especially when the children receive social support and therapeutic assistance to help them understand what happened and to express their emotions. When the traumatization is ongoing and unpredictable, and the child has no outside support or validation, the result is often a set of chronic posttraumatic conditions. These may occur concurrently with the abuse or be delayed in developing. Aftereffects and symptoms have an especially heavy impact on the immature child and become entangled in her ongoing development, potentially stunting and derailing it over time. This is in contrast to trauma that occurs in late adolescence or adulthood when the individual's personality is much more consolidated and less subject to deformation.

It is the occurrence of trauma in childhood and over the course of physical maturation and psychosexual development in a nonsupportive, nonvalidating social context that therapists believe explains the memory disturbance so commonly seen in clinical practice. The very nature of traumatization is implicated as well. Trauma impacts both the mind and the body, especially when the body is the locus of the trauma, as is the case in any type of sexual violation. Researchers conducting laboratory research on traumatized individuals (usually war veterans) have documented neurophysiological responses that, in turn, underlie and stimulate many of the physical and psychological reactions these people experience.

Memory disturbance has also been found to result from dissociation, a common psychological function that varies by degree from normal to pathological. In its normal form, it is more common in childhood than in adulthood and is often associated with children's imaginary processes: for example, children's propensity for imaginary companions, a process that diminishes as the child matures. Memory disturbance can operate as a defense mechanism in traumatic situations, allowing the victim to distance herself from the shocking event and to numb the associated emotions.

Dissociation now appears to be an especially likely response to chronic traumatization in childhood that, over time, becomes routine and automatic, interfering with the victim's conscious awareness. Pathological variants of dissociation (the dissociative disorders: dissociative fugue, depersonalization, psychogenic amnesia, dissociative identity disorder, and such disorders not otherwise specified) involve an alteration in the normal functions of personal identity, memory, and consciousness that leaves the individual with a lessened capacity for these functions. The memory disturbances of adults molested as children may therefore stem from dissociation used as a natural defense but which may entail loss of personal consciousness, including memory for the traumatic circumstances. Ironically, this formulation returns the mental health field to the work of Pierre Janet, a contemporary of Freud's, who emphasized dissociation as a response to trauma and whose work was eclipsed when Freud's emphasis on repression and on the oedipal theory took hold, effectively circumventing belief in the reality of sexual abuse.

One of the clearest contemporary examples of the dissociative process comes from the story of Marilyn Van Derbur Atler, the former Miss America who has described herself as having split or dissociated into "The Night Child" who knew about the abuse and the "Day Child" who was amnestic for it and who functioned outstandingly well in her everyday life. The split need not be so clearly demarcated for memory loss to occur. On the other hand, dissociative identity disorder (formerly multiple personality disorder) involves even greater demarcation through the defensive compartmentalizing of experiences and emotions; these experiences are so completely separated by partial or total amnesia barriers that one part of the self (or personality) may not know about the other(s). Its development has been strongly associated with a history of chronic severe child abuse (particularly sexual abuse), although a one-time overwhelming trauma may be etiological as well. Note that some of the same critics who challenge the reality of repression or amnesia and associated delayed recall in sexual abuse cases also take exception to the reality of dissociative identity disorder by insisting it is suggested and elaborated on by gullible or self-serving therapists.

Clinician-researchers studying chronic sexual abuse have come to understand the long-term effects as a posttraumatic condition that differs from adult-onset posttraumatic stress disorder in significant ways having to do with personality development in childhood and early adolescence. They have labeled the condition complex posttraumatic stress disorder or disorders of extreme stress, not otherwise specified (DESNOS) to account for these differences. Basically, this diagnosis incorporates the effects and symptoms long characteristic of posttraumatic stress disorder (PTSD) and found on Axis I of the *Diagnostic and Statistical Manual* of the American Psychiatric Association: depression, anxiety, denial/numbing, reexperiencing, physical dysregulation and hyperarousal, guilt, shame, rage; it supplements them with the developmental and personality dimensions found on Axis II and not incorporated in the current criteria for PTSD. Complex PTSD/DESNOS involves alterations in self-formulations and relations with others most often found in personality disorders but presents them as chronic adaptations to trauma that enter and influence the personality structure. Currently, field trials of this diagnosis are under way and preliminary data support differences between DESNOS and standard PTSD.

Many cognitive scientists and memory researchers are not impressed with the concept of dissociation or traumatic amnesia as an explanation for the compartmentalization of personal experience—and, by extrapolation, might not embrace a diagnosis such as DESNOS. They claim that such a process is not in accord with what is known about the processes of human memory. For example, repetitive events would be expected to be remembered rather than forgotten, some events might not have been encoded in the first place, and amnesia resulting from trauma is not adequately experimentally documented.

Their critics counterargue that studies of human memory undertaken in a laboratory setting on nontraumatized individuals are not adequate to explain the loss of memory so commonly reported clinically in traumatized groups. They also argue that clinical observations have validity and should be used to formulate research questions and thus inform research about the nature of traumatic memory. Both groups are in general agreement that dissociation has not been adequately studied as a possible aspect of human memory processes. Undoubtedly, studies and debates about these issues will be ongoing and will influence and enrich both the fields of cognitive psychology and clinical practice.

Meanwhile, we continue to work with clients who report abuse and must treat these individuals until new and more experimentally solid information on the processes of traumatic memory becomes available. The next section incorporates some of the information about memory processes and the critiques of flawed clinical practice with the everyday realities of clinical practice, illustrated by the four scenarios presented at the beginning of this section. The result is preliminary guidelines that may be helpful in assessment and treatment.

OVERDIAGNOSIS AND UNDERDIAGNOSIS OF SEXUAL ABUSE

Much of the current controversy arises from perceived overdiagnosis and misdiagnosis of sexual abuse by therapists who use suggestive questions and techniques and who do not conduct a comprehensive assessment before arriving at a "diagnosis" of abuse. In an egregious clinical example, the therapist determines that there is a history of sexual abuse based on a rather general list of symptoms that the therapist takes as conclusive "signs" of repressed or undisclosed sexual abuse—for example, a client who presents with an eating disorder, a food aversion, or a propensity to wear loose and baggy clothing. Another example is the therapist who makes such a "diagnosis" either over the phone without even meeting the client or within the first session. Obviously, these clinical practices represent very poor technique and serious flawed ethical practice. The potential harm of such therapeutic mismanagement is obvious, both to the client and to anyone accused of abuse on the basis of such shoddy assessment.

The opposite side of this story needs to be told as well since it tends to be omitted and neglected in the current debate: that of the therapist who pays little attention to evidence of past abuse. In these cases, the individual goes to therapy with an abuse history, whether (1) conscious and unresolved (and disclosed or not to the therapist) or (2) unconscious/unidentified due to dissociation or repression.

In the first circumstance, the individual might disclose and be met with a therapist who denies, rationalizes, or otherwise dismisses the significance of sexual abuse. Such a therapist might ignore the disclosure never to mention it again, or tell the individual to "put it all behind her and get on with her life," or be unable to tolerate discussion of abuse or sexuality, reacting judgmentally in a way that intensifies the individual's shame. In the second situation, the therapist might never consider an abuse history, even if the individual is symptomatic in some highly idiosyncratic ways suggestive of abuse.

When unresolved abuse and its effects and symptoms are not identified and treated, the effects compound and elaborate over time. These results can be lifelong and tragic for both the individual and for her social network. This side of the coin has been all too common historically. It has deprived many individuals of mental health and a peaceful resolution to intense personal distress. And in those survivors who cope with their abuse by repeating it and reenacting it with others (not the majority of survivors but a significant minority), the cycle of abuse extends as more victims are created.

We must expect that sexual abuse is among the problems clients present for treatment and may be etiologic of other treatment symptoms in a substantial proportion of our caseload. The proportion changes depending on the treatment specialties of the therapist and whether she works in an inpatient or outpatient setting. Approximately half of all individuals with a positive abuse history who seek treatment do not disclose their molestation history during intake and assessment. Rather, they make a disguised presentation for reasons such as the following:

- Failure of anyone to ask whether something of the sort had ever happened to them

- Their own naiveté or ignorance about abuse

- Their lack of awareness about abuse because of their repression or dissociation

- Their age and the chronicity of their symptoms (older individuals, on average, being less willing to disclose)

- Feelings of personal guilt, stigma, and "being crazy"

- Shame about liking the attention or sexual pleasure associated with the abuse

- Fear resulting from the means used to silence or threaten them

- Silence as protection of self or others

- Previous negative experiences with disclosure

- Mistrust of others and anticipation of ridicule and judgment

A presentation that fits Gelinas's now-classic description of the disguised presentation and which includes symptoms that match the documented aftereffects of abuse should raise the clinicians's "index of suspicion" of hidden or unacknowledged sexual trauma. Briefly, Gelinas advised the therapist to make note of the client who enters therapy with "a characterological depression with complications and atypical compulsive and dissociative elements" and who is difficult to relate to. Gelinas advised particular attention to the family background and functioning of such a client. Very often, abused children are emotionally neglected as they are required to parent their own mothers or fathers and siblings. The client who grows up in such a family role reversal usually presents a competent and responsible facade that covers massive depression and emotional neediness. Furthermore, clients of this type are intensely mistrustful of authority figures and so engage in a dance of "approach-avoid" as they repeatedly test the therapist or get close and then defensively push away.

In adulthood, the presenting concerns associated with previous molestation are, according to Gelinas and other clinician-researchers, the disconnected (and hence disguised) secondary elaborations of the untreated original aftereffects. This formulation is very logical and very likely for those individuals molested during "the age of denial," the time period when abuse was unacknowledged both societally and in the consulting room. The formerly abused adult whose core issues and symptoms did not remit spontaneously or through the influence of some mediating event or relationship was pretty much left to fend for herself. Sometimes, a therapy directed at the resolution of symptoms without knowledge of or attention to the traumatic antecedent proved to be useful. It was just as likely for such a therapy to "hold" temporarily until the individual was again cued in some way that triggered the return of the same or additional symptoms. As discussed in more detail below, normal life stage and developmental events, which on the surface appear benign, can create a cascading of effects and symptoms in the adult survivor.

These initial and long-term effects and their associated symptoms have been grouped into the following seven categories:

1. Posttraumatic reactions including the complex PTSD/DESNOS formulation described earlier

2. Emotional reactions including anxiety, fear, depression, guilt, anger, and self-destructive thoughts and behaviors

3. Self-perceptions that are predominantly negative and indicative of low self-esteem, shame, stigma, and a sense of malignant power

4. Physical and somatic effects that are the direct physical expressions of abuse or physical manifestations of emotional reactions

5. Sexual effects including dysfunctions, aversions, and obsession/compulsions

6. Interpersonal effects characterized by conflictual and mistrustful relationships with family members and others and difficulties with intimacy

7. Social effects ranging from superior functioning to a total inability to function socially or occupationally

Additionally, a history marked by depersonalization and periods of dense amnesia, repeated victimizations in adulthood (adult rape, relationships with abusive partners), repeated episodes of self-harm (cutting, burning, risk-taking), repeated suicide attempts or chronic suicidal ideation, and repeated unsuccessful attempts at therapy or reports of highly conflictual or abusive therapeutic relationships should all raise the "index of suspicion" for an abuse background.

Finally, some clients present in a crisis of symptoms and behaviors having a sudden and atypical onset. They often describe themselves feeling as though they had been hit by "a bolt out of the blue" and as having no idea what set off the sudden onset of symptoms. They are best understood using the posttraumatic formulation of delayed response cued by triggers in the individual's life or environment. Additionally, symptom formation and delayed onset can be understood from a learning theory perspective. The stimulus of the sexual abuse imprints or conditions positively or negatively on the victim. Symptoms associated with the imprinting return when the original stimulus is somehow recreated. These cues or stimuli may be completely idiosyncratic (such as smelling a certain men's cologne or seeing someone with a strong physical resemblance to the perpetrator) or may have to do with the individual's life stage or circumstance (such as the development of a committed relationship, the birth of a child, the death of the perpetrator, the loss of a special relationship). Whatever form they take, the stimuli can trigger reassociation of material that was previously dissociated or repressed defensively and which can lead to resultant symptom development. With the airwaves saturated with reports of abuse and other family violence as well as heated discussions of the false memory controversy, individuals are bombarded with innumerable cues that have the potential of triggering response.

The crisis presentation does not necessarily imply the return of cognitive memory of past abuse, however. Very often, the triggered individual becomes symptomatic in ways that have to do with the abuse and that can be traced by the therapist as potential clues to a repressed or dissociated abuse history. It is therefore important that the therapist not ignore these events. For example, a previously well-functioning and asymptomatic adult might develop a major sexual aversion or a sexual compulsion. The aversion or compulsion might include an exact repetition or a role reversal of the details and events of the original molestation. Other physical manifestations, emotional reactions, or behavioral patterns—the most common being flight, situational avoidance, guilt, and social isolation—might be observed, in which case their significance would need to be similarly assessed.

WALKING A FINE LINE: ASKING WITHOUT SUGGESTING OR ASSUMING

Good practice recommends that at the time of intake and assessment we provide clients with information (preferably in writing) about the therapeutic process and the therapist's style, requirements, and mutual rights and responsibilities. At this time, information can also be provided about repressed or forgotten personal memory that might emerge in the course of treatment and how such material is handled. In particular, you can introduce the idea of the malleability of memory and a therapeutic style that is exploratory without accepting all recall as absolutely factual.

We can also explain that the therapy process is geared toward helping the client make sense of her own reality and that it's not up to us to make such determinations. At this time we should also discuss the limits of confidentiality and third-party duties. As a condition of therapy, we can ask the client to agree not to make personal disclosures or confrontations or take legal action without first discussing these courses of action with the therapist.

Whatever the mode of presentation for treatment, questions about sexual abuse or about other difficulties and trauma in childhood should be incorporated into the routine intake and assessment procedure to provide a baseline of information. The assessment should follow standard practice and be comprehensive enough for the development of initial diagnostic formulations and treatment planning for the client's major symptoms. Whether in written or verbal form or both, questions about abuse signal the client that such experiences may be significant and are relevant to and *can be discussed in the therapeutic setting.*

The recommended approach is to ask in a straightforward and matter-of-fact manner about any sexual experiences with adults that occurred either in childhood or adolescence. Or you can ask more generally: "What was it like to grow up in your family?" or "How were things in your family when you were growing up?"

Sexual abuse, incest, victim, molestation, or other words with similar connotations should not be used initially unless the client uses them. Many individuals do not see themselves as victims or what they experienced as abuse. Others may be quite fearful about admitting to experience labeled in this way. However, it may be necessary for you to use these same words precisely for their exactness later in treatment to contradict or challenge a client's denial or minimization. Ethical clinical practice in this area requires us to tailor or modulate the approach according to the stage of treatment, the client's needs and capacities, and the client's defenses.

Some individuals will deny or not know about their positive history of abuse, others will deliberately not disclose, and still others will make a direct disclosure upon direct inquiry. It's important not to make assumptions about how the client will respond if a disclosure is made. For some, divulging abuse is very anxiety-provoking and threatening to the point that they might attempt suicide or make some other desperate gesture. For others, it is marginally uncomfortable or stressful and may even be accompanied by feelings of relief. At whatever point a disclosure is made, we should proceed with caution and sensitivity. Personal calm, listening, and reassurance are called for, responses empirically studied as among those that assist incest survivors to disclose.

As therapists, we must provide a context of personal support and general validation for the client yet remain cautious about overresponding, elaborating, or overvalidating the client's report, or conversely, about underresponding and not asking exploratory questions. Asking the client to disclose details and emotional reactions indicates our willingness to explore the material and its significance and to assist with developing an understanding of her personal history. What is needed here is a therapeutic stance of openness and neutrality to the possibility of abuse and the use of open-ended rather than closed and suggestive questions.

Paraphrasing Judith Herman on this matter, the therapist must be technically neutral while being morally cognizant of the prevalence and possibility of an abuse history. But technical neutrality *does not mean not asking* and cognizance does not mean that the therapist *assumes* sexual abuse to the exclusion of other issues. The therapist should be open to the possibility of other childhood events and trauma that might account for the symptom picture and should not prematurely foreclose these other possibilities. Most important, the therapist should not *tell* the client that she was sexually abused in childhood *and by whom* without actual memory on the client's part or without strong outside corroborative evidence, as a sole means of interpreting or accounting for the client's symptom picture.

The therapist must also be careful about making closed or assumptive statements that are overly suggestive or that put the client into a double bind. "You *must have been* sexually abused if you have *that (or those) symptom(s)*" or "You have a 70 percent chance of having been sexually abused due to your substance abuse/eating disorder—can you remember the abuse?" etc. The therapist *should* develop suspicions of abuse when constellations of primary symptoms are evident or when very idiosyncratic symptoms emerge in the crisis presentation as described above. Still, open-ended inquiry is needed rather than assumption or suggestion.

In contrast, when a client has disclosed some abuse memories (as in Scenario 2) and has forgotten having done so, or when strong outside corroboration of abuse exists and the client persists in denying any knowledge, we can take a more direct approach in questioning and can prod the client a bit. In this case, the therapeutic task is to ease the client's protective defenses enough that she is able to acknowledge the abuse and work it through. In my experience, the question "What do you have to lose or gain if you were abused, if the abuse is true?" is often useful. This question frequently brings tears and very poignant descriptions of losing one or more significant relationships, of admitting to a significant betrayal, or of having to deal with some of the core issues (usually the most disturbing and shame-laden) that have been long avoided. Gaining back a lost self or sense of personal reality are also often described. This situation is very typical of a large number of previously molested adults who resist rather than embrace memories of having been abused.

In another variation, the client tries to put the onus for belief or the determination of "reality" onto the therapist: "What do you think?" "Do you believe me?" "You do believe me, don't you?" "I *need to know* that you believe *everything* I tell you." Such statements and pleadings can be very stressful for the therapist and also very compelling. A therapist prone to rescuing or not doing anything that might upset the client or generate disapproval is likely to be very challenged by such a situation.

We must put the ambiguity back onto the client rather than offering blanket and unknowing reassurances. Instead, the need for outside confirmation can be presented as a therapeutic issue. While the therapist needs to maintain and communicate belief in the reality of abuse, it remains for the individual to struggle with identifying and admitting to the reality of her abuse recollections. We can help through strategies aimed at giving support, empathic confrontation, and reassurance. A client's struggle for understanding and acceptance of her own personal history is difficult and may involve ongoing testing of the therapist. We must support the client but also give back the responsibility for self-determination. The delicacy of the therapist's position and the client's understanding of its rationale are greatly assisted when they are explained to the client at the beginning of therapy as discussed above.

Situations such as the one in Scenario 4 may present us with the greatest challenge and calls for an assessment of the client's overall functioning and motivation. The client should be queried about possible outside sources of influence (exposure to media reports and personal accounts, the influence of friends or a support or self-help group), family functioning and conflict, and motivation for revealing an abuse history including potential secondary gain such as revenge, punishment, or special attention.

We can also assess whether the idea of abuse and a certain diagnosis are egosyntonic or attractive to the client and why. The more typical circumstance is for abuse to be egodystonic and for abused clients to struggle with accepting the reality of abuse—even when there is strong and even incontrovertible corroborative evidence—and to fight associated diagnoses (notably dissociative identity disorders). The client's belief system about trauma and memory must also be assessed, and any erroneous information and thinking must be challenged or corrected. Then the client can be evaluated on how she handles the therapist's queries and unwillingness to provide the client's requested confirmation. Some clients become enraged and leave therapy, often to find another therapist who they hope will provide the sought-after verification; others remain and struggle to explore their motivations and beliefs and to make sense of their history. In such cases, both therapist and client must "live with and tolerate the uncertainty" of not knowing whether abuse occurred, even when a number of potentially indicative symptoms exist. The uncertainty is difficult but necessary in the absence of corroborative evidence (such as witnesses, physical injury, other victims, or an admission by the perpetrator). In such a situation it may be useful for the client to seek out whether corroborative evidence is available. This should be done only if the individual chooses to do so without outside pressure or feelings of duress and is best done once therapy is well under way rather than at its inception. Should the client decide to search, the therapist should discuss search strategies and sources with her along with the various possible outcomes.

The client should also be encouraged to develop a personal network so as to have someone besides the therapist for support. A search may be extremely taxing and anxiety provoking, and may even involve danger or threat in some cases. Therefore it needs to be done in as well-planned, protected, and safe a manner as possible. Some sources to be investigated include the following:

- Childhood and family photographs and documents such as medical, mental health, school, and law enforcement records
- Journal, diary entries, poetry, or short stories written in childhood or adolescence
- Letters or other correspondence from the suspected abuser or others
- Relatives and significant others who can be questioned, starting with those who are potentially the most supportive up to and including the suspected abuser(s)
- Other victimizations by the same abuser(s)
- The locations where abuse is suspected to have occurred
- Newspaper or other public files

The accumulation of evidence or lack thereof then needs to be sifted and analyzed. In some cases, definitive confirmatory information is not available causing the individual to continue in her uncertainty and ambiguity.

Some of the current criticism directed at therapists has to do with their not including the alleged abuser or other family members in the assessment process. Whenever feasible, where relative safety can be insured and with the client's permission, such a strategy might prove useful. However, we must be prepared with knowledge of the family's abuse dynamics. It is not unusual for an incestuous family to appear to be functioning well or even to be exemplary, or to scapegoat the alleged victim as a liar, or to displace anger onto the therapist or the client. Therapists undertaking such sessions are advised to get specialized information and training; several books and manuals are now available on this type of assessment. They should also consider working in teams or with other professional consultation. This assessment strategy is not advisable if the therapist determines that the alleged abuser or other family members are potentially physically or emotionally abusive to a degree that would be unsafe for therapist or client.

Without evidence of ongoing abusiveness by family members, the therapist is also advised to be cautious about recommending that the client make a complete break or separation from the family. Instead, the therapist might help the client work toward newer and healthier methods of dealing with family members—for example, assertiveness, changing typical modes of interacting, asking for reciprocity, creating and adhering to boundaries, spacing family visits, or "fear of loss" strategies. We also recommend family therapy with a practitioner trained to understand and therapeutically challenge the dynamics of abusive families when this is necessary. Allegations of sexual abuse may, in some clients, serve as a screen for other forms of mistreatment or dysfunction in the family. They may be used to provide a catalyst for work on these other problems as well as for the assessment of sexual abuse.

When members of a family threaten or are emotionally, verbally, or physically abusive, or when the client suffers serious repercussions in the aftermath of a family contact (such as episodes of self-harm, suicide attempts, drinking binges), we have an ethical obligation to point out the ongoing interactional patterns and make suggestions for the client's safety; these can include the recommendation that the client limit or temporarily cease family contact. Ultimately, the client must decide whether to maintain an ongoing relationship or to terminate it completely.

When the abuse of minors is disclosed or strongly suspected, we also have the legal obligation to make a report or to encourage the client to report the situation to the appropriate child protection agency. Before reporting, the client should be informed of the various potential outcomes of such a report including a social services and police investigation, and removal of the alleged perpetrator from the home when the evidence is strong enough.

ASSESSMENT INSTRUMENTS AND DIAGNOSIS

Standard psychological instruments have not, for the most part, included the assessment of symptoms associated with traumatic response. As a result, such symptoms have either gone unrecognized or have shown up as elevated scores (and hence psychopathology) on standard instruments. The therapist should consider using both general and specialized types of assessment instruments while conducting a formal psychological evaluation. Obviously, information derived from these trauma-sensitive and symptom-specific instruments might provide data to support or counter an abuse history in the absence of clear memory in the client, although other trauma in childhood or adulthood might account for posttraumatic symptoms.

No well-validated instruments are available at present for sexual abuse or its aftereffects per se (although some are currently under development (such as the Early Trauma Inventory); but the therapist can choose from among a number of traumatic stress instruments to assess for major symptoms such as intrusion, numbing, dissociation, and hyperarousal (Impact of Events Scale; Everstine Trauma Response Index); anxiety, depression, anger, dissociation, defensive avoidance, sexual concerns and dysfunctional sexual behavior, intrusive experiences, and impaired self-reference (Trauma Symptom Inventory); trauma-related beliefs and assumptions (Jehu's Belief Inventory; McPearl Belief Scale). Additionally, a number of self-report instruments (Responses to Childhood Incest Questionnaire; Trauma History Questionnaire) and structured interviews and sets of questions (Incest History Questionnaire) are useful in eliciting detailed information about a remembered or more substantiated abuse history in an organized, straightforward way.

The assessment of symptoms of dissociation has similarly been omitted from most standard assessment instruments. When assessing a client for either traumatization or traumatic response, the therapist can consider using instruments developed specifically for this purpose. The most neutral of these is the Structured Clinical Interview, Dissociation (SCID-D). The Dissociative Experiences Scale (now available in adult, adolescent, and child versions) is a self-report screening instrument that can provide the therapist with preliminary information about the client's dissociative symptomatology. It can be supplemented by other instruments and sets of questions (Dissociative Disorders Interview Schedule; Diagnostic Drawing Series—Dissociation; Office Mental Status Examination for Dissociative Disorders/Multiple Personality Disorders; Dissociative Behaviors Checklist).

An extensive discussion of diagnostic issues is beyond the scope of this chapter so the focus here is on some major diagnostic and treatment plan considerations. Adults molested as children have traditionally carried a wide array of diagnoses (exclusive of posttraumatic stress disorder) and multiple diagnoses are often necessary to cover the full range of symptoms.

In recent years, posttraumatic stress disorder has routinely been used as an overarching diagnosis inclusive of the depression and anxiety symptoms so often seen in these clients, and the dissociative disorders have been diagnosed more as therapists have become more familiar with them. But, as discussed earlier, the criteria for PTSD as currently defined are not comprehensive enough to account for the multitude of symptoms (both Axis I and II and including dissociation) associated with childhood-onset chronic traumatization. The diagnosis "disorders of extreme stress, not otherwise specified" has been developed and field tested but was not included in the new *Diagnostic and Statistical Manual* (IV) of the American Psychiatric Association. Therapists therefore are likely to continue using a diagnosis of PTSD supplemented by other Axis I and II diagnoses.

The posttraumatic and dissociative diagnostic formulations are being challenged in the current controversy on the reality of delayed memories and dissociation. For example, in a recent article, PTSD was held to be an erroneous diagnosis when the traumatic antecedent is in question. The dissociative disorders (DD), particularly dissociative identity disorder, have been criticized by some as induced by the therapist or other social factors. Both PTSD and DD are seen as rather circular in terms of memory and, in fact, they are. Both have memory loss and amnesia among their aftereffects and diagnostic criteria. The therapist therefore counts the loss of memory as possibly being accounted for by the traumatized client's posttraumatic condition. The need for care in using suggestive questioning is obvious but so is the need to recognize memory loss as real and legitimate as a traumatic response.

Another challenge comes from a different source: managed care, with its emphasis on specific symptoms to be treated and detailed treatment plans. In some plans, the diagnoses of PTSD or DD are scrutinized more carefully than less controversial diagnoses and are subject to claim rejection when the therapist does not document specific symptoms to be treated and concrete treatment goals to be achieved.

In response to these challenges, we are well advised to be as careful in ascribing a diagnosis as in making an assessment of the client's concerns and circumstances. As we've emphasized earlier, the client is hurt equally when either a false positive or a false negative assessment is made and when she does not receive the appropriate treatment. Assessment that attends to the strategies and cautions presented above should reduce the risk of assumptions and erroneous diagnoses in either direction.

When the client remains uncertain or ambiguous about the past or in cases like Scenario 4, the therapist should be more cautious in making a diagnosis of PTSD or the dissociative disorders without documenting strong symptoms that meet the criteria of these diagnoses. The client should also be assessed as to outside influences or personality characteristics that might cause her to seek a particular diagnosis or to subscribe to a belief of sexual abuse in the absence of any memory. In cases of this type, it is certainly more conservative to diagnose Axis I and II disorders other than PTSD/DD and to highlight these as treatment foci. This strategy, in turn, allows the treatment to be symptom- and functioning-focused and sidesteps the criticism that some therapists are on a "fishing expedition" for trauma—or operate on a "no pain, no gain" philosophy about the treatment of traumatic circumstances, especially in the absence of memory for the trauma—at the expense of the client's current functioning and mental health.

In terms of managed care, whatever the history and whatever the diagnosis, treatment targets that are carefully selected and documented with their associated treatment strategy are likely to be those that pass utilization review. Therapy for formerly molested adults is generally not short term, so the therapist must be in a position to outline and provide rationale for the treatment goals and to document gains.

The treatment for the aftereffects of chronic traumatization is complicated. Current recommendations are that it be carefully sequenced, with the preliminary phases of treatment geared toward the stabilization of symptoms, the development of relative safety in the immediate environment and relationships, and the development of a working alliance with the therapist. All of these can be easily documented and help the therapist in goal setting in a treatment that requires a multitude of interventions and has complex demands and competing needs.

The assessment and diagnosis of adults molested as children requires both clinical acumen and extreme caution. Whereas child sexual abuse and other childhood traumatization were formerly grossly underdiagnosed, critics are charging that now these conditions are being overdiagnosed and even erroneously suggested to clients by therapists. Either situation does a grave disservice to the client and her family and social network. The goal of this chapter is to provide the working therapist some concrete assistance in "walking the fine line" in assessing for sexual abuse, especially when the client has no specific memory of the events or when recall or disclosure are delayed or develop during the course of treatment. The treatment of adults molested as children is a newly developed field, and therapists must remain current with the critiques of and new developments in this area if they are to offer the best service to their clients.

NOTES

P. 2, *secrecy and lack of awareness surrounding the occurrence of abuse:* Rush, F. (1980). *The best kept secret: Sexual abuse of children.* Englewood Cliffs, NJ: Prentice-Hall.

P. 2, *The treatment literature recently developed . . . as a source of stress:* Briere, J. (1989). *Therapy for adults molested as children.* New York: Springer; Courtois, C. (1988). *Healing the incest wound: Adult survivors in therapy.* New York: Norton.

P. 4, *sexual abuse constitutes a significant mental health risk throughout the life span:* Courtois, C. (1988). *Healing the incest wound: Adult survivors in therapy.* New York: Norton.

P. 4, *recommends that therapists routinely ask about sexual abuse:* Briere, J. (1989). *Therapy for adults molested as children.* New York: Springer; Courtois, C. (1988). *Healing the incest wound: Adult survivors in therapy.* New York: Norton.

P. 5, *Therapists have noted . . . or delayed recognition:* Harvey, M., & Herman, J. (in press). Amnesia, partial amnesia and delayed recall among adult survivors of childhood trauma. In K. Pezdek & W. Banks (Eds.), *Consciousness and Cognition,* special issue, The recovery of lost childhood memories for traumatic events.

P. 6, *experts on human memory:* Loftus, E. (1993). The reality of repressed memories. *American Psychologist, 48,* 518–537.

P. 6, *therapists have suggested or implanted false memories:* Yapko, M. (1994). *Suggestions of abuse: True and false memories of childhood sexual trauma.* New York: Simon & Schuster.

P. 6, *dialectic of trauma:* Herman, J. (1992). *Trauma and recovery.* New York: Basic Books.

P. 6, *innocent people are being falsely accused:* Loftus, E. (1993). The reality of repressed memories. *American Psychologist, 48,* 518–537; Yapko, M. (1994). *Suggestions of abuse: True and false memories of childhood sexual trauma.* New York: Simon & Schuster.

P. 7, *The treatment of sexual abuse is a new field:* Courtois, C. (1988). *Healing the incest wound: Adult survivors in therapy.* New York: Norton.

P. 7, *does not yet have strong empirical validation for its techniques or efficacy:* Briere, J. (1992). Methodological issues in the study of sexual abuse effects. *Journal of Consulting and Clinical Psychology, 60,* 196–203.

P. 7, *Traumatized clients are notoriously difficult to treat:* McCann, L., & Pearlman,

L. (1990). *Psychological trauma and the adult survivor: Theory, therapy, and transformation.* New York: Brunner/Mazel.

P. 7, *some criticisms . . . are valid:* Yapko, M. (1994). *Suggestions of abuse: True and false memories of childhood sexual trauma.* New York: Simon & Schuster.

P. 9, *the "disguised presentation":* Gelinas, D. (1983). The persisting negative effects of incest. *Psychiatry, 43,* 312–332.

P. 10, *partial or total loss of memory for experiences of sexual abuse . . . in clinical practice:* Harvey, M., & Herman, J. (in press). Amnesia, partial amnesia and delayed recall among adult survivors of childhood trauma. In K. Pezdek & W. Banks (Eds.), *Consciousness and Cognition,* special issue, The recovery of lost childhood memories for traumatic events.

P. 10, *It has many traumagenic characteristics:* Courtois, C. (1988). *Healing the incest wound: Adult survivors in therapy.* New York: Norton; Briere, J. (1989). *Therapy for adults molested as children.* New York: Springer; Herman, J. (1981), *Father-daughter incest.* Cambridge, MA: Harvard University Press.

P. 11, *traumatized children:* Terr. L. (1991). Childhood traumas: An outline and an overview. *American Journal of Psychiatry, 148,* 10–20.

P. 11, *traumatization is ongoing and unpredictable:* Herman, J. (1992). *Trauma and recovery.* New York: Basic Books.

P. 12, *Researchers . . . reactions these people experience:* van der Kolk, B. (Ed.). (1987). *Psychological trauma.* Washington, DC: American Psychiatric Press.

P. 12, *Memory disturbance . . . the associated emotions:* Spiegel, D. (Ed.). (1993). *Dissociative disorders: A clinical review.* Lutherville, MD: Sidran Press.

P. 12, *Dissociation now appears . . . chronic traumatization:* Putnam, F. (1989). *Diagnosis and treatment of multiple personality disorder.* New York: Guilford Press.

P. 12, *Pierre Janet:* van der Kolk, B., Brown, P., & van der Hart, O. (1989). Pierre Janet on post traumatic stress. *Journal of Traumatic Stress, 2,* 365–378.

P. 13, *Marilyn Van Derbur Atler:* Terr, L. (1994). *Unchained memories: True stories of traumatic memories, lost and found* (ch. 5). New York: Basic Books.

P. 13, *multiple personality disorder:* Putnam, *Diagnosis and treatment of multiple personality disorder;* Ross, C. (1989). *Multiple personality disorder: Diagnosis, clinical features and treatment.* New York: Wiley.

P. 13, *They have labeled the condition complex posttraumatic stress disorder:* Herman, J. L. (1992). *Trauma and recovery.* New York: Basic Books.

P. 13, Diagnostic and Statistical Manual: American Psychiatric Association. (1994). *Diagnostic and statistical manual of psychiatric disorders.* Washington, DC: American Psychiatric Association.

P. 13, *Complex PTSD/DESNOS:* Herman, J. (1992). *Trauma and recovery.* New York: Basic Books.

P. 14, *memory researchers:* Loftus, E. (1993). The reality of repressed memories. *American Psychologist, 48,* 518–537.

P. 14, *critics counterargue:* Brown, D. (in press). Pseudomemories, the standard of science, and the standard of care in trauma treatment. *American Journal of Clinical Hypnosis;* Harvey, M., & Herman, J. (in press). Amnesia, partial amnesia and delayed recall among adult survivors of childhood trauma. In K. Pezdek & W. Banks (Eds.), *Consciousness and Cognition,* special issue, The recovery of lost childhood memories for traumatic events.

P. 14, *critiques of flawed clinical practice:* Yapko, M. (1994). *Suggestions of abuse: True and false memories of childhood sexual trauma.* New York: Simon & Schuster.

P. 16, *repeating it and reenacting it with others:* Prendergast, W. (1993). *The merry-go-round of sexual abuse.* New York: Haworth Press.

P. 16, *they make a disguised presentation for reasons such as the following:* Courtois, C. (1988). *Healing the incest wound: Adult survivors in therapy.* New York: Norton.

P. 17, *disguised presentation:* Gelinas, D. (1983). The persisting negative effects of incest. *Psychiatry, 43,* 312–332.

P. 17, *initial and long-term effects:* Finkelhor, D. (1990). Early and long-term effects of child sexual abuse: An update. *Professional Psychology: Research and Practice, 21,* 324–330; Courtois, C. (1988). *Healing the incest wound: Adult survivors in therapy.* New York: Norton; Briere, J. (1989). *Therapy for adults molested as children.* New York: Springer.

P. 19, *aversion or a sexual compulsion:* Prendergast, W. (1993). *The merry-go-round of sexual abuse.* New York: Haworth Press.

P. 19, *Asking without Suggesting or Assuming:* Briere, J. (1989). *Therapy for adults molested as children.* New York: Springer; Courtois, C. (1988). *Healing the incest wound: Adult survivors in therapy.* New York: Norton.

P. 19, *we provide clients with information:* Yapko, M. (1994). *Suggestions of abuse: True and false memories of childhood sexual trauma.* New York: Simon & Schuster.

P. 20, *The recommended approach . . . childhood or adolescence:* Josephson, G., & Fong-Beyette, M. (1987). Factors assisting female clients' disclosure of incest during counseling. *Journal of Counseling and Development, 65,* 475–478.

P. 20, *Some individuals will deny* [Reasons for non-disclosure of an abuse history]: Courtois, C. (1988). *Healing the incest wound: Adult survivors in therapy.* New York: Norton.

P. 21, *Paraphrasing Judith Herman:* Herman, J. L. (1992). *Trauma and recovery.* New York: Basic Books.

P. 21, *cognizance does not . . . exclusion of other issues:* Yapko, M. (1994). *Suggestions of abuse: True and false memories of childhood sexual trauma.* New York: Simon & Schuster.

P. 22, *The therapist should develop suspicions . . . described above:* Briere, J. (1989). *Therapy for adults molested as children.* New York: Springer; Courtois, C. (1988). *Healing the incest wound: Adult survivors in therapy.* New York: Norton.

P. 22, *direct approach in questioning:* Courtois, C. (1988). *Healing the incest wound: Adult survivors in therapy.* New York: Norton.

P. 22, *can be very stressful for the therapist:* Chu, J. (1992). The therapeutic roller coaster: Dilemmas in the treatment of childhood abuse survivors. *Journal of Psychotherapy Practice and Research, 4,* 351–370.

P. 22, *We must put the ambiguity . . . unknowing reassurances:* McCann, L., & Pearlman, L. (1990). *Psychological trauma and the adult survivor: Theory, therapy, and transformation.* New York: Brunner/Mazel.

P. 23, *We can also assess . . . and why:* Yapko, M. (1994). *Suggestions of abuse: True and false memories of childhood sexual trauma.* New York: Simon & Schuster.

P. 23, *corroborative evidence:* Lawrence, L., & Reilley, M. A. (1993). Corroboration and evaluation of delayed memories of abuse. *Moving Forward, 2*(4), 15–16.

P. 25, *Therapists undertaking such sessions . . . professional consultation:* Kirschner, S., Kirschner, D., & Rappaport, R. L. (1993). *Working with adult incest survivors.* New York: Brunner/Mazel.

P. 25, *When the abuse of minors . . . is strong enough:* Herman, J. (1981), *Father-daughter incest.* Cambridge, MA: Harvard University Press.

P. 26, *Standard psychological instruments have not . . . traumatic response:* Briere, J. (1989). *Therapy for adults molested as children.* New York: Springer.

P. 26, *No well-validated instruments are available at present:* Stamm, B., & Varra, M. (Eds.). (1993). *Instrumentation in the field of traumatic stress.* International Society for Traumatic Stress Studies, Research and Methodology Interest Group.

P. 26, *Trauma Symptom Inventory:* Briere, J. (in press). *Trauma Symptom Inventory (TSI).* Odessa, FL: Psychological Assessment Resources.

P. 26, *Jehu's Belief Inventory:* Jehu, D. (1988). *Beyond sexual abuse: Therapy with women who were childhood victims.* New York: Wiley.

P. 26, *McPearl Belief Scale:* McCann, L., & Pearlman, L. (1990). *Psychological trauma and the adult survivor: Theory, therapy, and transformation.* New York: Brunner/Mazel.

P. 26, *Responses to Childhood Incest Questionnaire:* Donaldson, M. A. (1983). *Responses to childhood incest: A tool for self-assessment.* Fargo, ND: Village Family Service Center.

P. 26, *Incest History Questionnaire:* Courtois, C. (1988). *Healing the incest wound: Adult survivors in therapy.* New York: Norton.

P. 27, *SCID-D:* Steinberg, M., Cicchetti, D., Buchanan, J., Hall, P., & Rounsaville, B. (1993). Clinical assessment of dissociative symptoms and disorders: The structured clinical interview for *DSM-IV* Dissociative Disorders (SCID-D). *Dissociation, 6,* 3–15.

P. 27, *Dissociative Experiences Scale:* Bernstein, E., & Putnam, F. (1986). Development, reliability, and validity of a dissociation scale. *Journal of Nervous & Mental Disease, 174,* 727–735.

P. 27, *Dissociative Disorders Interview Schedule:* Ross, C., Heber, S., Norton, G., Anderson, D., Anderson, G., & Barchet, P. (1989). The dissociative disorders interview schedule: A structured interview. *Dissociation, 2,* 169–189.

P. 27, *Diagnostic Drawing Series—Dissociation:* Cohen, B., & Cox, C. (1989). Breaking the code: Identification of multiplicity through art productions. *Dissociation, 2,* 132–137.

P. 27, *Office Mental Status Examination for Dissociative Disorders/Multiple Personality Disorders:* Loewenstein, R. (1991). An office mental status examination for complex chronic dissociative symptoms and multiple personality disorder. In R. Loewenstein (Ed.), *Psychiatric Clinics of North America, 14* (Special issue on multiple personality disorder). Philadelphia: Saunders.

P. 27, *Dissociative Behaviors Checklist:* Armstrong, J., Laurenti, M., & Loewenstein, R. (1991). *Dissociative Behaviors Checklist-II.* Towson, MD: Sheppard Pratt Hospital.

P. 27, *"disorders of extreme stress, not otherwise specified":* (1992), Herman, J. (1992). *Trauma and recovery.* New York: Basic Books.

P. 27, *diagnoses:* American Psychiatric Association. (1994). *Diagnostic and statistical manual of psychiatric disorders.* Washington, DC: American Psychiatric Association.

P. 27, *PTSD was held to be an erroneous diagnosis:* Lindsay, S., & Read, J. (in press). Psychotherapy and memories of childhood sexual abuse: A cognitive perspective. *Applied Cognitive Psychology.*

P. 29, *"fishing expedition . . . no pain, no gain":* Yapko, M. (1994). *Suggestions of abuse: True and false memories of childhood sexual trauma.* New York: Simon & Schuster.

P. 29, *managed care:* Goodman, M., Brown, J., & Dietz, P. (1992). *Managing managed care.* Washington, DC: American Psychiatric Press.

P. 29, *Current recommendations . . . working alliance with the therapist:* Herman, J. (1992). *Trauma and recovery.* New York: Basic Books; Courtois, C. (1991). Theory, sequencing, and strategy in treating adult survivors. In Briere, J. (Ed.). *Treating victims of child sexual abuse.* San Francisco: Jossey-Bass, 47–60.

2

CRISIS INTERVENTION

Joan A. Turkus

Therapists working with adult survivors of childhood sexual abuse quickly become familiar with the triad of C's: "confusion, chaos, and crisis." To this I might add another C: challenge. This is challenging therapy for the survivors, who struggle with life and recovery, and the therapists, who struggle with containment of the work. Even a toothache may precipitate a major crisis for a survivor! In this chapter I present a problem-solving approach that matches the symptoms and level of impairment with a range of possible interventions. This decision-making process helps clinicians stay grounded in a therapeutic stance rather than being caught in the anxiety (and sometimes panic) that the work engenders. This discussion includes a conceptual framework for the management of crises exemplified by clinical vignettes (including the toothache), with strategic treatment planning for each.

Let's start with Anne's story:

CLINICAL VIGNETTE 1

Anne is a twenty-seven-year-old, single woman with a known history of childhood sexual abuse by her alcoholic stepfather, occurring when she was between the ages of nine and fifteen. She has had only occasional contact with her family since leaving home for college. Six months ago, with complaints of anxiety and difficulty sustaining intimate relationships with men, she started outpatient therapy with a female psychologist on a twice-weekly basis. She has been working in psychotherapy and maintaining her job as a nurse.

Two weeks ago, she returned to her hometown for her brother's wedding at which her mother and stepfather were present. In spite of her insistence that she was an adult and could handle the wedding and wanted to do so for her brother, she has been flooded by panic, flashbacks, and nightmares since the event. She is exhausted by the lack of sleep and is having difficulty concentrating at work. In her distress, she has been calling her therapist almost daily.

Anne and her therapist agreed to increase Anne's outpatient sessions to three times a week, but this has had little effect on the symptoms. The therapist is worried about her client in crisis, feels overwhelmed herself, and is wondering how to intervene before things get worse.

Anne's situation is a common scenario for a woman with a history of childhood sexual abuse. It contains elements of the aftereffects of childhood sexual abuse, such as anxiety and relationship difficulties. Then with the trigger of the family event, the acute symptoms of posttraumatic stress disorder (PTSD) are precipitated. Anne endured the pressure of seeing both her abuser stepfather and non-rescuer mother at the wedding and behaving as if "nothing had happened." Her ways of coping during the abuse were not effective, and she is overwhelmed by the intrusion of traumatic memories. Her therapist must rapidly decide on an appropriate response to the crisis. Before problem-solving the crisis, let's explore the three C's and see how Anne fits into the dynamics.

CONFUSION, CHAOS, AND CRISIS

Why is there confusion, chaos, and crisis in the lives and therapy work of women molested as children? Women survivors, despite having intelligence, resilience, and professional roles, are confused by the ongoing struggle with relationships, parenting, and the waxing and waning of their symptoms over many years. The more seriously affected survivors have a lifestyle filled with chaos and crisis. Therapists are not only taxed by the difficulty of the work and the nature of the traumatic material but also often feel helpless and overwhelmed in the face of continuing crisis. The therapy work requires staging, exquisite pacing, and containment to avoid further decompensation. However, in spite of our best technical efforts as clinicians, the three C's are still part of the work and are to be expected.

To start with, the symptomatology of the posttraumatic dissociative disorder spectrum of adult survivors is intense and destabilizing. It is not unusual for these clients to suffer from debilitating depression, suicidal ideation and behavior, self-mutilation, panic, flashbacks, hallucinatory reexperiencing of traumatic memories, body memories, nightmares, and dissociative experiences ranging from "spacing out" to internal ego states to discrete dissociative identities with amnesia. There are often relationship difficulties, questions about sexuality, and often sexual compulsion or avoidance. Substance abuse or an eating disorder are typical comorbid conditions. And then there may be concomitant medical problems, such as migraine headaches, chronic pelvic pain, or irritable bowel syndrome. A client may easily meet the criteria for six or seven DSM-IV diagnoses (how daunting for the therapist!). The symptoms interfere with these women's ability to function and are, in themselves, frightening and humiliating.

Anne's initial symptoms are moderate, but they escalate with the family visit in which she participates in a traumatic reenactment. There are strong psychological and physiological lures toward traumatic reenactment. Traumatic reenactment is the re-creation of the dynamics of the original trauma in the present. The simplest way to understand reenactment is with the Karpman Drama Triangle of *persecutor-victim-rescuer* in the family system. Karpman studied the family system of alcoholic families and discovered both the triangle and the shifting of roles by family members. Families in which there is sexual abuse follow the same pattern with the addition of a variant of the rescuer role, the "rescuer in denial." In Anne's story, the stepfather-Anne-mother lived out the persecutor-victim-rescuer in denial triangle in the past. At the family wedding, all three players probably performed with social grace, but Anne's ego defense of denial or repression didn't work. So she is now overwhelmed by traumatic memory.

Adult survivors may live out any of these roles in adulthood. They are often revictimized, for example, by rape or battering. Some years ago, I was the therapist for a small group of adult women with a history of childhood sexual abuse. Four of the five women had been or were battered wives, a condition that is surely not a coincidence. Survivors may follow the path of victim-to-victimizer (we don't yet know enough about women as perpetrators), but are more often nonrescuers of their own victimized children. And how many survivors are superb caretakers (rescuers) of others, then experience the resultant burnout as victimization? Survivors often live out reenactment in ongoing abusive relationships or internally with self-harmful acts. It is interesting, too, that clients with dissociative identity disorder (DID) have identities within the same triangle of roles. I teach the Drama Triangle of reenactment to therapists and clients. The only healthy way is to get out of the triangle.

There are a number of psychodynamic interpretations of traumatic reenactment including repetition compulsion, internalization of the "badness" (of the abuse), identification with the aggressor, and identification with part objects of the abusive or nonabusive parents. Although the psychoanalytic literature has many negative interpretations of repetition compulsion for women, modern thought emphasizes the desire for mastery, a need to make the ending come out different from what it was in the past rather than a masochistic wish for punishment. Perhaps Anne's unconscious wish for mastery shows itself in the participation in the wedding *as if* it were an ordinary life event, *as if* she had a normal childhood and adolescence. In work with survivors, it's apparent that there are many reenactment dynamics; these should be explored in the psychotherapeutic work.

The psychobiology of trauma as elaborated by van der Kolk shows us an "addiction to trauma" with an underlying complex neurobiology. In the midst of trauma, the mind-body reacts biologically to protect against or flee from the assault. The mind mobilizes many pathways of defense, which with repeated trauma become sensitized and overreactive. These reactions may explain the hyperarousal, numbing, and cascade of flashbacks or spontaneous abreactions of PTSD (when triggered as in Anne's case) as well as the biological pull toward reenactment. Reenactment can release internal opioids into the bloodstream. This creates a "high" in the person and potential for addictive reenactment behavior.

Many clients who cut or burn themselves report that they do it to "feel better." Indeed they do, particularly if they are adept at dissociating from the pain in addition to the rush of opioids. When I teach this addiction model of self-harm to survivors, it's accepted and understood with a sense of "Ah, ha!" It is helpful to use the principles of addiction treatment to help clients learn abstinence and the acquisition of healthy coping skills for the precipitating feelings. Our growing understanding of the psychobiology of trauma suggests appropriate psychopharmacology for PTSD—for example, the use of opiate blockers to interrupt the addictive cycle of self-mutilation.

As the medical director of an inpatient unit specializing in the treatment of posttraumatic dissociative disorders, I have been stunned by the incidence of ongoing abuse by one of the original abusers as well as revictimization in the present. I have treated adult women, ages twenty-five to forty-five, who are still involved in an incestuous relationship with their fathers. Our social workers estimate the rate of ongoing external abuse of all types at 25 percent of approximately eight hundred admissions over the past three years. So we are seeing continuing enactment of trauma as well as reenactment. Admittedly, our unit treats the more seriously ill survivors, but the incidence suggests that all of us need to increase our index of suspicion, particularly when treatment is crisis filled and frequently at impasse.

In my role as a consultant, the most consistent finding in the evaluation of crisis is that the trauma work is done *too early* in treatment. The beginning stage of treatment must focus on safety and stabilization. This is the stage in which the client's safety is addressed and secured; with the therapist, she must practice new coping skills, establish appropriate boundaries, put resources in place, learn a cognitive frame, and discuss crisis prevention. Anne probably did not solidify this therapeutic work or plan carefully enough for the trauma of entering the family system again.

This early stage may take from one to three years; there is nothing wrong with putting so much attention in this phase. I encourage you to take adequate time for this foundation laying, and would present the economic argument to managed care that it will save money in the long run.

Too often, however, both therapists and clients are eager to jump into the memory processing, which is mid-level work. Clients have a fantasy of "getting it out as quickly as possible"; there are also the psychological and physiological pulls toward flooding and reenactment.

If there is any lesson to be learned from the errors of the regressive trauma work we did a decade ago, it is this: "self work before memory work." Otherwise, the memory work is traumatic reenactment; it is not planned and contained as much as possible. In the best of clinical treatment, the metabolism of the trauma is destabilizing. The foundation for the work must be carefully prepared.

I have alluded to the training of the therapist as a factor in the precipitation of crisis. Very few of us had any training in the trauma field in our graduate or clinical work—and I am not included in the "very few." I had no such training in my psychiatric residency in the 1970s, nor did we have guidance in dealing with the assault of being an empathic listener to primitive, violent, sadistic sexual material. No one taught us how to protect ourselves from secondary trauma (vicarious traumatization), from which all of us suffer in doing this work.

We are learning together from seminars, reading, peer supervision, support groups, and clinical errors. At the same time, we are living through the crisis of constriction in health care resources, with its impact on the care of survivors who need long-term psychotherapy, as well as the media and legal attacks on our professional competence. We have to try to do good clinical work and take a neutral stance with regard to memory. We work in the midst of intense internal and external pressures, which generate significant trauma and crisis for us as therapists.

One last, but equally important, factor to add to this discussion of confusion, chaos, and crisis is countertransference. Every trauma therapist has the repeated experience of feeling deskilled and powerless, regardless of discipline or training. This is often countertransference, separate from a need for training or supervision (which each of us should get as part of our professional work). It is a projective identification with the client's helplessness. Is this what Anne's therapist is experiencing? It is amazing how contagious that helplessness can be, particularly if fueled by continuing chaos and crisis.

We, too, get caught in the Drama Triangle by our omnipotent rescue fantasies. After all, don't we become therapists to help others? Oh, to learn the difference between reasonable altruism and rescuing. When we are unable to rescue the client from her chaotic lifestyle and repetitive crises, we feel helplessness, guilt, and shame. However, the bottom line in this work is this: *The therapist cannot reparent or take away the pain of the abuse and abandonment. The survivor must take responsibility for her own recovery and grieve the losses.*

FRAMEWORK FOR THERAPEUTIC RESPONSE

With the understanding that crisis is a part of the psychotherapy of the survivor of sexual abuse, let's discuss the framework for therapeutic response. The building of the frame begins with the concept of *crisis prevention*.

In the initial phase of treatment (or backtracking now, if necessary), it is important that you do a comprehensive assessment. This should be done in an atmosphere of intellectual honesty and collaboration, reframing any issues that are shameful to the client as problems to be solved. This assessment includes not only the symptomatology, ego strength, and overall function, but a full range of questions about previous treatment (what worked, what didn't work); living arrangements; relationships and support network; safety of self, others, and from others; resources for funding of health care and living expenses; medical illnesses and preventive care; dental care; legal difficulties or plans for public disclosure and legal action. Don't forget to inquire about substance abuse and eating disorders. From this comprehensive assessment flows a plan for the early phase of treatment and emplacement of resources.

Let's take an overall look at the staging of treatment. The overarching principle here is *function*. As emphasized previously, the early stage of safety and stabilization is the most important stage of treatment. It is the stage of ego strengthening that supports the later trauma work; but even more important, it emphasizes the skills for maintenance of function for the survivor's entire life. In the middle stage is trauma metabolism, with its intense memory processing, affect, and grief work. The late stage—integration of memories and rebalancing—carries the survivor into the mainstream of normal life.

Crisis may intervene in any stage of treatment, although it occurs most commonly in the early and middle phases. Treatment often starts in crisis (since this is what pushes clients into seeking help), so crisis management becomes the focus within a longer-term plan. However, an unresolved issue may precipitate crisis and relapse in the late phase. *Crisis management is a collaborative treatment skill to be learned by both therapist and client.*

One of my most useful experiences was as a consultant psychiatrist to a case management practice. Clinical case management is the comprehensive management of mentally ill clients in the community. It "strives to bring order out of chaos, to stabilize the client in the community, and to encourage the highest level of function during treatment." The concept has much to offer us as trauma therapists. A client often brings too many current life issues for them to be ignored. We see a range of clients with a variety of skills and backgrounds. Many keep their lack of skills well hidden until a crisis develops. I have learned not to assume that survivors know "Normal 101." How can they, coming as they do, from such dysfunctional backgrounds? Case management takes a broad look at needs and resources, including the available health care. Case managers for insurance companies are often pleased with this broad-spectrum approach and the thoughtful conservation of resources. I try to integrate case management and mentoring with the psychotherapy of trauma survivors.

TREATMENT RESOURCES

Let's consider all possible resources to keep as a checklist for planning. Here is my personal list to which I encourage you to add others:

- Outpatient psychotherapy
    Individual therapy (including adjunctive hypnotherapy)
    Group therapy
    Current family/significant others
    Expressive therapies, particularly art therapy

- Psychoeducational groups
    Aftereffects of trauma
    Life skills
    Parenting

- Pharmacotherapy by a psychiatrist experienced in the trauma field
- Physician consultants (internist or family practitioner, gynecologist, neurologist, gastroenterologist)
- Dentist
- Consultant(s) in the trauma field
- Self-help and support groups (recommended selectively)
    Alcoholics and Narcotics Anonymous
    Overeaters Anonymous
    Survivors of Incest Anonymous
    Support groups facilitated by hospitals as community service

- Nutritionist
- Exercise counselor
- Allies at work, perhaps an employee assistance counselor
- Support network
- Vocational rehabilitation counselor
- Financial adviser/teacher
- Low-income housing

- Crisis beds or housing in the community
- Detoxification Unit
- Partial hospitalization program

  Trauma orientation
  Chemical dependency
  Eating disorder

- Residential program

  Chemical dependency
  Eating disorder

- Inpatient facility

  With experienced admitting psychiatrist and trained staff, if possible
  Specialty Trauma Unit

We will draw on these resources in responding therapeutically to crisis, but it's important to do a pre-crisis exploration of what is available in your community. This would be a worthwhile project for your peer supervision or support group. Check with colleagues, contact physicians and dentists, talk to case managers/social workers in community mental health centers and develop a comprehensive list of names and telephone numbers. It will be invaluable not only in times of crisis but in overall treatment planning.

If you are a nonmedical therapist, it is essential to find a trauma-knowledgeable psychiatrist with whom to work as part of an *outpatient treatment team*. In my experience, an internist, family practitioner, or neurologist is not the best choice. Many nonpsychiatrist physicians attempt to "help out," but may be overwhelmed in the midst of crisis. The best possible choice would be a psychiatrist who is also available for partial or inpatient hospitalization, if necessary. Then the client in crisis does not have to deal with a stranger. In the same anticipatory frame, it would be advisable to obtain a psychiatric evaluation at the start of treatment, even if medication is not indicated at the time. Having this knowledge would facilitate an emergency psychopharmacological consultation later in the course of treatment if the need for this arises. It is important to emphasize to clients that psychotherapy is the heart of the treatment, but that medications may be indicated as adjunctive treatment for periods of time. It's better to deal with any resistance—including your own—at the start of therapy.

There are no absolutes in the trauma field with regard to the use of psychotropic medication, but our clinical experience is growing. The general philosophy is to target specific symptoms, such as flashbacks, nightmares, panic, or depression. Autonomic arousal, which accounts for many of the symptoms of PTSD, can be reduced at different levels in the central nervous system with such medications as clonidine, propanolol, the benzodiazepines, and the selective serotonin reuptake inhibitors (SSRIs, such as fluoxetine, sertraline). The SSRIs are effective antidepressants, and as such can serve a dual purpose in the treatment of PTSD accompanied by significant depression. In addition, the SSRIs do not easily lend themselves to overdose, as do the tricyclic and monoamine oxidase inhibitor antidepressants, so they are safer to use with suicidal clients. Antidepressant medication may be necessary for a significant period of time in a difficult course of treatment.

Trazodone, another serotonergic antidepressant with sedative properties, is particularly useful in small doses to help clients sleep and to decrease nightmares. Trazodone is nonaddictive. Many clinicians are reluctant to use benzodiazepines because of their risk of addiction and dependence, particularly with clients who have a history of alcohol or drug dependence. However, the benzodiazepines are the best anti-anxiety agents available, and it is wise to weigh the benefits versus the risks carefully before discarding them in the face of debilitating panic or anxiety. It seems better to me to preserve function and to cope with slowly tapering (to avoid withdrawal) the benzodiazepine later. One empirical study indicates that the best choice of a benzodiazepine would be clonazepam, a long-acting medication with the qualities of mood stabilization as well. Clinicians also use other mood stabilizers, such as lithium, valproic acid, and carbamazepine, in the treatment of PTSD.

Most psychiatrists in the trauma field would agree that antipsychotic agents have little place in the treatment of posttraumatic-dissociative disorders. There has been confusion over the years between the pseudo-hallucinatory experiences of flashbacks or abreactions and true psychotic symptoms. Although antipsychotics are excellent anti-anxiety agents, they should be used for only the short term in crisis situations because of the long-term risk of tardive dyskinesia. Opiate blockers, such as naltrexone, may be useful in interrupting a resistant cycle of self-mutilation. Recently, I did an informal survey of the medication used on our specialty unit and found the most common treatment combination to be fluoxetine or sertraline with clonazepam.

Partial hospitalization deserves increased consideration as a resource in the acute care of the survivor. Representing approximately one-third the cost of inpatient hospitalization, it has creative possibilities for either day or evening treatment. It may be useful both in preventing inpatient hospitalization and as a step-down to shorten an inpatient stay. Chemical dependency programs have long used evening partial programs for after-work treatment; now eating disorder programs are following this model. Recognizing the numbers of trauma patients in treatment and their need for specialized treatment, administrators of many partial programs are developing a "trauma track."

Inpatient treatment is a useful resource for clients who need a safe, therapeutic structure in which to be treated for (1) active suicidality or self-mutilation, (2) debilitating depression, or (3) marked impairment of function from intrusion of traumatic memory or uncontrolled dissociation. This treatment is indicated when less restrictive interventions such as intensive outpatient treatment or partial hospitalization are ineffective. Inpatient hospitalization is best framed as a treatment resource, not a failure of either client or therapist. Clients sometimes need a safe place in which to regroup.

You may be asked to assist in the precertification of a hospital stay. In these days of case review by third-party payers, inpatient stays are short and focused on rapid stabilization, so it helps the inpatient team to know your goals for the client on admission.

Trauma clients sometimes have a difficult time on a general psychiatric unit in a community hospital. These units have a wide variety of patients from adolescent to geriatric age with all types of diagnoses. Trauma clients often complain that their needs are not met by the staff or group therapies. You may help your client by educating the staff, if they are receptive. Private psychiatric hospitals have become sensitized to the needs of this population and may have a trauma track or even a specialty unit that treats only the post-traumatic dissociative disorders of adult survivors. It's important to survey the closest resources, ask for tours to look at the accommodations (ambience, locked versus unlocked unit, policies with regard to your participation in hospital treatment). and talk to admitting psychiatrists *before* one of your clients is in crisis.

CLINICAL VIGNETTES/STRATEGIC INTERVENTIONS

The guiding principles in the therapeutic response to crisis are these:

- Rapid assessment by therapist and client of the level of impairment and potential dangers
- Strategic interventions that target the crisis symptoms
- Use of the least restrictive alternative
- Rebuilding of the treatment frame

To help clarify these, let's look at a number of clinical vignettes and strategic interventions. I will brainstorm the interventions in my clinical style, but please add your own creative solutions.

Let's return to strategic interventions for Anne, whom we've left in distress for some pages now. What is most important here is the preservation of Anne's function and privacy. In collaboration with Anne, I would suggest that she take a week off from work as vacation or emergency leave to give herself time to stabilize. I would try to avoid disclosure of her problem and treatment at work; in spite of the best of intentions, such knowledge often backfires.

Then I would arrange for an emergency psychiatric consultation for medication. Anne is overwhelmed by anxiety and flooded by flashbacks and nightmares. If I were the medicating psychiatrist, I would look at options with Anne. The options include (1) trazodone to help her to sleep, (2) clonazepam (small p.r.n. dose during the day, larger dose at bedtime), (3) clonidine during the day and at bedtime (clonidine lowers blood pressure, however, and this has to be monitored). These are all rapid-acting medications in contrast to the delayed action of antidepressants. Anne appears to be suffering more from anxiety and flashbacks than from depression.

Within the psychotherapy, Anne and her therapist need to work together to help Anne gain a cognitive understanding of what happened and to set healthy boundaries for the near future. The work should include reinforcement of her adult ego strength in contrast to the vulnerability of the child or adolescent. Anne should practice self-nurturing and self-soothing techniques to calm her hyperarousal. She might use her support network for playful activity or exercise. If the therapist is skilled in hypnotherapy and Anne gives informed consent—since the use of hypnosis may invalidate Anne's testimony in future legal action—hypnosis might be used for deep calming and to contain the traumatic memories with appropriate imagery.

This is also a time to reexamine the treatment plan. Perhaps, in addition to medication and individual psychotherapy, Anne might benefit from group therapy. She might start with a short-term group with a psychoeducational focus, then move into the long-term group. This is also a time to explore her work stresses (Is Anne working in a particularly stressful situation? Are there other choices?). Clients may have to make real adjustments in their work while they are under the stress of doing trauma therapy.

CLINICAL VIGNETTE 2

Barbara is a thirty-two-year-old single woman who works as a computer programmer. She is a known incest survivor whose father was the perpetrator; the abuse occurred during the years when she was seven to thirteen. She struggled with alcohol and marijuana in her late teens and early twenties, but with the help of Alcoholics and Narcotics Anonymous, she has been sober and clean for the past seven years. Because of troublesome flashbacks and retreating into deep silence when stressed, she decided on a course of psychotherapy with a woman social worker.

She has been in twice weekly therapy for the past two years and is now working through the traumatic memories. In spite of a pacing and containment approach, she is feeling overwhelmed at times. She has developed symptoms of gagging and aversion to certain foods as she works through memories of forced oral sex.

In the midst of all this, she develops a toothache and is suicidal at the thought of anyone inserting something into her mouth. She thinks that she would rather die. She knows her thoughts and feelings are out of proportion to the present, but she is unable to control them. She and her therapist agree on an emergency session to address the problems presented by the crisis.

Here is the ideal collaborative crisis management approach. Barbara and her therapist meet to solve the problems presented by the dental crisis. Within the session, Barbara needs time to verbalize her fears and thoughts and have them accepted within the PTSD framework. The thoughts of wanting to die are cognitive flashbacks, and what child would not feel this way in the midst of oral rape?

Only after this verbalizing and acceptance should the therapist move gently into how to manage the visit to the dentist. It is of inestimable value to have a sensitive and understanding dentist, one who knows survivor issues. Even so, advocacy is indicated. Barbara (or her therapist) might call the dentist and explain what she needs in the way of understanding and control. Control is critical; the dentist must be willing to explain exactly what he is doing, each step of the way, and be willing to stop for a short period if necessary.

Other interventions might include a p.r.n. anti-anxiety agent (which dentists can prescribe), self-hypnosis tape (relaxation with reinforcement of "now" in contrast to "then"), accompaniment by a friend, and check-in with the therapist after the dental visit. Barbara also agrees to work on her self-nurturing skills and return to Alcoholics Anonymous meetings "just in case." Assuming that the dental visit goes well, the therapist should be sure to reinforce the mastery of the experience. If not, Barbara and the therapist should continue to learn from the experience and to prepare for the next time.

CLINICAL VIGNETTE 3

Carol is a thirty-nine-year-old married woman with two school-age daughters, aged ten and seven. Carol is an artist who maintains a home studio. She is married to a physician. Three years ago, when her oldest daughter reached the age of seven, Carol began to have flashbacks of sexual abuse by a neighbor, the father of one of her closest childhood girlfriends. She ridiculed the reality of these memories, but with encouragement by her husband, she got in touch with the childhood friend.

Her friend told her that her father had died some years ago but that she had memories of incest by her father and vague recollections of "another little girl there at times." Both Carol and the friend recalled sleeping at one another's homes frequently. The friend was horrified and guilt-ridden about the possibility of Carol's having been abused too, but said she would discuss it in her own ongoing therapy.

Carol acted astounded by the information for a brief time, then reverted to denial and refused to consider psychotherapy. In the ensuing three years, however, she became increasingly depressed, less creative in her work, and sexually avoidant—which she attributed to general "lack of interest" at her age. The flashbacks became more frequent. She became obsessed with worry about her children when they left the house. Both her husband and children were becoming increasingly anxious.

Her husband finally insisted on a joint session with a male psychiatrist to look at what was happening to the entire family. In the joint session with her husband, Carol was confronted with her behavior and its effect on the family. With pressure, she agreed to a series of consultations with a woman psychiatrist, who specialized in trauma recovery. As the consultation progressed, Carol became more agitated and depressed and increasingly unable to function. She denies suicidality, and says that she "loves her children too much to even consider it."

Here is a client in diagnostic crisis. As the denial is undone, she becomes more symptomatic and unable to function. There are several issues to consider here, not only for Carol, but for her entire family. Let's start with Carol.

Carol has symptoms of posttraumatic stress disorder and major depression. I would think about a number of interventions: (1) outpatient psychotherapy twice weekly; (2) antidepressant medication, either an SSRI or tricyclic antidepressant (the latter may be more calming) plus p.r.n. clonazepam for a few weeks; and (3) a partial hospitalization program with a trauma track for two weeks for structure, support, and psychoeducation.

The antidepressant will not take full effect for some weeks, and Carol needs immediate help. We can hope that she will find the partial program helpful and at the same time develop a therapeutic alliance with her therapist. The focus of the initial work is stabilization and rapidly giving Carol a cognitive framework as well as a sense of hope in the process.

If Carol works well in the groups in the partial program, I would suggest a long-term therapy group as an adjunct to her individual work. Similarly, if art therapy is helpful to her in the partial program—and she is able to use the modality as a client, not an artist—it might be helpful to refer her for ongoing art therapy.

Carol's family is in crisis, too. Her husband needs support now and during the trauma work. The social worker in the partial program should probably meet with Carol and her husband. He might be referred to a spouse support group or to individual supportive therapy if a group is not available. Some thought will have to be given to the children. In most cases, children are reassured if they know that a problem is recognized and being addressed (which is good modeling). The social worker might have a family meeting if the parents want added support in talking to the children. If the children's anxiety does not rapidly resolve, or if they develop additional symptoms, they should be referred for evaluation.

CLINICAL VIGNETTE 4

Denise is a twenty-two-year-old woman who works in retail sales. She married a buyer in her store a year ago after a whirlwind courtship. Shortly after her marriage, she developed lower back and pelvic pain. Neither her internist or gynecologist were able to discern the cause of her pain, but it persisted and began to interfere with her life, particularly her sexual relationship with her husband. He became angry, and told her "to snap out of it." She tried, but over the months, became anxious and discouraged.

At her friends' urging, she entered weekly therapy with a woman psychologist. After some time in therapy, she revealed a history of sibling incest with a brother six years older. The incest had taken place between the years when she was seven and twelve. It stopped when the brother went away to college. She felt extremely ashamed and guilty about it and wanted to forget that it ever happened. She reluctantly agreed to try to work through the issues and increased her sessions to twice weekly. Denise was adamant about not telling her husband.

In the ensuing months, she became more and more depressed. She lost weight and began having difficulty sleeping. The psychologist referred her to a psychiatrist for antidepressant medication and she was started on desipramine (a tricyclic antidepressant). One weekend, several weeks later, she had a fight with her husband. He was angry about her problems and the lack of sex in their marriage. She, in turn, felt as if she were a failure as a wife. She impulsively took a significant overdose of the desipramine, then panicked and called her therapist.

This is the call each of us dreads, but it happens to all of us at one time or another, so be prepared with a plan. Let me put myself in the place of the psychologist.

The most immediate need is to get Denise to a hospital for emergency medical attention. If the husband is at home, I would ask to talk with them both and explain the need for medical attention. He will probably be furious, but agree to drive her to the nearest emergency room. If he is not at home or downplays the need for emergency attention, I would call 911. In either case, I would then call the emergency room to notify the staff that my client will be arriving and that I will be available to talk to the doctor on call. I would also notify the medicating psychiatrist about the overdose and discuss hospitalization to sort out the medical and psychological issues. Another issue that you must be prepared to face, if necessary, is involuntary hospitalization. It's essential to know the procedure in the jurisdiction where you practice.

Let's assume that Denise is appropriately treated in the emergency room, then admitted to a medical unit for twenty-four hours' observation. I would try to arrange a meeting with the client, psychiatrist, and myself to discuss a transfer to the psychiatric unit. Denise and her husband will probably be resistant to such a plan, but I would insist. This is a volatile situation with the factors of a yet unresolved major depression (too soon for therapeutic effect of the desipramine), a suicide attempt (or gesture), shame, secrecy, and marital discord. I think it would be unwise for her to return to exactly the same situation without strategic interventions. I would, however, make every attempt to protect Denise's privacy and try for a brief hospitalization.

Several critical issues appear here. The first one to be addressed has to do with the antidepressant. If Denise has been on the desipramine for perhaps two weeks, it might be restarted as soon as this can safely be done; then her blood level should be checked to determine whether the dosage is in the therapeutic range. It would be foolish to lose two weeks' head start on treatment, and it is possible to control the amount of medication that she has at one time. On the other hand, if her future safety is doubtful, the psychiatrist should consider changing to an SSRI such as fluoxetine.

The second issue to be thoughtfully addressed is that of the marital stress, which is intertwined with the shame, secrecy, hurt, and anger about the sibling incest. Denise's husband may be a good guy who is honestly confused and angry about what is happening to his wife. If so, Denise's willingness to give him some information now may help him to be an understanding ally in her healing journey. We can hope that she will agree to do so. He will need support in accepting and responding appropriately to the information—for example, not blaming his wife and suppressing his wishes to attack the brother. If he can accomplish this, the marriage can be strengthened. It would be wise to schedule several family meetings while Denise is still an inpatient, then refer her husband to a support group for spouses. Denise and her therapist might develop a plan in which the husband is included in a session every six to eight weeks to see how things are going and explain how he can be of help at this stage of the process.

In her individual therapy work, Denise needs reinforcement of the cognitive frame regarding understanding sibling incest, not blaming herself, and establishing a healthy boundary with the brother. Above all, she needs to work out a safety plan and contract with her therapist and psychiatrist.

CLINICAL VIGNETTE 5

Ellen is a twenty-nine-year-old single woman who remembers having been molested several times by a school janitor in junior high school. Some years later, after a number of complaints, the janitor was finally arrested and sent to prison. Ellen never revealed the molestation to her parents. She didn't think they would understand and thought they would blame her for not taking care of herself.

Ellen began partying and drinking in college, but managed to graduate with a degree in education. She enjoyed her school placement, then readily got a job teaching seventh-grade English. In the past five years, she has dated but has found it difficult to establish a long-term relationship. She parties a lot on weekends and sometimes calls in sick on Mondays.

Ellen's principal is concerned about her and refers her to an employee assistance counselor in the contract group for the school system. The counselor, in the assessment, is puzzled by Ellen's vague complaints of anxiety but refers her to a male social worker for short-term therapy with a focus on relationships. After a month in therapy, the therapist receives a Monday morning call from one of Ellen's friends. The friend reports that Ellen has been drinking heavily over the past four to five days and is unable to go to work.

Here is a "hidden" case of alcoholism in a woman with a history of sexual molestation. The therapist, knowing what resources are available in his area, asks the friend to take Ellen to the emergency room of a local hospital, which has a detoxification unit. He then calls the emergency room and asks for the client to be seen by a physician from the detoxification unit. This happens, and Ellen is admitted to the unit with a significant blood alcohol level. When she becomes clearer, a more accurate chemical dependency assessment is done. For the first time, Ellen reveals the history of sexual molestation and that she has been having flashbacks since she started therapy.

After detoxification and confrontation with the reality of her alcoholism, Ellen is referred to an evening partial hospitalization program, which specializes in chemical dependency. Her therapist is kept informed of the process and additional history. With permission, he talks to the employee assistance counselor who agrees to smooth things out at work and renegotiate treatment needs with the insurance company when a plan is determined.

So far, so good. But now the therapist is asked to participate in a treatment planning meeting with the staff of the partial program. What are Ellen's treatment needs at this point? We know that a history of sexual molestation and alcoholism frequently co-exist and that working through the trauma issues is important to long-term sobriety. But when does one work through them? We don't know all the answers yet, but sequencing of treatment is probably wise in the midst of acute alcoholism. It would be better to focus on sobriety; this includes using the support of the groups in the partial program as well as Alcoholics Anonymous meetings and finding a sponsor.

There is a choice between temporarily suspending individual therapy and continuing the development of a therapeutic alliance and supportive therapy. Ideally, the revelation of the molestation and the nonblaming acceptance by professionals will be helpful to Ellen in preventing additional unfolding of the PTSD. The therapist might do some very gentle psychoeducation with Ellen about sexual molestation and its impact, but focus more on supporting the struggle of sobriety. Teaching her relaxation and containment techniques might be useful. I would consider waiting for a year of sobriety before doing the trauma work, and then start with setting a secure treatment frame that includes relapse prevention and careful pacing and containment of the work.

CLINICAL VIGNETTE 6

Faye is a thirty-five year old married woman who had been in treatment on-and-off since she left home at age eighteen. She had had a number of diagnoses, including borderline personality disorder, bipolar disorder, and schizoaffective disorder as well as multiple hospitalizations related to suicide attempts and self-mutilation. She has "voices in her head" and periods of time that she doesn't remember.

During her last hospitalization, four months ago, she was given the diagnoses of dissociative identity disorder and posttraumatic stress disorder. She was referred for psychotherapy to a male psychologist who had some experience with the treatment of these disorders. During the hospitalization, she had been started on a new antidepressant, sertraline. The hospital psychiatrist agreed to continue her medication as an outpatient and work with the psychologist.

Faye's husband and two teenage children were familiar with her "personalities" and accustomed to her "changing." Faye did not know much about her childhood-adolescent history but thought "it was probably O.K. at home." Her parents were still living in the small country town in which she grew up. Her hometown was several states away, so she didn't see her parents often.

At this point in her therapy work, Faye is struggling to accept different parts of herself and encourage them to communicate and work together. So far, the parts seem to be mostly crying child parts with a few teenagers who can't keep things under control very well. The child and teenage parts are all very scared of "Blade," who keeps threatening to cut and has done so on numerous occasions in the past. The psychologist has tried to engage Blade in the therapy work, but "he" told the therapist to "go to hell." Faye often finds razor blades in her purse; she does not remember buying or putting them there.

Faye acts helpless and depressed most of the time. Her husband and children are exasperated with her. Her therapist is starting to feel the same way and wondering what to do. Then, Faye's parents send a note saying they are coming to visit next week. Faye becomes very agitated and Blade reacts with threats to "cut her throat this time to shut those wimpy kids up." Faye calls her therapist and tells him this on the telephone.

The psychologist calls the hospital psychiatrist and requests emergency admission for his client. He asks the husband to take her to the hospital immediately. This is an appropriate and therapeutic response. However, the next question is what to do with Faye in the hospital? To begin with, she should be placed on suicide precautions. She might be started on p.r.n. clonazepam to help her to calm down.

From a psychodynamic standpoint, Faye (the whole of Faye) achieved her goal of getting herself in a safe place. And she did it safely, by calling her therapist and asking for help. She did not cut herself before calling, so there is more of a therapeutic alliance here than the therapist may currently appreciate. We can hope the therapist can continue the psychotherapy on an inpatient basis for continuity of care, although he may feel that he needs a break, which is quite justifiable. The inpatient therapy has to center on internal system work, with the entire system of dissociative identities exploring what happened.

It appears that the parents' impending visit stirred up intense anxiety as reflected in crying by Faye's child parts. The teenage helper parts are probably unable to quiet them. Blade threatens with his method of stopping the crying. This is perfect, internal traumatic reenactment of the Drama Triangle. It may even be historical reenactment of the abuse.

This is an opportunity to make a breakthrough in the therapy work, and it's this positive frame that should be presented to Faye's internal system. It's an opportunity to do some important work in a safe environment. I would reinforce the decision to be in a safe place, although I would suggest a different strategy next time. I might say to Faye, "It is really O.K. to say that you are not able to maintain safety at this time and ask for help." The next step is to identify the letter from Faye's parents as the precipitating event and ask for one of Faye's parts to volunteer to explain what happened. If that doesn't work, several of them may be willing to put the sequence together.

Clearly, the major issue here is the so-far unstated history of the abuse. Faye, as the host personality, knows that dissociative identity disorder is associated with a history of childhood abuse. The Faye part has not yet been willing to talk about any of what happened, although she has flashbacks of sexual abuse by her father and remembers her mother's telling her to "stop crying." Other parts of Faye's internal system may have the cognitive distortion that Faye can't handle knowing. Indeed, she could not handle it as a child; that's the psychological purpose of defensive dissociation from the trauma.

This is all information to be shared in a psychoeducational confrontation, acknowledging the survival skills used by Faye's internal system and the wisdom of not overwhelming Faye with all the trauma history at once. The art of this therapy work is the pacing. Would her system now support Faye in knowing some of her history more clearly, so that a wise decision can be made about the parents' visit? Faye will also get support from the entire staff.

With luck, the internal system will be able to let Blade come out to talk in the safety of the hospital. Blade may come out roaring and cursing, but this is his "hello." The goal is to facilitate negotiation. Blade is sick of the child parts' crying, so they need to have internal safe places. If an art therapy group is available, I would ask the art therapist for some assistance in working on a picture of safe places for the children. Dissociative clients often generate rich internal imagery and can use this skill in recovery. The teenage helpers might find it easier to comfort the child parts in playrooms with pillows, toys, and rocking chairs. If the child parts stop crying, will Blade agree to a safety contract? Blade might also ask wisely for the parents to stop stirring things up.

There is long-term therapy work to be done, but it is surprising how much can be accomplished in a few strategic sessions in the hospital. This might also be a place to start on Faye's negotiating with her family. Faye has to work on getting out of her regressive dependency role; the family has to stop enabling the role. What do her husband and children need? What does Faye need? Her husband might help in setting a boundary with the parents. Couples therapy might be recommended as part of the discharge plan.

When Faye has worked out a solid safety plan and contract with her therapist, she can be discharged to step-down in a partial program for a few weeks of structure, then to outpatient therapy. Her clinical course will probably be stormy, but we can hope it will be successful. Her prognosis improved a great deal when the correct diagnosis was made.

These six clinical vignettes, Anne through Faye, represent treatment examples of women survivors of childhood sexual abuse. These survivors suffer from multiple aftereffects of the abuse; all have diagnoses within the posttraumatic-dissociative disorder spectrum. Each woman client is presented in the midst of crisis, for which strategic interventions are applied therapeutically. These interventions are creatively drawn from the list of resources to resolve the crisis and stabilize the treatment frame, so that the therapy work can continue on an outpatient basis. This is not only a worthwhile economic goal but one that respects a survivor's autonomy.

All of us who work with women molested in childhood are familiar with crisis in the lives and therapy of these survivors. A therapeutic response to crisis is thoughtful and draws on the full range of clinical interventions. The intensity of the client's symptoms and the level of impairment must be matched with strategic interventions to manage the crisis and stabilize the client as rapidly and economically as possible. I hope these clinical vignettes of clients within the post-traumatic-dissociative disorder spectrum are helpful as examples of this creative, problem-solving approach to crisis.

NOTES

P. 35, *clinical vignettes:* This and the following clinical vignettes do not represent any specific client but are a creative composite, based on the clinical experience of the author, to demonstrate specific problems and interventions.

P. 37, *symptomatology of the . . . spectrum of adult survivors:* Courtois, C. A. (1988). *Healing the incest wound: Adult survivors in therapy.* New York: Norton; Briere, J. N. (1992). *Child abuse trauma: Theory and treatment of the lasting effects.* Newbury Park, CA: Sage.

P. 37, *concomitant medical problems:* Laws, A. (1993). Does a history of sexual abuse in childhood play a role in women's medical problems? A review. *Journal of Women's Health, 2,* 165–172.

P. 37, *criteria for six or seven DSM-IV diagnoses:* American Psychiatric Association. (1994). *Diagnostic and statistical manual of mental disorders* (4th ed.). Washington, DC: Author.

P. 37, *Karpman Drama Triangle:* Karpman, S. (1968). Fairy tales and script drama analysis. *Transactional Analysis Bulletin, 7,* 39–43.

P. 38, *revictimized . . . by rape or battering:* Russell, D. (1986). *The secret trauma: Incest in the lives of girls and women.* New York: Basic Books.

P. 38, *internalization of the "badness":* Finkelhor, D., & Browne, A. (1985). Traumatic impact of child sexual abuse: A conceptualization. *American Journal of Orthopsychiatry, 5*(4), 530–541.

P. 38, *modern thought emphasizes the desire for mastery:* Herman, J. L. (1992). *Trauma and recovery.* New York: Basic Books.

P. 38, *The psychobiology of trauma . . . "addiction to trauma":* van der Kolk, B. A. (1987). *Psychological trauma.* Washington, DC: American Psychiatric Press.

P. 40, *"self work before memory work":* McCann, I. L., & Pearlman, L. A. (1990). *Psychological trauma and the adult survivor.* New York: Brunner/Mazel.

P. 40, *secondary trauma (vicarious traumatization):* McCann, I. L., & Pearlman, L. A. (1990). Vicarious traumatization: A contextual model for understanding the effects of trauma on helpers. *Journal of Traumatic Stress, 3,* 131–149.

P. 40, *neutral stance with regard to memory:* American Psychiatric Association (1993). *Statement on memories of sexual abuse.* Washington, DC: Author.

P. 42, *"strives to bring order . . . function during treatment":* Turkus, J. A. (1991). Psychotherapy and case management for multiple personality disorder. *Psychiatric Clinics of North America, 14,* p. 649.

P. 43, *particularly art therapy:* Johnson, D. R. (1987). The role of the creative arts therapies in the diagnosis and treatment of psychological trauma. *Arts in Psychotherapy, 14,* 7–13.

P. 45, *trauma field . . . psychotropic medication:* van der Kolk, B. A., & Saporta, J. (1993). Biological response to psychic trauma. In J. P. Wilson & B. Raphael (Eds.), *International handbook of traumatic stress syndromes* (pp. 25–33). New York: Plenum Press; Friedman, M. J. (1993). Psychobiological and pharmacological approaches to treatment. In Wilson, J. P., & Raphael, B. (Eds.), *International handbook of traumatic stress syndromes* (pp. 785–794). New York: Plenum Press.

P. 45, *empirical study . . . best choice of a benzodiazepine:* Loewenstein, R. J., Hornstein, N., & Farber, B. (1988). Open trial of clonazepam in the treatment of posttraumatic stress symptoms in MPD. *Dissociation, 1,* 3–12.

3

INDIVIDUAL PSYCHOTHERAPY

Mary R. Harvey and Patricia A. Harney

ANNIE

Annie is a forty-two-year-old married woman, a successful freelance artist and the mother of three children: Sam, who is eleven; Amy, nine; and Jimmy, four. She and her husband Jeff have been married thirteen years. Three-and-a-half years ago, Annie entered psychotherapy, saying to the therapist, "I need to deal with my history." That history includes a prolonged period of sexual abuse by the stepfather who married her mother when Annie was six, adopted Annie and her sister shortly thereafter, and began molesting her almost immediately. The abuse continued until Annie left home for college. She never really returned. Instead, she moved out of state, made her own way, and finally met and married Jeff, visiting her family rarely and briefly. For many years, Annie was able to distract herself from painful remembrances of her past.

Today, Annie has begun the process of termination. She is saying goodbye to the therapy and contemplating her future with optimism. As she and her therapist look back on their work, Annie is acknowledging the fact of her recovery and the role of psychotherapy in her recovery process.

This chapter considers the process of individual psychotherapy with women who were sexually abused in childhood. It examines the varied presentations that adult survivors bring to psychotherapy and considers the challenges to connection and recovery that arise in the clinical context. It looks at what Annie and other patients "do" in psychotherapy and uses their experiences to illustrate a theoretical framework for conducting psychotherapy with adult survivors of childhood trauma. Cornerstones of this framework include (1) an "ecological" view of psychological trauma, (2) a multidimensional definition of recovery from trauma, and (3) a "stages by dimension" view of treatment and recovery.

THE PSYCHOLOGICAL IMPACT OF CHILDHOOD SEXUAL ABUSE

A starting point for any discussion of psychotherapy with adult survivors is a consideration of the psychological effects of childhood victimization. These effects are variable and wide-ranging.

Many child victims and a significant proportion of adult survivors of childhood sexual abuse develop symptoms of posttraumatic stress disorder (PTSD). These symptoms include intrusive recollections, severely restricted or intensely experienced and labile affects, hypervigilance, sleep disturbances, and both nightmares and waking-state "flashbacks" in which salient aspects of the abuse are relived. PTSD symptoms may also include intense feelings of guilt, shame, and self-blame; a numbed responsiveness to the outside world, and a sense of isolation and existential separateness. Children who have been sexually abused may exhibit these symptoms immediately following an abuse incident. Adult survivors may become symptomatic many years later, often in response to developmental challenges and relational events that serve as triggers of traumatic remembrance.

Annie arrived at psychotherapy exhibiting multiple symptoms of decades-delayed posttraumatic stress disorder. For many years, she had successfully distanced herself from the past. She married Jeff and, after the birth of their first child, her life seemed particularly good. Amy's birth was a different story. A difficult and prolonged labor reintroduced Annie to a long-forgotten feeling of profound physical and emotional helplessness. The experience left her determined to exert control over her third pregnancy. When Jimmy was born and Annie had delivered exactly as she'd wanted to, something shifted for her. Later, she confided to her therapist: "I think it was the first time in my life that I took charge of my own body. I'll never forget it. And I'll never forget how different it was for me to feel in control."

Annie felt "triumphant" about Jimmy's birth. Psychologically, however, things had changed dramatically. She began remembering the many occasions on which she had felt no control. Nightmares, flashbacks, and fearful remembrances of the abuse intruded upon her consciousness with incredible intensity. She jumped at the slightest sound, had difficulty sleeping, and felt constantly afraid. Amy had just turned six years old—the age Annie was when her stepfather's abuse began. When she thought of the possibility of someone hurting Amy, Annie would feel a level of rage that startled and frightened her. She felt enraged with her stepfather and wondered where her mother had been at the time. She thought about finding a lawyer and suing her stepfather. One evening while driving home from a friend's, Annie became so flooded with her memories and fears that she parked her car, crawled into the backseat and curled up frozen in fear for hours. The next day, she decided to enter psychotherapy.

PTSD, as experienced by Annie and other survivors, is not the only long-term result of childhood sexual trauma. Early, prolonged, and repeated exposure to sexual violence has been linked to adolescent and adult histories of substance abuse, depression, suicidality, and self-mutilation, and to an intolerance of intimacy and an inability to negotiate and maintain safety in relationships. Aberrations of memory and consciousness are also relatively common among adult survivors, as are patterns of revictimization and diagnoses of multiple and borderline personality disorder. Judith Herman has proposed the diagnosis of "complex PTSD" to distinguish the sequelae of prolonged and repetitive trauma from classic PTSD. These sequelae include a multiplicity of somatic, dissociative, and affective symptoms, profound limitations in identity formation and self-representation, and severe disturbances in relational capacities. The following cases illustrate the wide range of presentations adult survivors may bring with them to psychotherapy.

JACKIE

Jackie is a twenty-seven-year-old single woman who recently completed her master's degree in economics. Throughout her academic career she has been involved in a series of stormy relationships with lovers, faculty, including faculty who became lovers, friends, and family members (including an alcoholic, manic-depressive father, passive mother, and extraordinarily abusive older brother). Jackie has a history of alcoholic drinking and episodic cutting. On occasion, she has made good use of twelve-step programs. Recently she has become preoccupied and flooded with memories of violent sexual assault by her brother. She's begun to attend a leaderless self-help group for incest survivors and through this network is looking for a woman therapist who "won't be overwhelmed by me," "can relate to me as a real person," and "will help me deal with the abuse." Jackie recently ended a relationship with her latest lover—a forty-three-year-old divorced man (and former professor) who is intensely jealous. Beneath her tough and flamboyant exterior, one senses a very vulnerable core. It is clear that Jackie is afraid.

Jackie's presentation is stormy and provocative. Her functioning in the world and her ability to make use of her considerable intellect is undermined by her impulsive, often self-harming and self-destructive behavior. Other survivors may enter psychotherapy with a much higher level of functioning, yet be plagued by inner worlds that are fragmented and chaotic. The next vignette describes a woman whose dissociative construction of self is masked by her impressive career accomplishments.

JULIA

Julia is a thirty-three-year-old African-American woman who attended college on scholarship, earned an M.B.A. in record time, and now earns a six-figure income as an area manager in a multinational corporation. At work, she is seen as a highly competent administrator who is close-mouthed about her personal life. Julia entered therapy shortly after being informed by her boss that she was a likely candidate for the first corporate vice-presidency to be offered to a minority woman (and the second to be offered a woman). After receiving this news, Julia barely made it to her office before becoming engulfed by panic. Later that night, she was awakened by nightmares. In the morning, she realized that she had been experiencing panic and having nightmares a lot lately.

Julia was born in the South to unmarried parents who were fourteen and sixteen years old when she was born. She was brought up at various times by her mother, her mother and father, their parents and, finally, by an aunt in Boston. In childhood, Julia both witnessed and suffered extreme physical and sexual violence. She was once beaten savagely by her mother for protecting a younger brother, and at eleven was raped by her father when he learned she'd been molested by an elderly white neighbor. It was after this incident that Julia's grandmothers arranged for her move to Boston where her aunt, a single woman employed as a school secretary, offered Julia a safe home and a model of economic self-sufficiency. She was determined not to burden Julia with talk about the past. Thus she never knew that Julia experienced herself "in parts": that Julia could look in the mirror and see someone else, that at times she wouldn't know who or where she was, or that sometimes Julia was quiet because she was searching for "the part that could talk to people" or, later, for "the part that could have sex without feeling it." After awhile, Julia stopped knowing it too.

Julia arrives at psychotherapy terrified by a new and growing awareness of the complex organization of her inner life. She is fearful that her impressive achievements may be at least partially founded on a now-dissolving amnesia for much of her childhood and on a now-compromised ability to wall off memories and awareness of the abuse. Other survivors, even those with relatively complete and continuous recall of childhood abuse experiences, may consciously or unconsciously recreate elements of their trauma history in their current life. The next presentation depicts a woman who finds herself reenacting elements of the traumatic script.

SONIA

Sonia is a thirty-two-year-old married woman. She is the mother of two children: an eleven-year-old son, Trevor, and a seven-year-old daughter, Christy. Sonia met her husband Mark when she was a freshman and he a senior at the local high school. They married as soon as she graduated and have been married for fifteen years.

Sonia and Mark like, respect, and care about one another. Nonetheless, their sexual relationship is emotionally painful and complicated for them both—with Sonia often being disinterested when Mark is interested, and both of them often disappointed after they make love. They attempted couple's therapy once, but did not find it helpful. Sonia has now inquired about individual psychotherapy for herself. She is still confused about her marriage, and deeply ashamed of the fact that throughout her marriage she has almost always had another lover. Since marrying Mark, and particularly since becoming a mother, Sonia has found it increasingly difficult to enjoy her sex life with Mark. Things are better when she initiates, but when she does so her motive is often guilt or a panicked sense that she might finally lose him.

In inquiring about psychotherapy, Sonia reports this material haltingly. Finally, she "wonders" to the new therapist if the duplicitous life she has been leading might not have "something to do with" the fact that her father had sexually abused her from a young age (perhaps as young as five or six) until she left high school to marry. The abuse included fondling and molestation in early childhood, and oral and vaginal intercourse from the time Sonia was twelve. What Sonia knows now is that she feels she cannot continue to live a lie. For two years she has been having memories of abuse that she never before "named" abuse and her reactions to these memories are deeply troubling.

Annie, Jackie, Julia, and Sonia illustrate the variety of clinical presentations that adult survivors of childhood sexual abuse bring to psychotherapy and the range of posttraumatic response and recovery patterns they may exhibit in their daily lives. Effective psychotherapy with adult survivors begins with a clinical assessment that takes into account the full complexity of individual lives and the interplay of person, event, and environment factors that underlie individual adaptations to childhood trauma.

AN ECOLOGICAL VIEW OF PSYCHOLOGICAL TRAUMA

Ecology is the science concerned with the interrelationship of living things and their environments. Within the field of community psychology, the "ecological analogy" suggests that psychological attributes of human beings are best understood in the ecological context of human community. The perspective recognizes that human behavior is multidetermined by the complex interrelationship of individuals and the communities from which they draw their identity, belongingness, and meaning. Applying these constructs to the phenomenon of psychological trauma, the ecological model presented in Figure 3.1 suggests that interactions among person, event, and environmental factors define the individual-community relationship and form for each survivor, a unique and changing context for adaptation to and recovery from childhood sexual abuse. The ecological model anticipates wide variations in individual response to childhood sexual abuse and equally wide variations in the clinical presentations of adult survivors who may seek psychotherapy.

Annie, for example, arrived at psychotherapy exhibiting PTSD symptoms after many years of effective occupational and social functioning. Jackie, on the other hand, has almost never been free of emotional distress and self-destructive impulses. Despite impressive intellectual gifts, she arrives at psychotherapy with a multitude of difficulties that challenge her safety in the here and now. Julia's adaptation to a particularly violent history is expressed in a remarkable contrast between the organization, continuity, and accomplishment of her external life and the chaos, fragmentation, and sense of powerlessness that are hallmarks of her inner world. Sonia enters psychotherapy relating her duplicitous relational life and her difficulties with sexual and physical intimacy to a childhood history of secrecy and violation.

The ecological model presented in Figure 3.1 also acknowledges that not all (or even a majority of) sexual trauma survivors will access

Figure 3.1
An Ecological Model of Psychological Trauma

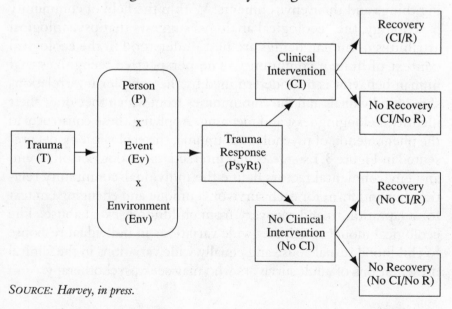

SOURCE: *Harvey, in press.*

and utilize clinical care. In fact, the majority will not. Few victims of childhood sexual abuse receive timely and appropriate care in childhood and many never seek treatment in adulthood. Those who do enter psychotherapy do so as the result of changing ecological circumstances, with different degrees of comfort and familiarity with professional care and psychiatric intervention and with or without the aid and encouragement of key support figures.

Much in Annie's ecosystem facilitated her access to clinical care. Her husband Jeff wanted Annie to seek professional help. Annie's closest friends include women and men who have made use of psychotherapy and who were able to offer her appropriate referrals. Annie and Jeff live in a community that is rich in clinical resources. She was able to interview a number of therapists before choosing the one that was right for her. Jackie's route to psychotherapy is more complicated. She is used to using twelve-step programs and self-help groups. She has long masked her discomfort with her father's erratic behavior and volatile emotional state with contempt for traditional clinical practice and an aversion to psychiatric medication. As she searches for a woman therapist who can be a "real person," she is likely to avoid more traditionally trained providers and to opt instead for alternative caregivers. Sonia's working-class origins and a not-so-helpful prior experience with couples therapy will combine with a paucity of clinical resources in her home community to complicate her search for a helpful psychotherapy. Julia's deep sense of privacy and her reticence to rely on white caretakers will interact with the limited availability of African-American therapists in her area to make her search complicated as well.

A third assumption of the ecological model is that clinical care in the aftermath of trauma is no guarantee of recovery. Indeed, any of four recovery outcomes is possible:

1. Ideally, psychotherapy will interact with other ecological influences to foster the survivor's recovery.

2. An ecologically ill-informed treatment may prove ineffective and actually impede recovery.

3. Recovery in the absence of clinical intervention is also possible, particularly when the naturally occurring ecosystem is supportive of resilience and repair and when the interrelationship of community and individual is positive. This is especially likely in the case of single incident traumatic events and may be more common among children whose abuse was perpetrated by someone outside the family system.

4. Finally, in the absence of clinical intervention, some individuals will not recover. As therapists consider the challenge of working effectively with those survivors who do seek treatment, they need also to be mindful of the need for public education activities and community resources that may ultimately lead currently untreated individuals to appropriate care.

THE ECOLOGICAL MODEL AS A GUIDE TO CLINICAL ASSESSMENT

The ecological model provides a framework for initial and ongoing clinical assessment. In this model, a wide variety of person, event, and environmental factors are understood to influence individual adaptations to childhood sexual abuse. Among these are some variables that clinicians routinely attend to in their assessment of client needs and others that they often neglect or ignore, including person variables, event factors, and environmental factors.

Person variables influencing posttraumatic response and recovery include, for example, the survivor's age and developmental stage at the time of the abuse, the severity of her initial distress, and the relationship (if any) between child victim and offender. Also important are the intelligence, creativity, vulnerabilities (such as physical or mental disabilities), and pre-traumatic coping capabilities of the survivor as child, an assessment of the adult survivor's mood, affect, personality, and coping style, and any number of demographic attributes (such as race, ethnicity and socioeconomic class). These variables are noted by most experienced clinicians and often figure significantly in diagnostic determinations and clinical formulations.

Ecologically significant person variables that may receive too little attention in traditional approaches to clinical assessment include the survivor's culturally based understanding of the experience of childhood victimization, her comfort and familiarity with various kinds of care, and the modeling of hope, tenacity, and resilience that may or may not have been provided by family, friends, and other significant figures. These are the persons and person attributes that help to define a victim's ecological relationship with the larger community and serve as important sources of strength and resilience. An effective psychotherapy will recognize these ecological sources of resiliency and will make use of a survivor's strengths.

Annie exhibited her artistic talents very early in life. Once her stepfather began molesting her, Annie used her imaginative skills to envision other realities. She learned to convert pain and unhappiness into a drawing or painting that would express her feelings without breaking her silence. Later, in psychotherapy, Annie often used drawing as a first step in sharing her history with her therapist.

Jackie, Julia, and Sonia will also bring strengths to the process of psychotherapy—strengths that arise out of the person attributes that define the ecology of their lives and histories. In Julia's case, for example, two concerned grandmothers arranged for her escape from a violent home. Her aunt in Boston then provided Julia with an experience of stability and a model of economic self-sufficiency that may have allowed her academic and career performance to flourish. Together these women also provided relational experiences that will enable Julia to develop trust and hope, capacities that she and her therapist will call upon as they work to establish and maintain a healing and helpful therapeutic alliance.

Event factors describe salient attributes of the sexual abuse the survivor experienced in childhood. Relevant variables include, for example, the frequency, severity, and duration of the abuse; the degree of physical violence and personal bodily violation that was inflicted; and whether the victim experienced the trauma alone or in the company of others. Ecologically relevant event factors also include any number of details to which the individual victim and his or her communities of reference may assign significance. We should not judge in advance what is or might have been the most traumatizing part of a patient's experience. Psychotherapists must listen for the subtleties, nuances, and idiosyncratic social constructions of the experience that provide insight into the survivor's unique response and adaptation.

Annie realizes now that for her one of the most difficult and shaming aspects of her experience was her silent compliance. If and when Jackie settles into a productive psychotherapy, she will confront the reality that early in childhood she often sought comfort and attention from the brother who abused her and who later terrorized and blamed her for his own actions. Julia, on the other hand, will contend with the extremity of the violence to which she was exposed. And Sonia will recall with enormous sadness the ways in which she tried —and failed— to make her father's abusive behavior known to her mother. Whatever these women have in common, each will revisit aspects of her experience that contributed in very particular ways to her understanding of and adaptation to childhood sexual abuse.

Environmental factors influencing a survivor's understanding of and response to childhood sexual abuse are many. They include the ecological context within which the traumatic events were experienced (such as the home, school, workplace, neighborhood, or other context); salient attributes of the victim's natural support system; the ability of that system to foster adaptive rather than maladaptive coping strategies; the degree of safety, credibility, and control afforded the child who was able to disclose; and the responsiveness of those who comprise an adult survivor's community of reference. Environmental factors of particular importance in an ecological framework include prevailing community attitudes and values, cultural constructions of race and gender, political and economic factors affecting the individual's vulnerability to victimization and access to care, and the nature, quality, and cultural relevance of victim services.

As Annie looks back on the environment in which she was abused, she recalls her mother's insistence that Annie's stepfather had replaced her father and that Annie and her sister show him the love and respect that a father deserved. She also recalls growing up in the South where everyone she knew went to church and where children were admonished to honor and obey their parents. It was not an environment that encouraged disclosure. Annie also remembers the role that school played in her life. Particularly, she remembers the teachers who encouraged her to develop her artistic abilities. Annie's creativity offered her a way to compartmentalize and survive sexual abuse. It also gave her a direction to pursue in college and later, in work.

Julia, Jackie, and Sonia, too, will also examine the environmental influences on their adaptations to abuse. Like Annie, Julia will recall growing up in the South and the roles that poverty, racism, and religious belief may have played in her early life. She will recall her aunt's readiness to help Julia "forget" the past. In the course of a helpful psychotherapy, Jackie will come to terms with the chaotic and alcoholic world into which she was born and with the extent to which family, friends, and almost everyone who comprised her early "support system" made alcohol and drugs available to her for "coping." She will look at the role of schooling as well and will remember that she grew up in a world where girls were supposed to hide their competencies. Even today Jackie is extremely ambivalent about her graduate school career and is often particularly self-deprecating about her intelligence.

Sonia will examine how separate the worlds of home and school were for her: how school provided a haven from the home life she dreaded, how school served as a "theater" for her pretense of a happy and caring family, and how the duplicity she lived for survival's sake then became the trap from which she is trying to extricate herself now. Each woman will look to the environment of her childhood for an understanding of the past; and each will look to the environment of her adulthood for a pathway to recovery and a way of making use of the psychotherapy she is offered.

The ecological model reminds us that a full exploration of person, event, and environmental influences and their interaction is essential to clinical assessment and thus to effective psychotherapy. Equally essential to effective treatment is a view of recovery that can give content and direction to the work.

ESTABLISHING TREATMENT GOALS: A MULTIDIMENSIONAL VIEW OF RECOVERY

In recognizing the complex ways in which person, event, and environmental factors interact to shape individually unique adaptations to childhood sexual abuse, the ecological model acknowledges the many ways in which adult survivors may evince resiliency, and the need for psychotherapy to interact with other ecological influences in order to facilitate recovery. In this model, recovery from sexual victimization is not limited to the absence of symptoms. Rather, a multidimensional view of recovery emerges, displaying as hallmarks the following outcome criteria.

Authority over the Remembering Process

A primary sign of recovery from the trauma of childhood victimization—and therefore a primary aim of treatment—is that the survivor develop new or renewed authority over the remembering process. Whatever their diagnoses, adult survivors of childhood trauma are often plagued both by the absence of salient information about their histories and by traumatic intrusions which disable and terrify even as they elude meaningful appraisal. The clinical vignettes presented earlier illustrate the many ways in which early exposure to sexual violation can wreak havoc with the adult survivor's ability to recall and make use of her history.

Jackie vacillates between chasing after memories that then destabilize her and seeking escape from traumatic remembrances in alcohol, drugs, and dangerous relationships. On the eve of entering psychotherapy, Julia is only beginning to understand and recognize the extent of her amnesia and the internal structure that enables that amnesia. And Sonia finds herself reenacting elements of her past. Each woman is at times plagued by nightmares, flashbacks, and intrusive remembrances of a past from which she has consciously or unconsciously sought distance. None has "authority" over what and how she remembers.

In contrast, the recovered survivor is able to choose to recall or not recall events that previously intruded unbidden into awareness, taking the form of frightening dreams or troubling flashbacks. In recovery, the amnestic aftermath of trauma is repaired. The balance of power between the survivor and her memories is reversed and she is able to call upon and review a relatively complete and continuous life narrative.

As Annie prepares to leave psychotherapy, her memories no longer take the form of flashbacks, nightmares, and intrusive thoughts. She remembers her experience and she has examined and remembered the context in which the abuse by her stepfather occurred. She is able to recall childhood experiences when she needs or wants to, and she is able to put thoughts of these experiences away when she chooses. She has placed the past in the past.

Integration of Memory and Affect

In the wake of one or a prolonged series of traumatic experiences, some victims will have clear memories of the events yet feel little or nothing as they recall these events. Others may feel waves of terror, anxiety, or rage in response to specific stimuli yet be unable to draw meaningful associations between these affects and their past or present precipitants. In both cases, memory and feeling are separate.

Sonia never forgot the occasions on which her father abused her, but her memories of these occasions have been held separately from her feelings. If she is able to review her past with the support of a safe therapist, an important goal of the treatment will be to revisit and recall the feelings that accompanied the abuse. Another goal will be to discover whatever feelings she may have about that experience as an adult. Similarly, an effective psychotherapy with Julia will not only help her remember the terror she felt when her father assaulted her, but it will also help her discover her anger and her sadness as she looks back.

In recovery from psychological trauma, memory and affect are joined. The past is remembered with feeling and memories of the past are linked both with feelings *from* the past and with contemporary feelings *about* the past.

Thus, Annie's remembrance of her stepfather's abuse has come to include remembrances of the affects and bodily states she experienced at the time—the fear, the frozen numbness, and the sense of powerless, inarticulate rage that washed over her and kept her still. Equally important, Annie has access to contemporary feelings about the past. She can feel profound sadness when she thinks about her experience as a child and she can feel and express her adult sense of outrage at her stepfather's exploitation of her.

Affect Tolerance

Recovery from psychological trauma implies that the affects associated with traumatic events no longer overwhelm or threaten to overwhelm the survivor. Feelings linked to the trauma have been deprived of their terrible immediacy and fierce intensity. They can be felt, named, and endured without overwhelming arousal, defensive numbing, or dissociation. In recovery, the survivor is relieved of undue alarm and dangerous impulse. Feelings are differentiated from one another and are experienced in varying degrees of intensity, reflecting a more measured response to traumatic recall and a greater capacity to manage contemporary stressors.

It has been a long time since Annie felt overwhelmed and out of control. She knows what she feels; she is able to feel her feelings in varying degrees and she is able to make productive and important use of her feelings as well. At one time, Annie would have avoided any form of "good-bye" to anyone she cared about. If she allowed herself to feel a sense of loss, the feeling could escalate into an overwhelming sense of despair and abandonment. It would have been easier and simpler to laugh off the loss or just disappear. Today, she is saying good-bye to her therapist, and allowing herself to feel the mixture of sadness and pride that this good-bye means.

On the eve of psychotherapy, as she goes from therapist to therapist and from group to group, Jackie knows little of affect tolerance. She is at constant risk of cutting herself and of drinking whenever she feels anxious. Her anxiety is diminished once she cuts, drinks, or uses drugs, but in doing so she deprives herself of important information about her emotional state.

Is she scared? Is she angry? Her anxiety blends these affects together. As she learns to tolerate her anxiety she will also learn to distinguish and tolerate the affects that so easily overwhelm her now. Affect tolerance is essential to safe and informed action. Until she can distinguish one feeling from the other and until she is able to experience each feeling in a range that can guide and inform her behavior, Jackie's safety will be impaired and her recovery impeded.

Symptom Mastery

In recovery, PTSD symptoms have abated or been rendered more manageable. Stimuli that serve as triggers for flashbacks, intrusive thoughts, or intense anxiety reactions are known, can be anticipated, and sometimes may be avoided. The recovered survivor may still experience symptomatic arousal, but she has learned and makes use of specific healthful routines to cope with and manage such arousal.

In order to manage her symptoms of fear, hypervigilance, and startle, Annie has learned to avoid particularly distressing stimuli (such as violent films) and she has mastered specific stress management techniques that help her contain her anxiety in the face of contemporary stressors. She exercises regularly and regularly practices meditation. She knows how to soothe herself and she knows when she is vulnerable.

The emphasis in symptom mastery is not on the abolishment of all symptoms, but on maximizing the survivor's ability to anticipate, prevent, manage, and contain symptomatic distress. Achieving symptom mastery may entail augmenting psychotherapy with adjunctive interventions.

In Jackie's case the goal of symptom management may be most achievable through a combination of psychotherapy and medication. Her family history is riddled with depression, suicidality, bipolar illness, and polysubstance abuse. Jackie's episodic drinking and drugging are suggestive of attempts at self-medication. These factors suggest that psychiatric medication could be helpful. However, Jackie will resist pharmacotherapy and any diagnosis that implies the need for it. In psychotherapy she will need to develop an investment in recovery that can help her take a different stance.

Self-Esteem and Self-Cohesion

Even single incidents of sexual abuse can have a devastating impact on a victim's sense of self and self-worth. Early victimization and prolonged and repeated exposure to sexual violation have been associated with severe identity disturbances, including a discontinuous and fragmented experience of self and the sense of oneself as fundamentally evil and deserving of harm. Recovery from psychological trauma thus entails repair and mastery in the domain of self-esteem and self-cohesion. The process requires a mastery over self-injurious behaviors and impulses and a replacement of these with healthful, self-caring routines.

In recovery, feelings of guilt, shame, and self-blame are examined and relinquished in favor of a new or newly restored sense of self-worth. Obsessive and self-critical review of the past is replaced by more realistic appraisal. The result of self-exploration and review is a more informed and coherent sense of self and an essentially positive view of self—as one deserving of care, for example, and as one capable of leading a self-caring, self-fulfilling existence.

Over the past three years, Annie has revisited the contempt she felt for herself as she adapted to her stepfather's demands. She has remembered how as a child she would pinch herself just before going to sleep and she has looked again at the ugly, self-hating pictures she once drew of herself. She has recalled her shy withdrawal during her elementary school years, the sexual acting out of her high school and college years, and the sense of self-hate that motivated both kinds of behavior.

Gradually, and with considerable effort, she has reviewed and acknowledged not only the many ways in which she once felt undeserving of care but also all that she did to cope with and survive her experience: how she used her creativity to transform her pain, how she tried—usually with success—to extend some measure of protection to her younger sister, and how she got away once she could get away. She has learned that she was not to blame for the abuse and she has learned to treat herself and her history with respect. She takes time for herself. As she extends care to her husband and children, she expects and anticipates that they will be caring toward her as well. A triumph of this therapy is that today Annie truly likes herself.

Sexual violation is an assault on the integrity and value of the self. In an effective psychotherapy, each survivor will cover the ground that Annie has covered and will chart a unique pathway to self-regard and self-cohesion.

Jackie's pathway will require that she learn to manage her many self-injurious impulses and that she replace self-harming behaviors with self-soothing ones. Getting and staying sober, controlling her impulses to cut, and taking action to ensure and safeguard her physical safety are the foundations on which Jackie can begin to construct self-esteem.

Julia's academic and career accomplishments express in her external life a sense of competence and mastery that is at complete odds with her internal sense of self. Consequently, Julia has never been able to internalize these accomplishments as her own. Instead, she has experienced herself as a fraud, someone not really as capable as she appears, someone not really deserving of the accolades she's received. Indeed, the harder she works and the more she accomplishes, the less authentic and the more panicked Julia feels. Her complex organization of self has served both to wall off her remembrances of brutal violence and to compartmentalize aspects of self that must now work together. At least one of Julia's many "parts" or personalities is able to observe what is happening to her and is able to take self-caring, self-protective action. Julia's first step to recovery lies in recognizing that the adaptations of her childhood no longer serve her well. Her recovery will be marked both by a sense of satisfaction and pride in achievements that are hers and hers alone and by the experience of herself as one self: multifaceted, yes; divided, no.

Sonia's self-esteem rests on her ability to disengage from the duplicitous sexual existence that has characterized most of her married life. An effective psychotherapy will help her to examine the sense of shame and self-blame that connects the life of secrecy imposed on her as a child to the life of secrecy she has repeatedly chosen for herself as an adult. As Sonia revisits her past, she will learn the many sources of her shame.

She will remember, for example, the day she knew that the price of a new sweater would be a nighttime visit from her father. She was thirteen; she wanted the sweater; she knew what it would cost her; and she thought to herself, "So, what's the big deal? It's just one more night like all the rest." In fact, she was wrong. That night proved to Sonia what she had long suspected: namely, that she was the one responsible for the abuse, not her father.

In psychotherapy, Sonia will look again at this and many other days and nights of her childhood. She will also look closely at the life she is leading today. As she takes control of her choices now and learns to live a life free of duplicity and deceit today, she will also be able to free herself from shame and finally to transfer responsibility for the abuse from herself to her father.

Safe Attachment

Self-imposed isolation from others and revictimization by them are for many survivors the polar consequences of trauma. Child sexual abuse entails a fundamental betrayal of trust that undermines the survivor's ability to develop and pursue feelings of safe and stable connectedness to others. Repeated abuse sorely compromises the ability to negotiate personal safety in relational contexts. In recovery from psychological trauma, these ruptures in relational capacities are repaired. The pull to isolation and detachment is replaced by a new or renewed capacity for trust and attachment. The recovered survivor is also able to negotiate and maintain safety in relationships with others and can view the possibility of intimate connectedness with hope and optimism.

Annie entered psychotherapy with many relational strengths. In retrospect, she sees that these strengths "saved" her. She attributes them to the caretaking she received—particularly from her biological father and her paternal grandmother—during her first five years. Later, after her stepfather was on the scene, Annie remembers comforting herself with images of her real father's smile and with remembrances of her grandmother's affection. These relationships offered Annie a means of envisioning caring relationships and supported the hope that she would someday leave home and construct a different kind of relational world for herself.

It was the sudden, inexplicable loss of these early relationships that devastated Annie and left her wary. While she always had at least one really good friend whose family provided an alternative to her own, she often held herself aloof from "too much" involvement. She also often attracted the interest of teachers who recognized her gifts and who responded to her need for encouragement. In psychotherapy, Annie used her relational strengths to develop a healing relationship with her therapist. She also relinquished much of her aloofness in favor of engagement and learned when and how to set aside her wariness in favor of trust.

Unlike Annie, Jackie will enter psychotherapy with little in the way of stable, safe, and nurturant caretaking in childhood. Jackie's father was out of control for much of her childhood. Her mother failed to protect

Jackie or any of her siblings from his violence and was totally unable to protect herself. Jackie's brother did offer her some degree of comfort until he began abusing her mercilessly. The violence and chaos of Jackie's family life left her totally unprepared to negotiate safety in a relationship. Consequently, Jackie's romantic career has involved one chaotic and violent relationship after another. If psychotherapy is to be effective with Jackie, it will need to provide her with a model of safety in relationship that she does not now have.

Establishing New Meaning

In recovery, the adult survivor will review and assign new meaning to the trauma of childhood sexual abuse, to the self as trauma survivor, and to the world in which child abuse occurs and recurs. Making meaning of childhood trauma is a deeply personal and highly idiosyncratic process.

Some individuals, as they discard the sense of a damaged self, will embrace instead the belief that misfortune endured can enhance personal strength and compassion. Others will renegotiate family relationships—grieving those that must be grieved, embracing and pursuing those that remain—and will assume a new, more genuine, and more empowered role in the family system. Still others will transform their personal experience into creative pursuit or determined social action—embracing a survivor mission as part of their recovery process. Whatever the process and its outcome, the recovered survivor will have named and mourned the traumatic past and imbued it with meaning that is both life-affirming and self-affirming.

Over the past three-and-a-half years, Annie has transformed her understanding of the abuse she suffered and has revisited many of the meanings she once made of her experience. Annie always hated herself for being compliant, for example, and saw in her passivity some responsibility for the abuse that began when she was six. She realizes now that as a child she understood "adoption" to mean that her stepfather had "bought" her, that her father had "sold" her, and that she had no right to resist any of her stepfather's demands. By the time she had laid this belief aside, Annie's pattern of compliance was firmly established. For Annie, making meaning of her experience and transforming her early understandings has meant taking action—action to undo the passive compliance that became her adaptation to abuse and action to undo the adoption that ushered in a childhood of abuse. She entered psychotherapy with thoughts about legal action and at times intently contemplated suing her now aging stepfather. In the end, she chose another kind of legal action. After reestablishing a relationship with her biological father, she successfully petitioned the court for a nullification of her stepfather's adoption.

Annie's efforts to transform and make meaning of her experience illustrate the deeply personal nature of the process. Jackie, Julia, and Sonia each has before her the task of discovering her own capacity and her own approach to the challenge. The role of the therapist in this process is not to guide and not to direct but instead to support and to bear witness.

Each of the foregoing recovery criteria in fact reflects an entire domain of experience that may or may not have been affected by the experience of childhood sexual abuse. Resiliency is evident whenever one of these domains remains relatively unaffected by the trauma, and whenever strengths in one domain are brought to bear on the task of healing and repair in another. Recovery is apparent any time change from a poor outcome to a desired one is realized. Together these domains describe a complex and multifaceted definition of recovery from psychological trauma; they offer to clinician and survivor a set of benchmarks against which individual recovery can be assessed and toward which clinical and nonclinical interventions can aim. These benchmarks can prove crucial to effective psychotherapy, particularly in an era of managed care, when clinicians are increasingly asked to provide focused treatment organized around well-articulated and operationally defined treatment objectives.

STAGES BY DIMENSIONS OF RECOVERY: A FRAMEWORK FOR MULTIMODAL TREATMENT

Effective psychotherapy with adult survivors also requires sensitivity to issues of timing and readiness. In clarifying ecologically appropriate treatment objectives, the therapist must carefully assess an individual survivor's readiness to undertake particular kinds of recovery work and consider the dangers inherent in a premature and poorly paced recall of the traumatic past.

The process of healing from psychological trauma has been described as unfolding in three broad stages, with one kind of work and one set of treatment goals providing foundation for the next. Early in recovery, the emphasis in treatment is on securing safety, achieving stability, and fostering self-care. Only when safety and self-care are reliably established should the survivor embark upon the second stage, a process of reviewing, exploring, and integrating the traumatic past. In the third stage, exploration and integration give way to the pursuit of intimate connectedness and the negotiation and renegotiation of important relationships.

In this section, case material is utilized to illustrate a "stages by dimension" framework for conducting effective, multimodal psychotherapy with adult survivors of childhood trauma. This framework integrates the attention to issues of readiness and timing implied by a stages-of-recovery model with a multidimensional conceptualization of recovery.

Stage One: Safety, Stability, and Self-Care

The first stage of recovery emphasizes attention to issues of safety, stability, and self-care. In whatever domain and to whatever extent the survivor's safety and stability are at risk, treatment must focus on the present with the aim of helping the survivor gain understanding and develop mastery of impulses, behaviors, sensations, and experiences that compromise safety.

Jackie exemplifies the client whose presentation demands multidimensional attention to these "stage one" issues. Despite her overt wish to "confront the past," Jackie has achieved no "authority" over her remembering process. She is unable to integrate the feeling states from which she flees with the memories she sometimes doggedly pursues. Her flashbacks have become more frequent now that she is attending a leaderless survivors' group. Her affect tolerance is fragile at best; her symptomatic distress is extreme. Her self-care is compromised by impulses to self-harm that intensify as she becomes flooded with memories of past abuse. Her former lover, who is possessive and obsessed with her, has a history of domestic violence. In all respects, Jackie's safety is at risk.

Early recovery tasks in psychotherapy with trauma patients include helping the survivor gain mastery over impulses to self-harm, developing and maintaining sobriety, and replacing self-injurious behaviors with self-soothing strategies. Depending on the needs and ecological resources of the survivor, treatments of choice might also include medication to secure symptom relief, involvement in one or another twelve-step program, enrollment in a behaviorally oriented group, and residency in a safehouse or shelter.

Intensive individual psychotherapy that encourages an exploration of the traumatic past is contraindicated for Jackie. Indicated instead are highly structured cognitive and cognitive-behavioral interventions to help her better understand her symptoms, and stress-management and stress-reduction techniques to foster mastery over her anxiety. For Jackie, early stage work also involves securing physical safety from a jealous and violent lover.

Work at this stage of recovery need not be accomplished solely in the context of a long-term individual psychotherapy. Highly structured and time-limited biobehavioral interventions (such as relaxation training) and equally structured time-limited groups that focus not on review of the past but on securing and maintaining physical safety are particularly cost-effective treatments of choice. It is also important to note that once a survivor achieves safety and stabilization in her daily life, she may elect to discontinue treatment for some time before embarking on the kind of exploration that ought be done in the context of an individual psychotherapy. The stages-by-dimensions model of treatment emphasizes responsiveness and flexibility. This flexibility not only honors survivors' variant needs but also addresses the changing ecology of mental health benefits and coverage constraints.

Stage Two: Exploring and Integrating the Past

When safety has been established, treatment can turn to the tasks of exploring and integrating the traumatic past. Memory retrieval and integration are most productively accomplished in individual psychotherapy where early, often quite idiosyncratic understandings of the abuse can be examined and relinquished in favor of more realistic appraisals.

It is in this context of intense personal review that the survivor will come to understand the full impact of childhood sexual abuse on her sense of self and self-cohesion and on a wide variety of personal and relational accommodations to terror, grief, and ruptured trust. The purpose of the work is not solely to remember and is certainly not to relive the past. Rather, the aim is to place the past in the past and to understand—and if necessary overcome and redress—the role that past events have played in shaping one's present life. The work may include exploring the past to fill in and examine amnestic gaps, integrate traumatic affects and memories, and clarify the traumatic origins of dissociative states and impulsive, poorly understood behaviors.

Sonia's case illustrates the psychotherapeutic work that exploration of the past can entail. As she reviews the past and accesses the feelings that were shut off when the abuse was taking place, she will enhance her capacity to feel both the past and the present and to mend the splits between affect and cognition that now enable her to lead a compart-mentalized existence.

Sonia's work in individual psychotherapy might be productively augmented by a trauma-focused survivors group in which she can finally learn that she is not alone—either in her history or in her secret and divided adaptation to that history. The relational impact of trauma can be substantively repaired in the context of the group. The aim of group treatment at this stage is not to recover, relive, and share new memories of past horror, but to learn that they are not and need not be alone in the world, that their history has not placed them beyond the reach of human company, and that others can understand.

Before moving to a consideration of the therapeutic goals that predominate in the final recovery stage, it is important to reiterate that treatment needs to be defined within a framework that is ecologically responsive and flexible. Psychotherapy is not a straightforward and linear process. Seldom are the goals of one stage fully accomplished before the goals of another are pursued. Rather, strengths suggestive of later recovery are evinced in some domains even as challenges to safety and stability persist in others. Often the work involves moving back and forth between stages to secure recovery across domains.

Julia's experience, for example, demonstrates the movement between stage one and stage two recovery tasks that many survivors undergo. Despite a very high level of functioning in her work, Julia is plagued by intrusive remembrances of her past and by a new awareness of her dissociative states. During the times when she is not sure who or where she is, she is clearly not safe. Her awareness that she has long experienced herself in parts is terrifying to her, as is the fact that she somehow has ways of calling upon this part or that to perform. As she establishes some faith in her ability to function in the ways she needs to function, she will be able to begin the work of exploring her past and learning the impact it has had on her construction of self. Whenever her anxiety intensifies in response to challenging situations, however, the treatment will need to refocus on safety and containment.

Getting first things done first is equally important later in recovery, when therapist and survivor choose between treatment goals that emphasize exploration and integration and those that emphasize relational repair.

Because Sonia has many relational strengths, her therapist may be tempted to recommend that she and Mark resume couple's therapy. The goals of this treatment might be to help Sonia and Mark examine and repair their marriage, to help Sonia find a safe way to disclose to her husband the secrets she is uncomfortably keeping from him, or even to treat her "sexual dysfunction" and help her derive greater sexual pleasure from a monogamous relationship with Mark. These goals aren't "wrong," perhaps, but they don't speak to Sonia's concerns. Moreover, there is no evidence that Mark is interested in resuming couple's therapy. Offering Sonia couple's therapy at this juncture might well repeat the message she learned in her family that the intactness of a marriage is somehow more important than the integrity of an individual. It was this message that kept Sonia's mother married to her father throughout her childhood.

Stage Three: Building and Repairing Relationships

It is in the final stage of recovery from psychological trauma that survivors turn to the tasks of building and repairing relationships. Work in this stage may involve furthering one's capacity for sexual intimacy, conducting family disclosure sessions, attempting to heal family relationships, or grieving the loss of relationships that cannot be repaired. In the realm of "memory work," the search for new information about the past gives way to acceptance and grieving and to a recognition that while the past can now be recalled at will, it cannot be erased.

At this stage, the integration of memory and affect means finding and experiencing new feelings; adult feeling about the past and the recovery goal of affect tolerance means bearing one's grief and knowing one's anger. These accomplishments witness the further development of self and the conviction that one is deserving of care and capable of caring. In this stage of recovery, the survivor reaches not only for relationship with others but also for relationship with self and for the meanings that these relationships can yield.

As Annie reviews her experience in psychotherapy, she recognizes it as a set of accomplishments she is able to acknowledge. She entered treatment frightened and overwhelmed, no longer able to distance herself from a childhood marred by sexual abuse. She leaves with her self-esteem firmly established and her capacity for intimate connectedness secure.

In the course of treatment, she reestablished a relationship with her father and disclosed her abuse history to her mother. Neither of these relationships is settled. Her mother has remained defensive and silent. Her father has welcomed her back in his life, but he is not the father she envisioned in her desperate and elaborate childhood fantasies. She is contending with her disappointment. She is also bearing the sadness of saying good-bye and learning through termination that sadness and loss can intermingle with optimism about the future and enthusiasm for whatever comes next. She is ready to leave.

The ecological framework reminds us that Annie, Julia, Sonia, and Jackie are different women, with different histories and different adaptations to these histories. It reminds us that recovery from trauma is a multidimensional phenomenon and that strengths and resiliencies in one domain can help to facilitate repair in others. The model cautions us that psychotherapy is not a straightforward guarantee of recovery. And it provides us with a set of criteria with which to begin defining appropriate treatment goals.

The issue of timing—specifically, the timing of traumatic exploration—is addressed by the attention to the three stages of recovery. The model honors the complexity of the experiences of survivors and the variations in the needs they present to psychotherapy. Moreover, the model fits well within a complex and changing mental health arena, one in which longer-term individual psychotherapy has become more and more difficult for people to afford.

Thus, the model offers a set of operationally defined recovery criteria, and paves the way for treatment-outcome research that will demonstrate the efficacy of treatment for survivors. Together with an ecological view of trauma and a multidimensional understanding of recovery, the stages-by-dimension framework provides therapist and patient alike with guidelines to fulfill the potential inherent in a solid therapeutic alliance.

NOTES

P. 64, *symptoms of posttraumatic stress disorder:* American Psychiatric Association. (1987). *Diagnostic and statistical manual of mental disorders.* (3rd ed., rev.) Washington, DC: American Psychiatric Association.

P. 65, *long-term result of childhood sexual trauma:* Briere, J. (1988). The long-term clinical correlates of childhood sexual victimization. *Annals of the New York Academy of Sciences, 52*(8): 327–334.

P. 65, *Aberrations of memory:* Harvey, M. R., & Herman, J. L. (in press). Amnesia, partial amnesia and delayed recall among adult survivors of childhood trauma. In *Consciousness and cognition.*

P. 65, *"complex PTSD" to distinguish the sequelae of prolonged and repetitive trauma:* Herman, J. (1992). *Trauma and recovery.* New York: Basic Books.

P. 69, *ecological model:* Harvey, M. R. (in press). An ecological view of psychological trauma and trauma recovery. *Journal of Traumatic Stress.*

P. 87, *Stages by Dimensions of Recovery:* Lebowitz, L., Harvey, M. R., & Herman, J. L. (1992). A stage by dimension model of recovery from sexual trauma. *Journal of Interpersonal Violence, 8*(3): 378–391.

4

GROUP THERAPY

Brian R. Abbott

The long-term consequences of childhood sexual abuse often leave adult survivors with a variety of intrapsychic and interpersonal problems that may have a profound negative impact on the individual's ability to function effectively. Recovery from these problems requires an intensive treatment plan, of which we consider group therapy an essential element.

Group therapy is an ideal environment in which to evoke and work through such issues as the survivor's interpersonal distrust, denial of or dissociation from the trauma, and feelings of self-blame, self-hatred, and isolation. Consequently, this chapter will discuss the issues and methods for conducting a weekly, outpatient, long-term therapy group for female adult survivors of sexual abuse.

PRELIMINARIES TO STARTING THE GROUP

As a group leader I must make a variety of decisions prior to initiating a therapy group for survivors of sexual abuse. This planning process provides the foundation on which a successful group therapy experience is built.

Prior to convening a therapy group, my co-leader and I must determine which method of group therapy we will use: a long- or short-term structure, or a dynamic versus symptom-specific approach; we must also decide the overall purpose of the group. This determination will influence other logistical elements of the group such as the criteria for selecting members, composition of the co-therapy team, and the size and length of time the group will remain in existence. Finally, I also find it important for the co-leaders to build in processes for ongoing evaluation of each group member, the overall group functioning, and the co-therapy relationship.

Theoretical Orientation

The method of group therapy that I prefer is dynamically oriented and operates over a long-term period. This kind of group is closed to new membership for a period of sixteen to eighteen weeks. As part of the termination process, the leaders and group members reassess the need to continue the group. At the conclusion of the group cycle, some members leave and new members join the group for another sixteen- to eighteen-week cycle. The choice of this method is influenced both by my theoretical orientation and the orientation of the clinic in which the group operates.

I also find that a long-term group therapy format offers several distinct advantages. First, it allows the development of intensive transference between group members as well as among group members and the therapists. Working through the transference relationships provides a corrective emotional experience regarding the dysfunctional or abusive family as well as other personal relationships the survivor has had; it also helps the members develop a stronger sense of self.

Second, survivors of sexual abuse seek treatment as a result of a variety of emotional and behavioral problems. These problems are symptomatic of repressed painful feelings and distorted cognitions the victim has about herself and others that are associated with the childhood history of sexual abuse. In these circumstances, the individual must have a high degree of psychological safety to access and work through these distorted cognitions and feelings. The trust and cohesion that forms during the course of long-term group therapy is conducive to building such a safe and supportive container in which these issues can be managed.

In some clinical settings, a long-term group therapy format is not feasible or consistent with policy and practice, such as within a managed health care environment. In these instances, short-term group therapy formats are available. Short-term therapy groups generally have from nine to eighteen sessions and focus on accomplishing specific tasks or alleviating certain symptoms. Short-term therapy groups offer the advantages of short time commitments, cost effectiveness, and containment of the regressive aspects of treatment. I believe that many of the methods and techniques discussed in this chapter can be utilized in or adapted to a short-term therapy group.

Screening Issues

Intense, painful emotions are evoked in group therapy with adult survivors of sexual abuse. Group members must be psychologically suited to functioning in such an emotionally charged atmosphere. In my experience, the screening process is critical in selecting those clients who are most able to function in the group setting as well as to determine which patients have sufficient motivation to participate in long-term therapy.

Typically the screening interview is most successful when both group leaders meet with each prospective group member. The screening process uses a semistructured clinical interview that ranges from forty-five to ninety minutes. Typical areas covered in the screening interview include the following:

- An assessment for specific psychopathology that would preclude effective participation in the group
- A determination of the client's motivation and commitment to participate in group therapy
- The ability of the client to discuss the sexual abuse
- The ability of the client to define her goals for the group

Once all clients have been screened, the group leaders must decide which ones are to be included in the group and which are screened out. All prospective members are informed of these decisions.

Over the years, I have routinely screened out several types of prospective group members. These included individuals who are psychotic, actively suicidal, brain damaged, very assaultive, and psychopathic. There are other prospective members who exhibit patterns of behavior that make them marginal candidates. These include clients with poor ego strength or who have a recent history of drug or alcohol addiction.

Individuals who demonstrate or have a documented history of decompensating under emotional distress are usually poor candidates for the type of group described in this chapter. Usually, I find these clients are diagnosed with borderline personality disorder or dissociative identity disorder. These patients become a management problem when the intense, emotionally charged environment of the group precipitates regular, acute episodes of decompensation—like splitting into subpersonalities or a severe regressive state—that require an inordinate amount of therapy time to manage.

During the screening process such behavior may not be readily apparent and the prospective group member may be allowed entrance to the group. But these patients must be asked to leave the group later if they become too disruptive to the group process. If allowed to continue in the group, these clients prevent the therapeutic work from moving beyond the management of their continual emotional crises or suicidal acting out. The more highly functioning members become irritated or angry with these members. When this problem cannot be managed or worked through, the group often comes to an impasse. The trust and cohesion diminishes as members come to resent the disruptive patient. Little therapeutic work occurs and often the more functional group members drop out.

Prospective group members who are actively dependent on substances should also be excluded. Substance-dependent individuals are unable to benefit from therapy when under the influence of drugs or alcohol. The group process will also activate emotions or memories related to the sexual abuse that will likely result in the use of substances as a coping mechanism. As a rule of thumb, a candidate for the group should have three to six months of sobriety prior to entrance. In addition, it's important for the recovering addict to have the psychological and social resources to cope with the group experience with a minimal potential for relapse into substance use. Group members with a history of substance abuse are likely to benefit from concurrent involvement in twelve-step programs.

Role of Individual Therapy

I find that it's advisable for all group members to receive individual therapy while participating in the group. The weekly group process evokes painful emotions and memories related to the sexual abuse that are likely to affect the survivor's day-to-day functioning. Individual therapy provides additional support and in-depth therapeutic assistance to help clients work through troubling feelings and thoughts.

Concurrent involvement in individual therapy raises the issue of who conducts this treatment, a topic that has attracted some debate. Some clinicians prefer the survivor to have the same group and individual therapist whereas others insist that either all or none of the group members receive individual therapy from the group leaders. A third viewpoint has found it advantageous for group members to receive concurrent individual therapy from clinicians outside the group. From the standpoint of clinical case management, I prefer but do not require that all group clients receive individual therapy from the group therapists or from other practitioners in the clinic where the therapy group is conducted.

When individual and group therapy are being conducted concurrently, the hazard exists that the two therapies will work at cross purposes and the patient will resist therapeutic work in group by taking issues to the safer domain of individual therapy. This situation can be more easily managed when the individual therapists for group members are the group leaders or clinicians from the setting where the group meets.

I don't automatically screen out clients, however, who have individual therapists outside the group or clinical setting. Instead, I suggest that the client's participation in group therapy be contingent on an agreement of regular communication between the treating clinicians. If this does not occur in practice, it may be necessary to terminate the client's participation in group or to arrange a transfer for individual therapy to a group leader or someone within the clinic where the group operates.

Guidelines for the Selection of Group Members

Once a potential pool of candidates is defined, the leaders select the group members. I have found it generally desirable to compose a group of sexual abuse survivors who are heterogeneous in their problem area—with similarities in types of psychiatric diagnoses, problems in expressing anger or other feelings, interpersonal conflicts, and level of self-disclosure regarding the sexual abuse—but homogeneous in their degree of ego strength. Other factors that I take into account have to do with the diversity of group membership including age, ethnicity, marital status, educational level, sexual orientation, and income.

Heterogeneity of the group membership must not occur at the expense of creating a group isolate. For instance, one twenty-two-year-old single female may find little in common with the issues facing a group of middle-aged, married women. I have seen an isolate group member feel so different from the majority that she experiences an acute exacerbation of preexisting feelings of isolation or shame related to the victimization experience: "I am the only one who feels this way or has this problem." When this happens, the person will often drop out of the group or become an inactive participant.

Co-Leader Issues

Given the intense nature of the therapeutic work in a weekly female survivor group, I always advise having co-therapists to lead the group, preferably a male-female team. The adult survivor experiences conflicts and troubling emotions toward both mother and father as well as other male-female relationships. Consequently, the male-female co-leader team helps to evoke these transference issues, which then become one of the focuses of therapeutic work in the group. It can also be a corrective emotional experience for the group members to observe the male-female co-therapists working together with mutual respect. This can be an effective antidote to the destructive competition, mutual derogation, exploitation, or pervasive sexuality that has characterized the survivors' prior experience of male-female relationships.

An all female co-therapy team is a second choice when a male-female pairing is not possible. An all male co-therapy pairing is inadvisable for working with an all female survivor group. As the representation of the victimizer, the all male team can evoke considerable fear and anxiety in an all female survivor group. This reaction can become insurmountable to work through or may prevent effective functioning of the group over its duration. Before we initiate the group, my co-leader and I work together as a team during the planning process, which includes the screening and selection of group members. Once the group has begun, we meet before and after each group session. Before the session, we have a ten- to fifteen-minute meeting to plan strategy for the upcoming group, to provide updated information regarding any of the group members, to identify any countertransference issues any leader might have that could affect his or her participation in the group, and to provide support to clear the air of any tension that might have developed from the day's activities.

After each session, we meet for fifteen to twenty minutes to critique the group. The focus of this meeting is to share our impressions of each member, to discuss the overall group process, and to revisit the co-leader relationship. This meeting helps us to reach a mutual understanding of problems or issues related to the group process itself or with individual members. Based on this agreement, we can plan strategy for upcoming group sessions. A critique of our co-leader relationship helps us detect or prevent interpersonal problems that can negatively impact the effective functioning of the group. Equally important is our reinforcing positive ways the co-leader team works together.

With the preliminaries completed, it's time for the leaders to start the group. The remainder of this chapter presents the stages of forming the group through its conclusion. This discussion assumes the reader has a working knowledge of group process and thus focuses specifically on critical issues related to conducting weekly, outpatient, long-term group therapy with female survivors of childhood sexual abuse.

BEGINNING THE GROUP

The goals for the early stages of our group process are to build trust and cohesion among members and to develop a positive peer culture where work on the sexual abuse issues is the norm. To achieve these goals my co-leader and I rely on the modeling of appropriate behavior, shaping or reinforcing positive behavior by group members, and establishing a structure that facilitates cohesiveness among the members.

Group Structure

Therapeutic work on the sexual abuse evokes acute feelings of distress. In order for the survivor to access and work through these feelings, she needs a safe, predictable environment. The structure of the group can be manipulated to mediate the level of anxiety associated with the therapeutic work. There is ample documentation that a moderate level of anxiety is conducive to effective therapeutic work in the group setting. As described below, my co-leader and I provide structure to sustain such a moderate level through the use of a consistent group format as well as through specific interventions in any one group session.

The group is conducted on a weekly basis, on the same day every week. Each session lasts two hours. The duration of the group ranges from sixteen to eighteen weeks. The group leaders make a determination as to the exact length of the group, including any breaks for holidays or other events. During the screening process, the prospective members should be informed of the day, time, length, and duration of the group meetings and make a commitment to attend for the full duration. During the first session, we re-affirm this commitment with each member.

If any members renege on this agreement, we handle it in the group setting; we clarify the discrepancy between the client's expressed commitment during the screening interview and her currently stated uncertainty. Sometimes an uncommitted member may have to attend several sessions before she makes a genuine commitment to stay with the group for its entirety. Such issues must be resolved because an uncommitted member is usually perceived as being untrustworthy by other group members, and this perception can inhibit everyone's level of disclosure. Because of the imbalance she can cause, a member who maintains a reluctance to commit to the group probably should be asked to leave it.

Group Ground Rules and Goals

Also in the first session, the leaders state the overall goals and the ground rules, which may vary from group to group. The statement of goals and ground rules provides a means for members to have a mutual understanding of the function of the group, as illustrated in the following dialogue:

> *Brian (group leader):* To make this group a safe place to work on the sexual abuse issues, we have a few simple ground rules to follow. Most important, what is said in this group stays in this group. You can certainly share with a significant other what you said in group or what you learned about yourself. But it's very important for the safety of the group that you do not divulge the identity of any group member or discuss what other members say outside of the group. In a group like this, some of you may want to discuss outside of group

what went on or to talk about what other members have said. I think the group should come to a decision on this issue. So let's discuss it. What do you think? (The group discusses this issue and comes to a decision.)

Martha (group leader): O.K. now that we have settled that, I want to finish the group ground rules. There is no eating or drinking in group; you must come to the group sober; there is no smoking; and physical violence between group members is not acceptable. Any questions or comments?

Other ground rules may be specified as necessary, but I usually try to keep them to a minimum. If problem areas emerge that require a ground rule, my co-leader and I will discuss the need for it with the group. The group leaders act unilaterally if the group members cannot agree on the ground rule and the co-leaders decide that one is necessary for the group to continue functioning well.

The goals for the group are generally set by the therapists and by the setting in which the group is conducted. Short-term therapy groups normally have specific or concrete goals, such as to alleviate a certain problem or symptom. Long-term groups are likely to have broader, process-oriented goals; an example is to identify and work through the trauma associated with the sexual victimization. The group leaders delineate the goals of the group during the first session.

Starting the Group: Introductions

We ask each group member to state her name and offer some details about the sexual abuse, like the identity of the offender, her age when it occurred, the length of time it occurred. Then we ask each one to set personal goals to accomplish in the group, and to state any issues they would like to discuss during the group session.

This introduction is the beginning in breaking the feeling of shame and isolation associated with the sexual abuse. Hearing other members share their own experiences about sexual abuse helps to alleviate distorted thoughts such as "I am the only one this happened to," or "I was sexually abused because I am worthless and deserved it." Introductions of the members and group leaders take place during the first session.

In subsequent group sessions, a check-in occurs during the opening of the group. Each member makes a brief statement (one to three minutes) about how they're feeling and to state if there is an issue that they want to discuss. This check-in also provides a means for the group leaders to assess each member's mental status. Once the check-in is complete, the leaders may respond in several ways. Based on strategy previously discussed, we may pursue a specific issue or topic brought up during the check-in. Or, after the check-in, we may sit silently and allow the group to determine its course.

Methods and Issues

The beginning stage of group is a time for the co-leaders to shape the behavior of the members toward the development of a positive peer culture. A positive peer culture is characterized by a supportive environment where group members feel safe to work through painful emotions related to the sexual abuse and its long-term impact. The group leaders shape the behavior of members and the overall group process through various interventions including modeling, group process comments, direct questioning of members, positive reinforcement, confrontation and interpretation with individual members, and structuring of interactions among group members.

Like other types of dynamically oriented groups, during the beginning phase of a survivors' group, members will make tentative forays toward meeting the purpose and goals of the group. For example, it is common for a group member to discuss a problem related to sexual abuse with little affect. The group leaders may initiate the shaping process by asking the individual to identify and express her feelings.

> *Brian (group leader):* Maria, can you tell me how you felt when your mother did not believe you when you told her that your stepfather was sexually abusing you?

Maria: I feel like she had no choice because if she left my stepfather, she would have no one to support her financially.

Martha (group leader): I understand. I wonder, though, how it felt as a young child not to have your mother believe you?

Maria: Like I said, what could she do? She had no choice.

Jane: (in an irritated tone of voice) What did you feel? As I listen to you, I would have been pissed off at my mom and would have felt hurt, too.

Martha: Do any of those feelings ring a bell?

Maria: Yes, I recall feeling really hurt and all alone.

Brian: Yes. And, instead of allowing yourself to have those feelings, you tend to hide behind this belief that your mother had no choice because of her financial dependence on her husband. That may have been true but you still have a right to feel hurt and lonely.

A similar problem arises in this stage of the group development with the "yes, but" member who solicits and rejects advice given by group members. As other group members begin to feel frustrated and angry, the leaders respond with a group process comment describing the interactions that are going on.

Martha (group leader): I notice that as Sherry has been asking for advice from group, it appears that she rejects all of it. As this is happening, I also observe that some group members appear to be reacting to this. Can some of you tell Sherry how you are feeling? (silence among group members) How about you Sue, and Maria, too?

Sue: I really get pissed off at her.

Brian (group leader): (points to Sherry) Please tell her how you are feeling.

Sue: I feel angry when I see you rejecting any help that I offer. At this point I don't even feel like responding to you because I know you are going to say yes, but.

Maria: When I see you rejecting the advice of other members, it reminds me of how my mom didn't support me when the sexual abuse happened.

Martha (group leader): What are your feelings when you have this association?

Maria: I feel angry too, but I also feel a lot of hurt.

Brian: Good! Thanks for expressing those feelings. I know that is hard to do. You may fear that Sherry will be mad at you or that you'll hurt her feelings. In a minute we will ask how Sherry felt when she heard your feedback. Part of being in this group is helping each other. Expressing your feelings like you did shows that you care about Sherry and want to help her. Also it prevents her from feeling resentful. Resentments toward others build up when you don't express your negative feelings toward others. O.K., now I would like to hear from Sherry. How did it feel to get this kind of feedback?

The goal of this intervention was directed toward the development of behavior among group members that supports a positive peer culture. Also, when these types of interactions occur, we always allow time for the member who was confronted to discuss her reaction or feelings. This process can often be used as a bridge to elicit and discuss similar problems the individual has experienced in childhood or other relationships. For example, after Sherry has discussed her reactions to the feedback the group leader asks:

Brian: I wonder if this pattern of seeking help but ultimately rejecting it is a familiar pattern in your life?

Sherry: I think it is. I can recall times when I was in college or in jobs when I would reach out for help and reject it when it was offered. I guess I can now see why my advisers at college or supervisors at work seemed frustrated or didn't want to help me. I always thought they were mean or didn't like me.

Brian: So you can see how this has caused problems in other relationships with females. It seems to be a pattern that is not working. I wonder, then, what is the pay-off to you? What do you gain from such behavior?

Sherry: I'm not really sure. Maybe it has to do with the feelings I have toward my mother for not protecting me when I was molested. (She goes on to explore her disappointment with her mother, how this has led to the expectation that she can't depend on others to help her and, consequently, how she fears that if she accepts the advice or help she will then become too close and eventually be rejected.)

As such interventions increase the trust and cohesion among group members, you will notice an increased level of self-disclosure regarding the sexual victimization as well as a commensurate expression of genuine affect. This is our cue that the group is entering the second or middle phase of the group process. This is the stage where the in-depth or primary therapeutic work takes place.

THE MIDDLE STAGE OF THE GROUP

The long-term impact of child sexual victimization has been classified in several categories including symptoms of posttraumatic stress, cognitive distortions, avoidant behavior, impaired social relationships, and a damaged internal representation of self. Managing these forms of symptomatology is the primary work of the middle stage of the group. The following section presents therapeutic group interventions used to handle these problems and discusses some general methods of group process.

Methods of Group Process

There are several common methods of group process that may be used in conjunction with any of the therapeutic interventions discussed in the next section. This type of intervention involves at least several group members who share thoughts, feelings, and reactions in relation to therapeutic interventions.

Therapists recognize that therapeutic work occurring with one or more group members usually affects nonparticipating group members. As part of the structure of intervening with one or more group members, you'll need to allocate time to handle reactions of group members to any one piece of therapeutic work.

These reactions may not always be readily apparent. Some group members may withdraw or dissociate without displaying obvious affective responses, so it's important for group leaders to observe nonverbal reactions that may indicate a member is feeling disturbed. To handle the emotional reactions of group members, we build a structure that is followed at the conclusion of each therapeutic intervention. On closure of a therapeutic intervention, we ask the group members not directly involved in the intervention for their thoughts, feelings, or reactions to the therapeutic work. In some instances, specific group members who displayed obvious or subtle signs of distress may be called on to discuss their reactions. The use of this method is essential so that clients don't leave the group without closure to their emotional reactions.

At the conclusion of therapeutic work with a group member, that client may feel highly vulnerable, embarrassed, or even concerned about what other members think of her. To counteract these reactions, my co-leader and I solicit supportive comments from other members. We also encourage group members to make these comments directly to the vulnerable member. Once this feedback is completed, the vulnerable group member is asked to share her reaction to this information. This method not only alleviates anxiety but also helps to validate or universalize the group member's feelings.

During an intervention a client may exhibit a defensive reaction. For instance, a member may talk about a particularly brutal instance of sexual victimization without apparent feeling and, furthermore, go on to justify or excuse the offender. When such defenses are shown, the group leaders may structure a supportive confrontation of that client. The following exemplifies this process.

Brian (group leader): Maria, I noticed that as you talked about how brutal your father was during the sexual abuse, you said it as if the abuse were an everyday experience. And you seem to believe that you should have no feelings about what he did because he was abused as a child. I'm wondering if any of the group members who had a similar reaction can share what they think about this.

Sheila: When I listened to what you said, I felt furious with your father . . . like I wanted to kill him. I can't understand why you aren't angry at him.

Maria: Well, how can I blame him? (group leader interrupts)

Brian: Excuse me, Maria. Now Sheila, I can understand how you are feeling but I recall that earlier in this group you responded in a similar way about your father. Can you share with Maria how you handled that issue and tapped into your feelings toward your father?

Sheila: Well . . . my father and I were real close even before the sexual abuse happened. He was really the only one who gave me love in the family. A few months ago I realized I could not get angry with him because I was afraid that he would abandon me. I know that is how I felt as a child and I was still carrying that with me. My anger really came when I saw how he manipulated my trust, a child's trust in her father, to coerce me into the sexual abuse and that I don't have to be fearful of his rejection. (in angry and tearful tone) He was the adult and I was the child. He shouldn't have taken advantage of me!

Maria: (in an irritated tone of voice) I can see what you mean but I think my situation is different.

Martha (group leader): O.K., Maria, I notice you are getting a little defensive about the feedback. I am not expecting that you accept for yourself the experience of Sheila. I would like you to take what she has said and think about it after you leave group. The idea is to think about feedback for awhile rather than rejecting it outright. Maybe when you think about this later, you'll find that what Maria said makes sense.

This type of supportive confrontation combines several elements. First, the group leader describes the defensive reaction. Second, the leader asks members for feedback about it. The idea is for group members to share with the defensive member how and why they had similar defensive reactions, how they worked through them, and what was the positive outcome of this work. This procedure is akin to the therapist's making an interpretation of the client's defenses. In fact, an alternate or additional intervention may include the therapist's actually interpreting the client's defenses.

Survivors experience a feeling of isolation related to the psychological consequences of the childhood sexual victimization. In essence, the survivor believes that she is the only one who is experiencing these feelings, thoughts, or problems.

This feeling of isolation serves to exacerbate the survivors' emotional pain—the self-blame, the self-hatred. The group process provides a wonderful opportunity to diffuse this feeling of isolation. When specific problem areas are discussed, the group leaders facilitate disclosure by other members who experience the same problems. The resulting discussion acts to universalize the problem, which helps to decrease the group member's feeling of isolation. By understanding the commonality of her problems with those of other group members, the survivor will exhibit increasing levels of disclosure both in content and affect.

Posttraumatic Stress

Survivors of sexual abuse often experience intrusive and disturbing recollections of the victimization experiences. These recollections can be visual, tactile, auditory, and/or olfactory. Memories of the sexual victimization range from fragmentary to coherent and detailed. Flashbacks are precipitated by various cues such as sexual stimuli, interpersonal relationships, information about abusive behavior received through the media, the disclosure of sexual victimization by others, and talking about one's sexual victimization. The goals for discussing the flashbacks in the group are to alleviate the anxiety associated with them, to seek affective catharsis related to the memory and, in some cases, to gain a more complete memory of the sexual abuse experience. These goals can be accomplished in several ways by utilizing the group process.

Typically, flashbacks are elicited by some type of situational cue, such as engaging in a specific sex act with an intimate partner. At times the victim may not be aware of the events that precipitate the flashback. In such instances, the group leaders can facilitate discussion among members who can verbalize the precipitants of their flashbacks.

Judicious questioning by the group leaders may help the member become aware of the factors that set off the flashbacks. Survivors often experience a great deal of distress associated with the flashbacks including the perception that her experience is idiosyncratic. To alleviate this anxiety, we facilitate discussion of the issue among members. As group members discuss the frequency and nature of their flashback experiences, the problem becomes generalized, and this helps to reduce the anxiety the survivor experiences. In addition, through supportive comments or discussion among group members, the troubled member can learn how to manage the precipitants of the flashbacks as well as their psychological and interpersonal effects.

Members with tactile or sensory flashbacks, such as gagging or pain in the genital area, often feel this is a peculiar experience. Group discussion can reveal it to be common, a realization that helps to alleviate the feeling of shame or anxiety associated with this experience. Imagery techniques can also be used to help members associate feelings or visual memories with the sensory flashbacks.

You can ask the member to close her eyes and to focus on bodily sensation. The client may be asked to assign a shape or color to the sensation and then intensify this experience, that is, make the shape bigger or deepen the color. As emotion arises, the client is asked to express whatever words or sounds are associated with the image. This technique not only helps in expressing repressed affect but may also bring a visual memory of the abusive event.

Cognitive Distortions

Negative attributions that the victim holds about herself appear to be a by-product of the sexual victimization. Cognitive distortions are most often symptomatic of low self-esteem. The child victim not only feels helpless and powerless when she is being sexually abused, but she also develops a characteristic way of rationalizing the occurrence of the abuse. A perception of self-blame is the primary way the child victim rationalizes why a "trusted adult" would commit an act that is harmful to a child.

Self-blame manifests in such cognitive distortions as "I'm worthless." The survivor may also exhibit negative assumptions about the amount of danger and adversity in the world, including interpersonal relationships. These cognitive distortions not only have a negative influence on the manner in which the survivor relates to her world, but they also affect the manner in which she presents herself in group and relates to others.

The primary goal of intervening with distorted cognitions is to provide feedback or information that corrects this distortion. We can accomplish this in several ways.

Abuse survivors normally accept their negative self-attributions without question. The following intervention introduces a way to challenge the negative self-perceptions.

At a time the survivor is exhibiting the negative self-attribution, one of the leaders invites her to stand up and to approach several group members one at a time. As the client goes up to each member she repeats the negative self-perception: "Sherry, I want you to know that I am a no-good, worthless person." The members who are approached are asked not to respond.

After repeating this process several times, the client usually will manifest an affective response—like sadness, hurt, or anger. This response is explored by the group leaders who seek to tie the negative self-perceptions to the experience of being sexually abused. At times, the group leader may have to verbalize the process, showing that the negative self-perception was the only way the child could cope with knowing that a trusted adult acted in a harmful manner toward her.

The goal is to help the survivor gain insight into the fallacy of the negative self-perception and begin to reverse these thoughts by placing responsibility onto the offender. As the survivor gains this understanding, a second step in the process occurs.

The survivor is invited to take the next step.

> *Brian (group leader):* O.K., Jane, now you have heard how as a child the only way you could make sense of being molested by your stepfather, whom you loved and trusted, was to believe there was something wrong with you. Now, imagine that your stepfather is sitting in this chair (places chair in front of Jane). I want you to say to him: "I'm a worthwhile person. It was not my fault that you molested me; it was only your fault." Go ahead and say it.

The leader asks the member to repeat the statement with increasing emotional intensity. This intervention helps the member internalize a positive self-statement as well as tap into feelings of anger directed toward the offender.

Once the client has gone through this process, the leaders solicit group members to provide feedback that supports the positive self-statements made by the client.

Avoidant Behavior

Survivors of sexual abuse manifest high rates of depression and anxiety. Often these and other distressing emotions related to the sexual victimization are expressed consciously or unconsciously through avoidant behavior. Common avoidant behaviors include dissociation, substance abuse, suicide or self-mutilation, indiscriminate sexual activity, or eating disorders. The goal of our group interventions is to identify and express the feelings underlying these forms of acting out. Catharsis helps to diffuse the emotional pain. If the pain is experienced and expressed directly, there is less chance for it to be discharged covertly through the avoidant behaviors.

Role-playing and regression work are two group interventions that are helpful in eliciting the release of emotional pain. While these interventions focus on one or several group members at a time, it is common for nearly all group members to be affected by this work. Once the intervention is completed with individuals, the group leaders expand their focus to the reactions of the other group members. If proper closure is not provided, group members can leave the group emotionally wounded. To avoid this problem, the group leaders must assure adequate time—ranging from thirty to sixty minutes—to complete the intervention fully. In addition, member feedback, as described earlier in the chapter, is provided to the clients who were involved in the role-play or regression.

Role-playing is used to enact certain interpersonal relationships that allow the survivor to express and resolve emotional pain associated with those relationships. This technique is commonly used to help the survivor identify and work through troubling feelings regarding the offender, the non-offending parent, or others in a close interpersonal relationship to her. For instance, a woman who feels angry and sad about the non-offending parent's rejection and abandonment may use a role-play to express these feelings.

In this situation, expressing the anger and sadness helps to alleviate the survivor's feelings of low self-worth related to the perception of being rejected by this parent, the sense that "I was not worth much because my mom did not protect me."

Usually the leader has to set up the scenario for the group member. The goal is to develop a situation that allows the client to identify and express feelings that she has repressed. Since these feelings may be unconscious, the client may have difficulty in understanding or getting into the role. Encouragement by the group leader can help to overcome this reluctance.

In the following example, the group leader intervenes with a member who appears to have a great deal of anger directed at her mother for leaving her alone with the offender. The group member is avoiding this feeling by rationalizing that her mother had no idea that the sexual abuse was occurring while she was gone.

Brian (group leader): Mirabel, I want to stop you here for a moment. I know you think your mom had no idea that the sexual abuse was occurring. That may be absolutely correct. But I also think that, as a child, you weren't able to perceive it so objectively. Children assume their parents are all-knowing. I wonder what it felt like, as a child, to have your mother not there to protect you? So what I'd like to do

is to have Martha (the co-leader) play the role of your
mother. Then imagine yourself as that seven-year-old child
who realizes that her mother is about to leave and dreads
what will happen with her father.

Mirabel: But I don't think that's the issue. My mom really wasn't
aware of what was happening.

Brian: I know that is how you see it now. I just want you to try
this role-play and let's see what happens, O.K.?

Mirabel: All right.

Brian: Good. Now, Jane, you will be Mirabel's mother who is
getting ready to leave to visit a friend. Remember you are to
act as if you have no idea the sexual abuse is going on.
Mirabel, I want you to close your eyes for a moment and
imagine yourself at the age of seven, in your home; your
mother is about to leave and you have that feeling that you
know what your father will do once she leaves. When you
open your eyes, I want you to express fully what you are
feeling and what you want to tell your mom.

If the client has difficulty expressing feelings or thoughts in the role-
play, the group leader may ask her to repeat a specific statement. For
example, using the above scenario, "Mom, don't leave me, I need
you to protect me to keep dad from molesting me." As an alternative, one or more group members can act as an alter ego to the
client. The following example illustrates this method.

Martha (group leader): O.K., Mirabel, I notice that you are having a hard time expressing yourself. I would like one of the
group members to stand behind you and to speak for you.
Elisa, go ahead and stand behind Mirabel and express your
feelings and thoughts as she interacts with her mother.

The therapist or members may also offer the alter ego other feelings or thoughts to verbalize. The alter ego technique provides sufficient psychological distance that the client can consciously
experience affect that had been denied or repressed.

Once the role-play is finished, closure occurs. The group leader first spends time helping the client discuss her reactions to the role-play. Next the antagonist is asked to give feedback to the client about what it was like to play the role and to hear what the client said. The group leader then broadens the discussion to elicit thoughts and feelings from the observing group members.

Regression Work. Regression is a therapeutic intervention that is often used in individual therapy but also may be used in the group context. It is a method that allows the survivor to relive various traumatic events psychologically and to express the feelings she experienced at the time they occurred.

Regression may occur spontaneously as survivors talk about abuse-related issues. The group therapist may also use a regression technique to help a survivor access and express denied or avoided affect. In both these circumstances, the group therapists guide the client through the regression and bring her back to the adult state.

In a group setting, I use regression work judiciously. As a guiding principle, I will use regression work on those abuse-related issues that are common to at least several other group members. In so doing, I try to avoid performing primarily individual therapy in a group setting.

Regression to a former mental state can be precipitated in various ways. In one method, the survivor speaks from the abused inner child. Imagery can also be used to have the client visualize herself at a certain place and time of her life. Whatever intervention is used to elicit the regressed state, the therapist follows specific guidelines in facilitating the process. The group leader encourages the client to verbalize what she is thinking and feeling. The therapist may ask specific questions of the "inner child" or direct the "inner child" to act in a certain manner. Again, our goal in this process is to help the survivor become conscious of and to express feelings and thoughts that have been denied, repressed, or avoided.

Regression work by one client will activate responses in other clients, including regressed states. Normally these reactions are apparent. Once the regression work is completed the therapists must attend to those members who were affected by it. The leaders call upon those members who exhibited visible reactions. Other group members are also encouraged to share thoughts and feelings evoked by the regression.

Disturbed Relations and Impaired Sense of Self

The occurrence of sexual abuse may interfere with the ability of a survivor to refer to and operate from an internal awareness of personal existence that is stable across contents, experiences, and affects. This lack of a sense of self may lead to problems in identity, to difficulties in maintaining boundaries, to feelings of emptiness, and to difficulty in separating the needs and feelings of others from their own experience. Such problems often lead to impaired social relationships.

Some survivors may isolate themselves from close relationships out of distrust or fear of vulnerability or revictimization. Others may develop relationships that are characterized by the following:

- Overdependence or idealization of the other individual
- Multiple, brief affiliations with a superficial level of intimacy
- Hypersexual relations that usually end when intimacy is expected
- Choosing partners who act abusively toward the survivor

The symptoms of disturbed social relations and impaired sense of self are acted out in the transference relationships that develop in the group. Labeled as abuse-related transference, its psychological mechanisms can be seen in three broadly defined and overlapping domains:

- Primitive responses to current interpersonal relationships where the responses are based on chronic distortions that reflect a general worldview influenced by childhood experiences
- A current interpersonal exchange that restimulates childhood trauma and results in the acute, intense display of emotion

- An ingrained pattern of perception of a significant person in adulthood that is based on certain similarities to a psychologically important person in the survivor's childhood

Abuse-related transference may manifest in various forms including one or more of the following common situations:

1. The male therapist is perceived as the offending parent. Or alternatively, the female therapist or another female group member is perceived as the critical or rejecting non-offending parent. Mannerisms, speech pattern, ways of relating to females, and so on, may remind the female survivor of her abuser or the non-offending parent.

2. The female survivor devalues the female therapist in ways such as rejecting interventions or not responding while acting in an eager-to-please manner with the male therapist. Children whose abuser was also a primary source of nurturance and emotional closeness often develop overidealized relationships with males and project anger onto the non-offending parent. This split can be played out in the group setting.

3. A power dynamic may develop between the female survivor and the female therapist or other group members. In this situation the female survivor sees herself in competition for the male therapist's attention. The female client may exhibit jealousy and bitterness toward the female therapist or other members as well as vie for the attention of the male therapist.

4. An analogous power dynamic may occur in the relationship between the female survivor and the male therapist. The client attempts to gain control in the therapeutic relationship using sexual or feminine behavior to negotiate for acceptance or attention.

As presented above, transference relationships can develop between group members and the therapists as well as among group members. Transferential responses in the group setting are often identified by the disproportionate reaction to an identified stimulus, as in the following examples:

- Sheila, age forty-two, was sexually abused by her biological father for five years, beginning when she was eight. Her father reinforced her cooperation in the abuse through his increased nurturing behavior toward her. In the group setting, Sheila perceives the nurturing behavior of the male therapist as the manipulation used by her father to elicit her cooperation in the sexual abuse. This results in a rageful vilification of the male therapist.

- Fran, age thirty-eight, was sexually abused by two stepfathers and one of her mother's boyfriends when she was between the ages of six and seventeen. Fran's mother was aware of the sexual abuse but took no action to protect her daughter. A group member acts in a way that Fran perceives as rejection. Fran responds to this perception of rejection with the anger that she feels toward her mother for not protecting her during the sexual abuse.

Other forms of transference may be subtle as they represent habitual patterns of relating to others that the survivor learned as a result of the abuse. For instance, the female survivor may engage in acquiescent or eager-to-please behavior with a male therapist while simultaneously maintaining a distrustful attitude toward him. Such a dynamic can dilute or obviate the effectiveness of therapeutic interventions by a male leader.

The identification of transference provides valuable feedback to the client and gives my co-leader and me insight about the nature of the survivor's relationship with the offender, non-offending parent, and other significant adults. Whatever form the transference manifests, we may proceed in two ways. First, I may respond in a therapeutic manner without interpreting the nature of the transferential relationship. Second, we may bring the nature of the transference to the consciousness of the survivor before starting the therapeutic work.

In the latter instance, we noncritically and neutrally point out the nature of the interaction that is symptomatic of the transference. Alternatively or in conjunction with this interpretation, group feedback or confrontation (as described earlier in the chapter) can be used as a powerful tool to help the client identify and understand the nature of the transference reaction. Several transferential interactions may have to occur before the group member understands and accepts this reaction. Once the group member is aware of the basis of the transferential reaction, we encourage the client to express her thoughts and feelings toward the actual person from her childhood. This can be readily accomplished through the role-playing technique discussed earlier.

Another method of intervention allows you to structure group member and leader interactions in a way that facilitates the resolution of the transference. This technique of working through the transference is premised on recapitulating the dysfunctional relationship and responding to it in a manner that provides a corrective emotional experience for the client.

This is a process intervention that occurs over time in the ongoing therapeutic relationship between the group leaders and members or among group members. The major goal is for you to respond or to facilitate group member interactions in a way that counteracts the survivor's expectation of engaging in an exploitive or violent relationship. The ongoing nature of this relationship helps the survivor to repair her feelings and thoughts that underlie the problems associated with disturbed relatedness and impaired self-reference. The benefits of this process are seen when the survivor begins to direct the transferential emotions to the significant adult from her childhood. At this stage of the intervention, the role-playing or regression techniques discussed in this chapter are useful in working through these emotions.

THE TERMINATION PHASE OF THE GROUP

The termination phase of the group is a time when both practical and therapeutic issues arise. The goals of the termination phase include first introducing the ending of the group to assess whether the group will continue for another sixteen to eighteen weeks and, if so, which members will continue; next we manage therapeutic issues that are activated in group members as a result of termination.

Group members are reminded of the termination date of the group when first entering, then I usually remind them two to three times during the latter part of the middle phase of the group. In the course of a sixteen- to eighteen-week group, we initiate the termination phase when three to five weeks remain. The timing of the introduction of this phase is guided by our knowledge of the group members' ability to handle termination issues. The more difficult we anticipate this process to be, the longer we allow for it.

How group members handle the termination phase depends on several factors:

- Whether a member expects to continue in the group for another cycle
- Whether the group member will continue in individual psychotherapy on termination
- Whether on termination the member will no longer receive therapy

Normally termination under the first and second circumstances proceeds without major complications. But termination can be a difficult process when a client will no longer receive individual or group treatment.

Two common termination themes typically emerge in a survivor group. Members may experience a reactivation of loss and abandonment issues and fears related to post-treatment regression.

Members who plan to leave the group may experience loss/abandonment feelings, and these may spread to the other members who plan to stay with the group. These feelings may be communicated overtly or expressed covertly, such as through avoidance or withdrawal behaviors. We help members who express their thoughts and feelings about these issues. The use of group feedback is helpful. Similarly, group confrontation helps the member who is avoiding these issues. When abuse-related abandonment or loss issues are reactivated as a result of the group termination, we use the various therapeutic interventions—role-playing or regression—and group process methods discussed in this chapter to manage these problems.

When leaving the group, members may verbalize concerns regarding their inability to function without the support of the group. This anxiety about post-treatment regression can be managed by you and group members providing reassurance. Through the use of group feedback, anxious clients can be helped to see their progress to date and to realize that only they have the ability to prevent regression. This may also be a time to examine what problems a client may have difficulty handling in the future and to develop a plan of action to deal with these problems if they emerge.

The process of termination also involves a specific structure. In a group of six to eight members, one session is devoted to a self-assessment process. Each member provides an analysis of her progress or accomplishments in group, issues they did not work on, and for group members who plan to continue in the next group cycle, a statement of personal goals to accomplish in the next group. After each member provides the self-assessment, you and group members respond with feedback or, if necessary, confrontation. Generally, this self-assessment is intended to validate or support the gains a client made in group. For members who make little progress in the course of group, the group confrontation can help to engender motivation to participate more fully in future groups.

All or part of the final group session is devoted to some type of ceremony that helps bring closure to the group. Members and leaders are allowed to express feelings and thoughts or to reminisce about the group experience with one another. There is a reciprocal exchange of good-byes among group members who are not returning and those who will continue to stay with the group. In some instances, group members may want to have a social event with food or soft drinks.

RESOLVING FEELINGS TOWARD OFFENDERS AND NON-OFFENDING PARENTS

A final termination issue emerges where survivor groups are conducted in clinics using the Giarretto model of comprehensive community-based treatment. At the conclusion of a sexual abuse survivor group cycle, some members may be appropriately included in an orientation group. The orientation group is composed of adult incest offenders and non-offending parents who are newly referred to treatment and adult survivors who have been through a period of individual and group treatment and have been approved by treatment staff to participate in this group.

An adult survivor is presumed to be appropriate for the orientation based on the following criteria:

- The survivor expresses an interest in participating in the group.
- She has exhibited the ability in the survivor group therapy to express a range of affect toward the offender and non-offending parent.
- The survivor can benefit by working through feelings regarding her offender or the non-offending parent.

In the orientation group, we structure confrontations between adults molested as children and offending and non-offending parents. Adults who were molested by father-figures who continue to deny and whose mothers refuse to acknowledge that the abuses occurred are permitted by the offenders and their partners to engage them in role-playing exercises in which they act as surrogate parents. The survivors are thereby enabled to discharge and resolve their frustration and anger. In addition, as offenders talk about the manner in which they groomed the victim, manipulated the victims to keep the secret, and engaged in sexual fantasies toward their victims, the survivor comes to understand the deliberateness of the offender's behavior.

This recognition is beneficial in correcting the distorted cognitions that underlie the victim's guilt and self-blame. The victim realizes that she did not cause or act in a way that led the offender to commit the sexual abuse. Often this insight is followed by the expression of repressed or denied feelings toward the offenders.

Through these experiences, many survivors eventually come to respect offenders and non-offending parents for their support of the victims and their willingness to cope with the consequences of the abuse therapeutically. In fact, a healing transference may develop in which the surrogate parents from the group can make supportive comments to the survivor, such as "I am sorry that you were so deeply hurt," "You deserved to be protected," "You have every right to feel the way you do," and so on.

The experience of a supportive parental relationship provides a profound healing experience for the survivor whereby both good and bad aspects of the mother and father introjects are integrated. This healing greatly assists in developing more functional interpersonal relationships as well as improving self-worth.

I have found that long-term, dynamic group therapy is not only an effective mode of treatment with female adult survivors of sexual abuse but is also a professionally rewarding experience. The support provided by group members, the effect of a positive peer culture, and the facilitation of the healing process by the group leaders has a profound beneficial impact. I am continually awed and gratified by the power of group process to promote growth and long-lasting change among severely traumatized individuals.

I also want to express my gratitude to the many survivors of sexual abuse who have received treatment through the Giarretto Institute. Without your courageous and inspiring work I would not have had the professional and personal learning experiences from which to communicate the concepts and methods presented in this chapter.

NOTES

P. 95, *Recovery from . . . an essential element:* Briere, J., & Runtz, M. (1993). Childhood sexual abuse: Long-term sequelae and implications for psychological assessment. *Journal of Interpersonal Violence, 8*(3), 312–330.

P. 95, *Group therapy is an ideal environment . . . self-hatred and isolation:* Briere, J. (1989). *Therapy for adults molested as children.* New York: Springer; Carver, C. M., Stalker, C., Stewart, E., & Abraham, B. (1989). The impact of group therapy for adult survivors of childhood sexual abuse. *Canadian Journal of Psychia-*

try, 34, 753–758; Cole, C. H., & Barney, E. E. (1987). Safeguards and the therapeutic window: A group treatment strategy for adult incest survivors. *American Journal of Orthopsychiatry, 57,* 601–609; Courtois, C. A. (1988). *Healing the incest wound: Adult survivors in therapy.* New York: Norton; Giarretto, H. (1989). Community based treatment of incest families. *Psychiatric Clinics of North America, 12*(2), 351–361; Gil, E. (1988). *Treatment of adult survivors of childhood abuse.* Walnut Creek, CA: Launch Press.

P. 96, *First, it allows . . . and the therapists:* Briere, J. (1989). *Therapy for adults molested as children.* New York: Springer; Courtois, C. A., & Leehan, J. (1982). Group treatment for grown-up abused children. *Personnel and Guidance Journal, 60,* 564–566.

P. 96, *The trust and cohesion . . . issues can be managed:* Cole, C. H., & Barney, E. E. (1987). Safeguards and the therapeutic window: A group treatment strategy for adult incest survivors. *American Journal of Orthopsychiatry, 57,* 601–609; Goodman, B., & Nowak-Scibelli, D. (1985). Group treatment for women incestuously abused as children. *International Journal of Group Psychotherapy, 35,* 531–544; Herman, J., & Schatzow, E. (1984). Time-limited group therapy for women with a history of incest. *International Journal of Group Psychotherapy, 34,* 605–616; Schadler, M. (1992). Brief therapy with adult survivors of incest. In M. McKay & K. Paleg (Eds.), *Focal Group Psychotherapy.* Oakland, CA: New Harbinger Publications; Swink, K. K., & Leveille, A. E. (1986). From victim to survivor: A new look at the issues and recovery process for adult incest survivors. *Women and Therapy, 5,* 119–141.

P. 97, *In these instances, . . . formats are available:* Abney, V. A., Yang, J. A., & Paulson, M. J. (1992). Transference and countertransference issues unique to long-term group psychotherapy of adult women molested as children. *Journal of Interpersonal Violence, 7*(4), 559–569; Gil, E. (1988). *Treatment of adult survivors of childhood abuse.* Walnut Creek, CA: Launch Press.

P. 97, *Short-term . . . alleviating certain symptoms:* Briere, J. (1989). *Therapy for adults molested as children.* New York: Springer; Herman, J., & Schatzow, E. (1984). Time-limited group therapy for women with a history of incest. *International Journal of Group Psychotherapy, 34,* 605–616.

P. 98, *If allowed to continue . . . suicidal acting out:* Yalom, I. D. (1975). *The theory and practice of group psychotherapy.* New York: Basic Books.

P. 99, *The weekly group process . . . day-to-day functioning:* Courtois, C. A. (1988). *Healing the incest wound: Adult survivors in therapy.* New York: Norton; Vanicelli, M. (1989). *Group psychotherapy with adult children of alcoholics.* New York: Guilford Press.

P. 99, *Concurrent involvement . . . conducts this treatment:* Abney, V. A., Yang, J. A., & Paulson, M. J. (1992). Transference and countertransference issues unique to long-term group psychotherapy of adult women molested as children. *Journal of Interpersonal Violence,* 7(4), 559–569.

P. 100, *heterogeneous in their problem area:* Yalom, I. D. (1975). *The theory and practice of group psychotherapy.* New York: Basic Books.

P. 100, *homogeneous in their degree of ego strength:* Yalom, I. D. (1975). *The theory and practice of group psychotherapy.* New York: Basic Books.

P. 101, *It can also be . . . of male-female relationships:* Yalom, I. D. (1975). *The theory and practice of group psychotherapy.* New York: Basic Books.

P. 102, *The structure of . . . mediate the level of anxiety:* Shapiro, J. L. (1978). *Methods of group psychotherapy and encounter.* Itasca, IL: F. E. Peacock.

P. 108, *The long-term . . . representation of self:* Briere, J., & Runtz, M. (1993). Childhood sexual abuse: Long-term sequelae and implications for psychological assessment. *Journal of Interpersonal Violence, 8*(3), 312–330.

P. 117, *Regression is a . . . in the group context:* Briere, J. (1989). *Therapy for adults molested as children.* New York: Springer.

P. 118, *The occurrence of . . . experiences, and affects:* Briere, J., & Runtz, M. (1993). Childhood sexual abuse: Long-term sequelae and implications for psychological assessment. *Journal of Interpersonal Violence, 8*(3), 312–330.

P. 118, *Others may develop relationships that are characterized by the following:* Briere, J., & Runtz, M. (1993). Childhood sexual abuse: Long-term sequelae and implications for psychological assessment. *Journal of Interpersonal Violence, 8*(3), 312–330.

P. 118, *Labeled as abuse-related transference, . . . three broadly defined and overlapping domains:* Briere, J. (1989). *Therapy for adults molested as children.* New York: Springer.

P. 123, *Giarretto model of comprehensive community-based treatment:* Giarretto, H. (1982). *Integrated treatment of child sexual abuse.* Palo Alto, CA.: Science and Behavior Books.

5

COUPLES THERAPY

Victoria M. Follette and Jacqueline Pistorello

ALEXIS

Alexis first presented to treatment after Bill called on a weekend requesting an emergency session. Although no openings were available in the clinic at the time, they were able to secure an immediate appointment for an intake with the clinic director. Their resourcefulness and assertion in relation to the treatment community, as well as Alexis's entering therapy with her husband's support, provided important information about the case. In particular, it foretold both some of their strengths and some of the difficulties they would encounter in the course of therapy.

Alexis was experiencing suicidal ideation, and they were both concerned for her safety in view of the husband's imminent trip out of town. The couple reported that they had just recently moved from out of state, where the client had been in intensive individual psychotherapy for approximately three years, mostly addressing current problems associated with her history of child sexual abuse. Bill had been an integral part of this treatment, especially in helping Alexis cope with flashbacks and keep herself safe. Because of their recent move and large psychiatric hospital bills, the couple had limited financial resources. Alexis reported that soon after she got married, she began experiencing dreams and flashbacks about her biological father molesting her. The memories ranged in clarity, content, and her age at the time the recalled events occurred. Her descriptions of the abuse involved aggressive sexual acts by her father, including intercourse and a wide range of emotionally abusive behaviors. At the urging of her husband, she entered individual treatment. Alexis describes her first therapy as a very positive experience, in which she stabilized after experiencing extreme depressive cycles that included serious bouts of suicidal ideation. Moreover, she gained a great deal of confidence in herself. While her father denied having abused her, she remained adamant in her allegations and chose to limit her contact with her family for the time being. She was ostracized by her family and blamed for causing them distress. Later in Alexis's treatment, the issue of contact with her family of origin was to be revisited, with some different conclusions on her part.

Alexis quickly formed a good relationship with her new therapist. Although she was clearly very distressed, feeling depressed and having thoughts of killing herself, her strengths also emerged early in therapy. In a sense, Alexis was a true "survivor." Despite having lived through a particularly abusive family environment, she had emerged with a kind and gentle disposition. Her strong intellect and quick wit were to prove valuable assets over the long and difficult course of treatment.

Alexis reported problems with intrusive thoughts and images about the abuse as well as actual flashbacks and dissociative episodes, symptoms similar to those associated with posttraumatic stress disorder (PTSD). In an attempt to avoid feelings related to the trauma, she reported engaging in some self-injurious behaviors, including bulimia and compulsive hair pulling. Individual treatment focused initially on presenting complaints that the client often linked back to her childhood history. Bill continued to be a resource in treatment and attended therapy a few times at crisis points that occurred during the first year. Within one year, Alexis stabilized: she obtained a regular job and reported increased ability to cope with her suicidal ideation. Intrusive thoughts and self-destructive behaviors also reduced in frequency. The client demonstrated an inordinate amount of insight and commitment to treatment, setting the stage for facing the difficulties that would later arise in her therapy.

Throughout individual treatment Alexis attributed her improvement, at least partially, to Bill's encouragement and advocacy. She frequently contrasted her husband with her father. During flashbacks Bill would be a steadying force, grounding and supporting her. At that point in treatment, both spouses acknowledged that the client's abuse history was a central part of their lives, be it through flashbacks or due to a focus on Alexis's current psychological treatment.

Approximately eighteen months into individual treatment, Bill revealed to the client a history of sexual contact with his younger sister during their late teenage years. Alexis vacillated between a great deal of hurt and anger, feeling betrayed. The extent of her feelings of betrayal were clear in her statement, "I didn't know that he was one of 'them.'" Although Bill reported that the nature of the contact between him and his sister was voluntary, Alexis reported feeling misled because he had waited so long before revealing this history to her. In a great deal of turmoil, Alexis found herself struggling, confusing issues specific to her husband with those related to her abuse history.

At that time, while continuing her individual treatment, Alexis entered couples treatment with her husband, led by another therapist in the clinic. Although Bill's history with his sister was the presenting problem in marital therapy, a number of other issues were discussed in marital sessions, including finances, communication patterns, and sexuality. Concurrently, Alexis struggled with her own issues, increasing her sense of power and ability to communicate her wants and needs in healthy ways. Alexis's pregnancy and the subsequent birth of their baby daughter gave rise to discussions of parenting issues. In particular, they explored how each of their histories interacted with the presence of a female child in the household. After three years of individual therapy and close to two years of marital treatment, Alexis has cut down her individual therapy to twice a month and their marital therapy has been terminated. Bill has started individual treatment in order to better understand his own history and to avoid repeating some of the patterns of interaction that had occurred in his family of origin. Because of our extended clinical contact with this couple, particularly with Alexis, and the fact that this case depicts some typical and some atypical clinical scenarios for couples in which one of the partners has been sexually abused, we have chosen to elaborate on this couple in some detail. Additionally, both Alexis and Bill have made significant improvements in their lives and in their marital relationship.

The overall focus of this chapter is on issues that frequently arise in a relationship in which one of the partners is a survivor of child sexual abuse. After a brief examination of some of the rationale for couples therapy with survivors, we move on to a general description of our treatment approach, noting some special issues related to couples in which at least one member of the dyad is a sexual abuse survivor. At that point, we return to the case of Alexis presented above, describing issues related to her treatment in more detail. Subsequently, we introduce a second case history that illustrates other possible treatment presentations for survivors and their partners.

The cases presented in this chapter are discussed primarily from the survivor's point of view. In general, the pronoun *she* is used in reference to the survivor while her spouse is referred to as the partner or husband. However, this discussion should also be relevant to unmarried and same-sex couples. The choice of language reflects the reported higher frequency of sexual abuse of girls than boys. It also draws from our clinical background; the materials discussed in this chapter are a product of our research and clinical experiences with individual, marital, and group psychotherapy for women sexually abused as children.

THE ROLE OF COUPLES THERAPY IN THE TREATMENT OF SEXUAL ABUSE SURVIVORS

The clinical and scientific literature clearly suggests that survivors tend to experience an inordinate amount of distress and dissatisfaction in their couple relationships. Survivors' childhood experiences often lead to a disruption in trust that hinders their ability to develop and maintain emotionally intimate interpersonal relationships. When compared to controls, survivors are more likely to be separated or divorced, demonstrate higher rates of conflict and fear of their partners, and report lower relationship and sexual satisfaction. There is ample evidence that sexual functioning may be impaired in this population. Additionally, survivors appear to be vulnerable to revictimization in adulthood in the form of emotional, sexual, or physical abuse.

The inherently interpersonal nature of the aftermath of child sexual abuse has led to a focus on group treatment for survivors. Although this form of treatment has been generally successful in reducing the amount of distress reported by the survivor, one study found that married survivors did not benefit as much from group psychotherapy as did those with no partners. The impact of the couple relationship in a survivor's recovery is underscored by the finding that rape survivors who were in a stable intimate relationship had a speedier recovery than those who were not. In a study of group therapy for sexual abuse survivors, the few clients who deteriorated after group treatment were experiencing severe marital problems, as measured by both self-report standardized measures and clinical observations.

The prominent role of interpersonal relationships in psychological treatment for this population is also underscored by the assertion that those in the trauma survivor's social network "have the power to influence the eventual outcome of the trauma." It follows that the greatest impact of treatment gains would be felt on the woman's primary intimate relationship.

There are several rationales for using couples therapy with this population. Sexual abuse frequently occurs in the context of an intimate interpersonal relationship. Therefore, a couples relationship can be a particularly powerful working context because it offers some approximation of the original family setting in which the abuse occurred. Additionally, areas such as communication, partner abuse, and sexual issues are best addressed when both partners are present. As suggested above, the inclusion of the survivor's partner may also help prevent possible therapeutic iatrogenic effects on the relationship.

To provide a framework for the discussion of cases and to expand on treatment implications, we present below a brief overview of our general theoretical and treatment approach.

ACCEPTANCE AND COMMITMENT THERAPY (ACT) APPROACH

ACT, Acceptance and Commitment Therapy, was developed by Steve Hayes and his associates; it is a contextually based approach that emphasizes treating emotional avoidance and helping the client make behavioral changes that will result in more value-congruent life choices. The basic premise in this approach is that clients presenting for therapy have been avoiding certain thoughts, feelings, or memories that they evaluate negatively. Avoidance strategies can cover the gamut of clinical problems, including dissociation, substance abuse, eating disorders, affective disorders, and relationship problems. These avoidance methods are counterproductive to the clients' own goals in life.

At a technique level, ACT combines some traditional behavioral strategies (such as exposure, self-monitoring, and goal setting) and Gestalt experiential exercises, using metaphors to exemplify key concepts. We believe that ACT is particularly well suited to treating survivors for a number of reasons. First, the emphasis is on exploring the current function of the presenting complaints, a strategy that moves away from mere blaming or pejorative analyses. Second, the therapy is a collaborative effort between client and therapist in which power hierarchies are minimized. Finally, the ultimate goal of the treatment is to empower the client to take control of her own life, defining goals and values and making a commitment to herself to do what will help her attain those goals.

ACT and the Treatment of Survivor Couples

In couples work, ACT can be relevant to treatment in a number of ways. Specific problems reported by couples in which one partner has been sexually abused seem to have an underlying theme of the avoidance of intimacy. For example, while interacting with her partner, an environmental stimulus, such as a hug from her partner, triggers a memory of the abuse and the survivor experiences fear, anger, or anxiety. She may then attempt to get rid of these feelings (or private events) by dissociating. Notice what happens to the interaction between the survivor and her partner when she engages in this behavior. This avoidance strategy functions to temporarily eliminate the anger, fear, or anxiety the survivor was experiencing. However, there is also a significant cost: the emotional and psychological distancing of the survivor from her partner. In treatment, the clinician is presented with a complaint of lack of intimacy in the relationship.

Without understanding the historical aspects of this behavior, the clinician could be puzzled by the couple's interaction around issues related to affection. Naturally, this clinical scenario can be complicated by other issues, such as the avoidance strategies used by the partner, the partner's purposeful or inadvertent reinforcement of the avoidance strategies used by the survivor, or the safety of the survivor in the current intimate relationship. Therefore, it's critical that the therapist conduct a contextual analysis of the behaviors present in the relationship.

Therapy proceeds with a review of ways in which both individuals have dealt with negative thoughts, memories, or feelings and having the couple outline goals for treatment. Outlining these goals in itself has therapeutic importance, as often survivors and their partners have not thought about what their goals are, either as individuals or as a couple.

In couples treatment, we would suggest that initially both spouses carry out this assignment independently in order not to contaminate either individual's perspective. It's not uncommon for the survivor to be less autonomous, to be excessively other-directed, and therefore to be more likely to subjugate her needs to those of significant others in setting the direction for her life. After the individual goals are stated, the couple shares them in treatment, a task that functions on both a content and a process level. At a content level, it is important for the couple to find some shared couple agenda, not only for treatment but also for life goals. At a process level, this task represents a first step in increasing communication and developing more emotional intimacy in the relationship.

At this early phase of treatment, we can present our treatment rationale, particularly emphasizing the role of acceptance in the change process. Articulating different domains of acceptance may be useful for the clinician and the couple alike during treatment planning. For purposes of treatment clarification and utility, acceptance can be broken down into acceptance of internal events, such as thoughts, feelings, or memories; acceptance of one's history; acceptance of self; and acceptance of others. Although all these domains inevitably converge back to acceptance of one's own thoughts and feelings, this distinction may be helpful in clarifying the treatment implications of an acceptance approach with couples where one partner is a survivor of child sexual abuse. It is important to note that the term *acceptance* does not pertain to acceptance of past or current abuse; neither does it suggest condoning of the perpetrator's behavior. Acceptance refers solely to acceptance of the individual's own reactions to events.

Acceptance of One's History

In the current verbal cultural and social context, which supports explanations of behavior in terms of personal history, clients frequently come to therapy wanting to get rid of their past histories. The survivor may have tried to "forget" her history by engaging in any of a number of behaviors, such as becoming a perfectionist or working excessively ("If I do this well, then I'll be OK"). This nonacceptance that the abuse occurred may lead to a range of behavioral consequences such as substance abuse or avoidance of truly intimate relationships. The more the survivor is unwilling to accept these past experiences, the more likely she will be to repel any thoughts or behaviors that may serve as reminders of the abuse.

For example, sexual intimacy with her partner may be too reminiscent of abuse experiences; thus, she will avoid such intimacy at all costs. When an event is unchangeable, as in the case of past abuse, the change that we call acceptance (of the survivor's reactions to that event) is essential for her to set the stage for behavioral change.

A distinction between acceptance of past behaviors and current behaviors may be useful here. At times, the survivor may realize that she withdraws from intimate contact in particular situations (as in gatherings of her family of origin), and she may choose to accept her actions in view of her goal to reduce the likelihood of being revictimized. In ACT, we work to help clients establish control in areas where conscious, purposeful control works. That control works in the case of current behavior but not in eliminating events from one's history.

Acceptance of Self

Although this topic can be discussed in great length, the point of interest here is to draw a distinction between self as content and self as context. Zen Buddhism suggests that there are two types of awareness: one is observing our feelings and actions; the other is to do so from a consistent locus or point of view. The former type of awareness can be equated to self as content and the latter to self as context.

Acting from a self as context perspective is useful in the process of acceptance of private events such as thoughts and emotions. This perspective allows the survivor to experience events belonging to the same class as the abuse, such as a flashback, without having to act on that experience in familiar ways, such as dissociating. Taking the content of private events derived from aversive experiences as if they are literally happening often leads the survivor to activate her defenses. During flashbacks, for example, the survivor may feel as if she is experiencing the event all over again.

In couples work, the survivor may describe experiencing a flashback during sexual intercourse with her husband and then pushing the husband away. The partner may experience this as a hurtful rejection. When the survivor can observe herself experiencing the flashback, she has the choice of behaving in ways that further her goals in life, such as by talking to her partner about her experience and increasing the intimacy and sharing in the relationship. A goal of treatment would be to define ways the couple could enhance their sexual relationship without additional trauma to either partner. Operating from the perspective of the observer can allow not only the survivor but also her partner to gain some distance from difficult experiences.

In treatment, experiential exercises and metaphors that help the client gain an "observer perspective" are used to facilitate acceptance. One metaphor we use frequently is a chessboard, with all the pieces on the board representing thoughts, feelings, and memories that are in immediate contact and yet are separate from the board itself. The board is equated to the observer self, which provides the context in which these internal experiences occur. We emphasize that while there might be an ongoing struggle between the black and white chess pieces, the board can still move in whatever direction it chooses to go.

Acceptance of Others

This domain of acceptance of others might be the most relevant within couples treatment of the survivor and her partner. However, *acceptance of others* is a deceiving term. In actuality, it pertains to the acceptance of private events that, at a content level, refer to other individuals. Acceptance in this form does not pertain to "approval" or "condoning" in any way. Moreover, the accompanying public behavior may take different forms. For example, the survivor, accepting that she married someone who is abusive, may decide to leave the relationship.

Acceptance also refers to a partner's ability to "have" his wife's history. Many survivors report that their partner will tell them to "forget" their history. After all, "it happened so long ago and I am nothing like that." Of course, she may have spent a good part of her life trying to do just that and his advice serves only to increase her sense of inadequacy. We believe that a partner may say these kinds of things not only to be helpful to the survivor but also because he cannot accept his own thoughts and feelings about his wife's abuse. Thus, we work with both members of the couple to accept historical aspects of their lives.

While this chapter is focused on sexual abuse, you should also note that both partners may have other difficult historical issues. Survivors in our groups often report that their partners have experienced child physical abuse, witnessed domestic violence, or struggled with PTSD as a result of wartime traumas. These observations underscore the need to clarify to both members of the dyad that couple problems are inherently a product of the interaction of two people's histories, not just one.

ALEXIS

Having outlined the general approach we take in the treatment of survivors and their partners, we turn to a discussion of some of the issues and treatment implications illustrated in the introductory case history.

In the Alexis case, the amount and type of support provided by the partner was unusually high. For the first eighteen months of individual therapy for the survivor, Bill played a crucial role in helping her cope with suicidality, flashbacks, and dealing with her family of origin. During flashbacks, which were equated to "having guppies" due to the gradual and painful nature of the process, the survivor reported that her husband would stay next to her, reassuring her of her safety while making her aware of her present surroundings. In this initial phase of treatment, Bill attended periodic couples sessions, where general issues (for example, communication) were discussed.

Balancing Power within the Relationship

An area of concern the therapists addressed during treatment planning was the central focus awarded by the couple to Alexis's history of sexual abuse. Although for the time being this attention had treatment utility in terms of aiding the survivor in coping with immediate needs, we were aware of the stigmatizing and pathologizing potential of focusing so intently on the survivor's history.

During the initial periodic couples sessions, the partner at times took the role of a co-therapist, repeatedly emphasizing that he would do anything to help his wife. A goal in treatment was to balance the power within the relationship and set a context for the de-stigmatization of the survivor—and hence lessen the burden on the partner. To the extent that the survivor had strong support by the therapist, the partner would have less need to take on a therapist-like role himself.

Benevolent Blame

It is not uncommon for partners of survivors to engage in some form of "benevolent blame"—that is, to behave in a supportive way while delegating the responsibility for the couple's troubles to the survivor and her history. This point has important treatment implications. Obviously, this attitude perpetuates the stigmatization and power-lessness frequently experienced by adult survivors of sexual abuse. In couples treatment, the issue needs to be taken seriously as there is always the danger that therapy will slowly become about fixing the "broken" survivor. By alternating the focus of treatment between the survivor's and the partner's histories and issues, the therapist conveys the message that both histories contribute to current marital problems.

During the treatment of another couple, Joan, who had been in group therapy, and Dan, we noticed a tendency for him to bring up her childhood history when in fact there were more pressing current relationship difficulties in need of attention. At other times, this avoidance of couple issues can be a function of an interaction between both members of the dyad. For example, Mary complained that her partner treated her like a fragile object, suggesting that she could not adequately deal with her own life. However, her husband reported that whenever he would confront the survivor about her behavior in any way, she would "fall apart," threatening suicide, binge drinking, or running away from home. Interrupting these patterns was greatly facilitated by having both members of the couple present in therapy.

In the Alexis case, Bill demonstrated a keen ability to refrain from engaging in blame under circumstances that could easily lend themselves to a "benevolent blame" approach. For example, he frequently referred to Alexis's psychiatric hospital bills as "our bills." However,

Alexis reported that she had only an experiential understanding of how each of their histories contributed to their marital difficulties when she became aware of her partner's history of incestuous contact with his sister.

Currently, there is a marked difference in how Alexis and Bill present and discuss their relationship issues, and more recently Alexis has talked about periodic role reversals in their relationship in terms of who seeks help from whom in dealing with individual, historical issues. Although in this particular case the partner's history also revolved around sexual issues, there is some anecdotal evidence documented by individuals working in Veteran's Administration settings of a high prevalence of dual survivor couples, particularly couples consisting of a female survivor of sexual abuse and a war veteran suffering from posttraumatic stress disorder (PTSD).

Contact with Family of Origin

Alexis's husband has always been her most important source of support in dealing with her family of origin. When she decided to confront her father about her memories of abuse, Bill remained by her side, being supportive without interfering. In the last year, Alexis has increased her contact with her family of origin, speaking periodically with her mother and at times with her father. Her partner's reactions have been characterized not only by emotional support but also by a willingness to adjust to the level of contact desired by Alexis.

In the survivor's dealings with her family of origin, this flexibility combined with support on the part of the partner tends to be supplanted by either indifference or overinvolvement. Because a great number of survivors presenting to therapy have been molested by a close family member, contact with in-laws becomes quite complex with couples in which one partner was sexually abused as a child. Conflict within the dyad stems mostly from a discrepancy in the desired amount of contact with the survivor's family of origin. One likely scenario is that the partner will be so outraged by the abuse that he refuses to have any contact at all with her family, or, alternatively, the partner may wish to have more contact with the family than the survivor feels willing to have.

These difficulties may be affected by the extent of the partner's knowledge of the abuse as well as by concern over the safety of the couple's children. Couples therapy provides an environment where both partners can discuss these issues, and unrealistic expectations by either partner can be accurately assessed.

Flashbacks

In addition to the support provided during contacts with Alexis's family of origin, the process of increased intimacy between Alexis and Bill was also intensified by their joint sharing of her flashback experiences. Although flashbacks may occur outside the sexual realm, in general they tend to be triggered by some external stimulus in the environment that reminds the survivor of the abuse. Obviously, events surrounding sex tend to be very reminiscent of those associated with the abuse experience.

A flashback may be very distressing and is always intrusive, disconnecting the survivor from the immediate experience (for example, a sexual encounter with her partner) while taking her back to a time in which she did not feel safe (as in being touched by her perpetrator). With support and practice, the survivor may become able to recognize flashbacks and to overcome their disorienting effects. The partner may play a significant role in this process.

Although in the Alexis case the survivor and her partner spontaneously developed a style of interacting during these flashbacks that grounded and reassured her, the therapist may be called on to intervene in such cases, by educating the couple or helping them cope with the aftermath of flashbacks.

While it might be useful for the therapist to have the partner read books such as Davis's *Allies in Healing* or Hansen's *Survivors & Partners* as a form of bibliotherapy, general guidelines for partners on how to respond during flashbacks include being supportive and gentle, orienting the survivor to time and space, and reassuring her of her safety. It is important not to judge, not to ask probing questions, and not to show disgust in any way during or after the flashback episode. In addition to dealing with feelings of embarrassment and shame, the survivor may need time to adjust to the intensity of these recollections. At this point, some flexibility is required on the part of the partner as survivors vary in the amount of interpersonal contact and discussion they desire after a flashback.

The flashback experience may impact the partner as well. He may feel confused, frightened, or angry about these experiences. He may have heard new details of the survivor's abuse experience that he did not know and he may have difficulty coping with his own reactions. Therapeutically, preparing the partner for the possibility of flashbacks, even if the survivor has never experienced them previously, becomes of utmost importance. Alexis and Bill tended to process their joint experience after the flashback incident and discuss their respective reactions. However, as previously suggested, not all individuals cope with flashbacks by increasing the amount of contact with significant others. The couple's plan of action is contingent on each individual's choice.

Dissociation

Although dissociation was less an issue for Alexis than for some, it is frequently identified as a problem by survivors. Flashbacks may occur in conjunction with dissociative episodes. That is, the flashback may serve as a discriminative stimulus for a dissociative response. When describing dissociation during sex, some of our clients alluded to "numbing," "shutting down," "turning [herself] off," "being miles away," "wanting to be elsewhere," "making up a grocery list," or "body going through the motions but mind not being there." The survivor may also focus on some environmental stimulus, such as ceiling or lamp, or feel that she is an observer of the sexual act rather than a participant.

Partner/Perpetrator Association

In addition to flashbacks and dissociation, survivors may experience a range of sexual issues. For example, some survivors fantasize about some aspect of their childhood abuse while having sex with their partners. The association of sexual pleasure with the abuse can be very confusing to survivors and partners alike and may generate negative attitudes toward sex in general in the survivor, and feelings of betrayal and lack of desire in the partner.

Similarly, the survivor may confuse the partner with the perpetrator. This confusion may occur during sexual relations or it may interfere with other interactions between the partners. Distinguishing between reactions to the perpetrator and reactions to the spouse becomes a target area in couples treatment. The partner's knowledge of this difficulty can help resolve these conflicts. The therapist, however, must be alert to the possibility that the partner might be eschewing responsibility for his behavior by encouraging this identity confusion. In fact, some clinicians have suggested that survivors may often find themselves with partners who share similar characteristics with the perpetrator, especially when the latter was a parental figure.

Low Desire and Fluctuations in Libido

Other sexual difficulties reported by survivors pertain to the level of their sexual desire. Although low desire is a particularly prominent issue with survivors of sexual abuse, extreme fluctuations in desire are also commonplace. Alexis reported alternating between extremes in her sexual desire, which led to considerable confusion and frustration in her partner. This vacillation is not an unusual phenomenon, and it has been documented that many survivors experience periods of intense and frequent sexual contact followed by periods of low desire. These dramatic changes tend to confuse the partner, and it is important for him to understand that this is not necessarily a reflection on him or his performance. As with many issues presented in this chapter, even after undergoing treatment, the survivor's libido may continue to fluctuate and it will be up to the partner to accept some of these variations in sexual desire.

The "Dialectic of Trauma"

As illustrated by the discussion of sexual cycles, several issues reported by Alexis and other survivors in treatment tend to have a common theme of significant alternation in behaviors, from one extreme to the other. Some therapists suggest that these cycles serve the function of distracting the survivor from negative affective states, such as depression or feelings of emptiness. There appears to be a tendency for different survivors, or for the same survivor at different times, to experience difficulties that lie at opposite extremes of a continuum. In addition to sex, some of the areas of extreme fluctuation often reported by survivors and their partners include mood, control, and intimacy, among others. Alexis reports experiencing drastic fluctuations in mood according to seasons, varying from feeling extremely depressed in the fall to seeking perfection in weight, work, and looks in the summer.

More than simply revealing the survivor's ambivalence, this pattern seems consistent with what Herman labeled the "dialectic of trauma." As with other behavioral manifestations, this alternation between two extremes may be maintained because "neither the intrusive nor the numbing symptoms allow for integration of the traumatic event." From our point of view, coping strategies that either distract or numb the survivor function similarly: they preclude the individual from fully experiencing the feelings, thoughts, and memories associated with the traumatic event.

This "abuse dichotomy" pattern tends to generalize to interactions within the dyad. The survivor may evaluate herself, her partner, and the relationship in extreme ways—either all good or all bad. As an extension of their childhood history, adult survivors may perceive any relationship problem to be their fault, and hence, unacceptable. This perception may result in a constant preoccupation with perfecting the relationship and ridding it of any conflict. The survivor struggling with this issue typically reports trying to please her partner all the time, doing most of the chores, smoothing and avoiding conflicts, and neglecting most of her own needs.

We view this tendency to dichotomize as emerging within a context of nonacceptance. Often survivors view thoughts such as "I am bad" as core aspects of themselves rather than as thoughts and feelings associated with an abusive history. Indeed, when thoughts such as these are taken literally, clients may find themselves engaging in behaviors congruent with the *content* of those cognitions. Therefore, if the survivor sees herself as unacceptable, she will take steps to destroy herself by attempting suicide, self-mutilating, or engaging in more subtle forms of self-destructive behaviors, such as substance abuse or unprotected sex.

The dichotomy of the survivor as all bad and her partner as all good is another clinical presentation. It is the task of the therapist to alter this polarized perspective, helping the couple to see that they are not together by accident. That is, the partner's history fits with the survivor's history in a comprehensible manner.

For example, someone whose history generated the rule "I must be perfect to be worthy" may find herself with someone whose own rule is "I need to be with someone who must be perfect to be worthy of me." Partners may reinforce activities by the survivor such as excessive cleaning, perfect care for the children, or excessive control over her body in terms of exercise or food intake. Therefore, to the extent that therapy impacts the survivor's worldview, the couple will inevitably be impacted. In the case of Alexis, as she became more self-reliant and independent, the relationship as a whole underwent significant changes in terms of relationship roles.

Parenting Issues

Parenting, a generally challenging experience, poses particular difficulties for survivor couples. With the birth of their baby daughter, Alexis and her partner had to deal with several concerns associated with parenting and trust. A pervasive and unsettling issue is the survivor's concern that the child will be sexually abused, either by strangers or by her partner. This fear can have a very deleterious effect on the relationship if unmanaged, and may push trust issues to their limit. The survivor may become hypervigilant about the child's safety. Clinically, the therapist must maintain a delicate balance: he or she must provide support for the survivor, helping her examine historical factors that contribute to her suspicion; at the same time, the therapist must be cognizant of the possibility that abuse could actually occur.

This issue was a particularly difficult one for Alexis and her partner. Although Alexis had a warm and caring relationship with her partner, she was keenly aware of his history of sexual contact with his sister, and she was concerned about being so distrustful of her own perceptions that she would find herself overlooking evidence and therefore not protecting her child. Her husband, on the other hand, also articulated some fears, inquiring about the accuracy of the stereotype that individuals abused as children become perpetrators as adults.

In couples treatment, our focus is on discussing the predicament of both partners, acknowledging the difficulties involved and outlining a course of action should either partner become suspicious. Recently, Alexis acknowledged that because of their respective histories, she has had to accept that, at least at this time, she is not completely trusting of Bill as far as their child is concerned. Having this thought, however, does not prevent her from acting with love and consideration toward him.

Some survivors also report feeling jealousy toward their children. It is not unusual for survivors to express sadness and hurt about their lost childhoods. This is contrasted with the attention and love that is lavished on their own children. Issues of triangulation, which were often present in the survivor's family relationships, may arise among the mother, father, and children. The therapist must work toward establishing an environment with both the survivor and her partner that would tolerate the disclosure of socially undesirable feelings, such as distrust toward partner or anger and jealousy toward children.

In spite of all the issues confronting them, Alexis and her husband have managed to establish a loving family environment and are currently looking forward to adding to the family. The progress made by Alexis and her husband is no doubt attributable to their individual and relationship strengths. Amid their struggles, an unwavering commitment to treatment and to the relationship has been their greatest ally.

GISLAINE

Gislaine presented initially as an individual to our clinic. However, after extensive therapy, she came to think that continued change in her life would be hindered without changes in her marriage. She initially sought psychological treatment at the urging of the only friend who knew of her abuse history. Although she had always remembered the abuse, the therapist was the first person with whom she discussed her childhood experiences in detail.

Gislaine reported extensive sexual abuse by her biological father that lasted for a number of years. She was also abused by her older brother in later years. Her home environment was marked by paternal alcoholism, maternal depression, the presence of a mentally handicapped sister, and severe domestic violence. These trauma experiences were exacerbated by a date rape experience that she also had never disclosed to anyone for fear that her father would "kill" her.

Gislaine experienced an inordinate amount of shame, guilt, and self-blame regarding the abuse, never disclosing the maltreatment until she was an adult. Despite these difficulties, she excelled in school, was quite athletic, and developed some close friendships. At twenty, she married to leave home. She reported that her husband, Michael, whom she supported through professional school, was a kind and gentle person. However, he was mostly emotionally unavailable in the beginning years of their marriage. For years, she felt that Michael would not accept her if he knew about her history and inner feelings. Her husband's own emotionally detached style allowed her to remain hidden from him in the relationship.

Gislaine was one of those clients who attain a special significance in our lives. Her shy, gentle style was contrasted with a quick wit. She was extremely bright, a quality that she minimized. Despite the extensive trauma in her family of origin, she had emerged with a love for people. This love was particularly evident in her relationship with her two children. Thus, even though she presented for treatment with a great many problems, she showed from the start that she was capable of significant change and growth.

She entered therapy without telling her husband. For a period of time, Gislaine paid for treatment with money that she saved from her household account and when she finally disclosed her therapy to her husband, she did not tell Michael why she had sought treatment. During the first year, therapy dealt with dissociation, nighttime flashbacks, substance abuse, and self-mutilation. She made significant gains in therapy and eventually felt that she needed to tell her husband about her abuse in order for him to have some understanding of who she "really" was. This event marked one of many turning points in the relationship. Both Gislaine and Michael made significant changes in their style of interaction in the course of the years. She eventually identified the goal of completing her college degree. Currently Gislaine does volunteer victim advocacy work, takes care of her growing family, and will soon begin graduate school.

Disclosure

In Gislaine's therapy, one of the key factors influencing her ability to trust Michael involved his reaction to her disclosure of having been abused. Many survivors have also identified disclosure as a critical event in their relationship history. Some of the typical negative reactions exhibited by partners are confusion, hurt, frustration, and anger. The partner may either blame or doubt the survivor, or alternatively, may overidentify with the survivor's pain—in this case sometimes expressing uncontrolled anger toward the perpetrator. Either pattern of reactions invalidates the survivor's experience.

Thirty adult incest survivors who were interviewed reported that the therapist interventions they found most helpful included validation, advocacy, empathic understanding, and absence of derision or contempt. If a parallel can be made between reactions by therapists and significant others, these results provide some suggestions for partners.

In Gislaine's case, the husband looked to the therapist for guidance in his response to her. He was somewhat bemused, but in a kindly manner was able to provide some of the reassurance and acceptance that she had feared he would not communicate. The therapist plays a crucial role in helping both members of the couple to accept their own feelings and reactions during this transitional period in their relationship.

A particularly complex situation arises if the partner does not know about the survivor's history, and they wish to have couples therapy. Before proceeding, the therapist and the survivor should have a thorough discussion regarding repercussions of disclosure, possible reactions by her partner—both positive and negative—and possible settings for telling the partner. The decision to disclose or not to disclose lies with the survivor. We should limit our input to empowering the client to do what she thinks best. Under no circumstances should the therapist demand that the client tell her partner about the abuse. This would greatly lessen her sense of empowerment, and most likely would be counter-therapeutic.

Reaction to Therapy

A similarly important aspect of the survivor's treatment is her partner's reaction to therapy. It is not unusual for individuals to feel threatened when their partners are in treatment and they are not. Partner reactions to therapy may influence how much the client is able to benefit from treatment. Providing couples therapy is one way of overcoming this barrier. However, partners' willingness to be involved in treatment varies. For example, the partner may agree to come to couples therapy only "to help her."

If the partner is not willing to attend therapy at all, he can still affect the survivor's treatment in a multitude of ways. In its more obvious form, lack of support can be expressed by refusing to listen to the survivor's issues, or overtly denigrating her for undergoing psychotherapeutic treatment. We found that partners can negatively impact treatment in profound ways through passive-aggressive means such as failing to provide child care when the survivor has a therapy session or getting drunk and picking a fight on therapy days. It is important that the therapist recognize these behaviors for their function and not just their form.

Trust

Trust and emotional intimacy are inextricably intertwined and represent critical issues for survivors. Childhood abuse of any sort tends to lead to a disruption of trust. If the abuse involved an immediate family member, lack of trust or intimacy avoidance may be especially evident in the survivor's adult couple relationships. All survivors interviewed in one study reported difficulties with intimacy and a tendency to withdraw and isolate themselves from others.

Gislaine reported a great deal of ambivalence about being more intimate with Michael, at times actively distancing herself when her partner began to get closer to her. This difficulty is central to a number of other couples issues described in this chapter. In our experience, enhanced intimacy is not possible until basic issues of trust have been resolved. In some cases, a number of tears in the fabric of the relationship (related to trust violations) must be mended before the survivor is willing to risk increased vulnerability. Treatment interventions should target not only an increased level of intimacy and trust in the relationship, but also acceptance of the survivor's coping style with regard to intimacy. Herman suggests that partners should expect and to an extent tolerate trauma survivors' "fluctuating need for closeness and distance".

Self-Reference

Some survivors believe there is something fundamentally wrong with them that they will never be able to change. At times, the sole goal of treatment with Gislaine was to lend her some of the therapist's hope that she could in fact "get better." Other clients have a negative sense of self, describing this feeling of having a "big black blob" inside.

Mary, a group client, talked about the "blob" quite literally, and as she progressed in her recovery, she reported that the blob was getting lighter and lighter in color. This presentation, previously labeled the "damaged goods syndrome," most likely reflects a disruption of the survivor's sense of self based on a history filled with violating experiences.

We view this type of presentation as a metaphor for the survivor's inability to accept herself. The lack of self-acceptance may spring from the survivors' difficulties in having internal experiences they find unacceptable, such as fantasies about their abuse, or it may reflect an unwillingness to accept their history, with all its pain.

Attractiveness/Femininity

Over the course of therapy, Gislaine also struggled with issues of attractiveness and femininity. This topic is frequently discussed in our group sessions, with members commenting on their discomfort with dressing attractively, looking feminine, or being complimented on their appearance. At times, these feelings seem related to fears of being thought too forward and provocative. For Gislaine, however, this difficulty with appearance seemed to be another facet of her sense that she was a fundamentally bad and even "ugly" person. While this issue seemed to diminish in strength as she dealt with her internal experiences, it was the therapist's impression that Gislaine would never see herself as others saw her—a very attractive woman.

Communication

It is not surprising, given the extensive levels of dysfunction in Gislaine's family of origin, that she was very reticent in expressing herself. A history of oppression and dismissal of the survivor's thoughts and feelings tends to lead to great difficulties in the area of assertiveness, especially within intimate relationships. Working to get Gislaine to express her needs and desires in her individual therapy was an ongoing task. As noted by Kohlenberg and Tsai, it is critical that we remain aware of the emergence of the clinically desired behaviors in session (such as assertion), being careful not to punish behaviors that are not recognized as improvements.

For example, in treating a client with assertion deficits, the therapist, whenever possible, should accommodate her request for a session change resulting from reasonable scheduling difficulties. Doing so reinforces the client's sense that her needs are legitimate and that others will heed the expression of those needs. Couples therapy is a particularly suitable setting for increasing the survivor's assertiveness. We have the opportunity to empower the client to be assertive with her partner in session, where the survivor can feel safe and obtain feedback that is moderated by the therapist's input. Working on this issue in couples therapy is particularly important in that the partner may initially be resistant to these changes in his spouse and thus might extinguish her assertive behaviors. It is the therapist's role to shape the husband's response, working with him to recognize advantages in her communication changes.

Confusion was a recurrent problem for Gislaine, both in and out of therapy sessions. This confusion manifested itself on both process and content levels. With regard to content, Gislaine was often very unsure of herself on a number of matters. Survivors may report being confused about issues such as sex, family, intimacy, dating, or parenting. The client may report either "being confused" or "not knowing" what she thinks or what she should do about these issues. This confusion is not at all surprising when one considers the interactions that occurred in the family of origin.

In Gislaine's case, her observations of events were consistently denied in her family. She was told that things she had witnessed had not occurred and that she was crazy. This invalidating environment leads to severe disturbances in the sense of self that is normally formed in very young children. Therefore, an ongoing aspect of therapy was to provide an environment in which Gislaine's ideas were treated respectfully and "I" statements were reinforced on a consistent basis.

On a process level, Gislaine's confusion arose during times of emotional arousal. She often experienced this confusion after emerging from brief dissociative episodes and being unsure of what had occurred in the last few minutes. However, the confusion seemed to also serve as a coping mechanism, functioning to slow down or control intense interactions. Therefore, the therapist must work to expose the client slowly to increased levels of emotional arousal, providing grounding and a sense of safety. After this process has been established in the individual therapy, it should be generalized to the partner relationship by continuing the work in couples therapy.

The problem of communication may occur at different levels and in different settings. In addition to common difficulties in general communication, survivors tend to report specific problems when communicating their private emotions, feelings, and thoughts, particularly as they relate to the abuse. The survivor may report that she herself is, or they as a couple are, unable or unwilling to discuss feelings, thoughts, or emotions with each other. She may also report feeling "unsafe" or otherwise dissatisfied after sharing her feelings with her partner. Thus, communication is an important target for treatment.

Baucom and Epstein have provided useful treatment guidelines for communication training that are well suited for survivors' therapy. Exercises that assist the couple to label and discuss emotions, as well as training in problem-solving techniques, are appropriate interventions. These treatment strategies, based on a social learning approach, were useful tools for Gislaine and her husband in expanding their repertoire of communication skills.

Sexual Issues

After a great deal of relationship therapy, Gislaine and Michael were ready to address the sexual aspect of their relationship. Because of the nature of sexual abuse, the survivor may associate sex with shameful, guilty feelings. She may see sex as "dirty" and "unclean," and may report experiencing negative feelings, emotions, or thoughts about herself or her partner during or after having had consensual sex. Therefore, work using traditional sex therapy, with graduated safe exposure to sexual contact and arousal, is an essential aspect of treatment for many survivors.

As noted earlier, survivor adult couple relationships have been characterized by a lack of adequate communication. Sometimes sexual difficulties merely reflect relationship difficulties in general; nowhere is this consideration more noteworthy than in the area of communication. If the couple has problems communicating in general, they will definitely run into difficulty in the sexual realm as well. However, for some couples, sex is a particularly difficult subject to discuss. The survivor may report being unable to convey to her partner her sexual desires, wishes, turn-offs, general reactions to sex, or how sex with her partner reminds her of the abuse. We have found the work of Heiman, with the special recommendations by Maltz and Holman, to be especially useful in providing effective guidelines for treatment.

Coordination of Treatment

A final note on Gislaine's case relates to the coordination of treatment. It is not unusual for the survivor to be in individual or group psychotherapy concurrently with couples therapy. In these cases, all therapists working with the client have a special responsibility to communicate effectively so as not to work at cross-purposes. While this caveat may seem obvious, we have frequently observed cases in which differing therapist agendas have resulted in negative effects for the client. However, Gislaine's individual and couple therapists had a great deal of respect for each other, stayed in regular contact, and avoided issues such as triangulation and blaming that can disrupt therapy relationships. Although this issue was not generally discussed in the therapy, the clients seemed to be aware of the general tenor of the therapists' relationships and thus were not distracted by inter-therapist problems.

Gislaine and her husband recognize that work on a relationship is never truly over, but rather that the work takes a different form as the relationship evolves. Their commitment to personal growth, and to each other, exemplifies the strengths and values that we see in many couples. Thus, they continue striving to define a relationship that is supportive and loving, one in which neither of them is subject to the kind of pain and trauma that characterized Gislaine's early years.

SPECIAL ISSUES

A number of special issues emerge during couples therapy when one partner has experienced childhood sexual abuse.

Physical Abuse and Social Isolation

One of the sequelae of sexual abuse most often articulated is revictimization. It may take the form of adult rape, domestic violence, or both. The prevalence of domestic violence in this population has been well documented in the literature. Consequently, we must always be sure to conduct a thorough assessment for the presence of emotional, physical, and sexual abuse within the relationship. The assessment must be detailed enough to identify milder forms of abuse. A number of our clients describe circumstances that suggest an attempt by the partner to socially isolate the client from other support networks. Partner abuse, as outlined in the domestic violence literature, may have a severe impact on psychological treatment for the survivor, regardless of treatment modality. If domestic violence is present, it is critical that the therapist develop a safety plan with the survivor and inform her of local services, such as shelter facilities.

The decision of whether or not to work on the relationship in the presence of domestic violence is complex. A great deal has been written about this issue and a review of those writings is beyond the scope of this chapter. However, three matters are critical in relation to this issue. First, the therapist must do everything in her power to make the survivor aware of the risks and dangers associated with domestic violence. Second, the therapist must be careful to avoid taking a patriarchal stance in relation to the survivor, thus invalidating her own needs for autonomy. Third, the issue of current child abuse must be thoroughly assessed, with clients informed of legal and ethical considerations with regard to reporting issues.

Managed Care

The increasing reliance on third-party payment for therapeutic services calls for a reevaluation of the allocation of time in treatment. Although both cases discussed in this chapter had the advantage of long-term and multiple modality treatments, this abundance of time and resources is quickly becoming a rarity in settings other than nonprofit, university training sites such as the ones in which these cases were treated.

Within the current social-economic climate, two points warrant clarification. First, the content of this chapter is in no way intended to suggest that all couples in which one partner was sexually abused need to undergo couples treatment. In fact, there is documentation of successful treatment of survivors in group modalities. We recommend that only those couples who have not been able to deal successfully with difficulties such as the ones presented in this chapter, and who are willing and able to commit to treatment, be encouraged to pursue couples therapy. For these individuals, couples treatment might be the most useful psychotherapy modality for the reasons discussed throughout this chapter.

Second, a frequent concern articulated by therapists committed to short-term treatment is the lavish allocation of therapy time to the discussion of childhood issues. In fact, it would not be cost effective to spend five of six total couples sessions discussing the survivor's past history. In our approach, the starting point in treatment is the outline of current relationship concerns and the couple's goals for the future. However, as behavior occurs in a context that includes both individuals' histories, treatment might be more effective, and no less cost effective, if it is historically informed. The importance of conducting an extensive assessment of the survivor's sexual abuse history will vary depending on the relevance, type, and severity of the issues the couple presents in treatment.

De-stigmatizing the Survivor

It is fitting that we close this chapter with a discussion of the paradox of promoting the de-stigmatization of the survivor as the identified patient within the context of a chapter whose main emphasis is that one of the partners has had a history of childhood sexual abuse.

We hope that by now the reader has come to some of the same conclusions reached by the authors on this subject. Operating from a contextual perspective, we believe that all contributing variables must be considered in the treatment of couples. However, the sexual abuse history need only *inform* the treatment of the couple, not become the focus of treatment. For example, knowing that survivors are vulnerable to revictimization in the form of physical violence does not mean that when domestic violence is present, treatment would involve explaining that vulnerability to the couple or trying to understand why it came about. Instead, the intervention would target behavioral change that would ensure the woman's safety and be congruent with the value and goal of stopping the violence.

As emphasized throughout this chapter, the knowledge of sexual abuse in the survivor's history should not obscure the equally relevant contribution of her partner to relationship difficulties. All concerns arising in a dyadic context are the result of an interaction of two individuals and their histories. The critical and essential aspect of treatment is working to provide a context that is not only free of violence, but is also life-enhancing to both members of the couple.

NOTES

P. 132, *The overall focus . . . survivor of child sexual abuse:* It may very well be the case that both partners are survivors. Although this factor would add to the complexity of the phenomenon, the issues discussed in this chapter would still be applicable and would not deviate considerably. Hansen (1991) suggests in his book *Survivors and Partners* that being a partner as well as a survivor often improves the partner's ability to understand the other person's issues.

P. 132, *The clinical and scientific literature:* Briere, J. N. (1988). The long-term clinical correlates of childhood sexual victimization. *Annals of the New York Academy of Sciences, 528,* 327–334; Briere, J. N. (1992). *Child abuse trauma: Theory and treatment of the lasting effects.* Newbury Park, CA: Sage; Johnson, S. M. (1989). Integrating marital and individual therapy for incest survivors: A case study. *Psychotherapy, 26*(1), 96–103.

P. 132, *Survivors' childhood experiences:* Briere, J. N. (1992). *Child abuse trauma: Theory and treatment of the lasting effects.* Newbury Park, CA: Sage; Browne, A., & Finkelhor, D. (1986). Impact of child sexual abuse: A review of the research. *Psychological Bulletin, 99,* 66–77; Harter, S., Alexander, P. C., & Neimeyer, R. A. (1988). Long-term effects of incestuous child abuse in college women: Social adjustment, social cognition, and family characteristics. *Journal of Consulting and Clinical Psychology, 56*(1), 5–8.

P. 132, *When compared to controls . . . separated:* Russell, D. H. (1986). *The secret trauma: Incest in the lives of girls and women.* New York: Basic Books.

P. 132, *fear of their partners:* Meiselman, K. (1978). *Incest.* San Francisco: Jossey-Bass.

P. 132, *lower relationship and sexual satisfaction:* Waltz, J., & Jacobson, N. S. (1992). *Effects of childhood sexual abuse on female survivors' and their partners' relationship and sexual satisfaction and communication patterns.* Paper presented at the annual meeting of the Association for Advancement of Behavior Therapy (AABT) in Boston.

P. 132, *sexual functioning may be impaired:* Briere, J. N. (1988). The long-term clinical correlates of childhood sexual victimization. *Annals of the New York Academy of Sciences, 528,* 327–334; Maltz, W., & Holman, B. (1987). *Incest and sexuality: A guide to understanding and healing.* Lexington, MA: Lexington Books; Polusny, M., & Follette, V. M. (in press). Long term correlates of child sexual abuse: Theory and review of the empirical literature. *Applied and Preventive Psychology.*

P. 133, *vulnerable to revictimization:* Briere, J. N., & Runtz, M. (1991). The long-term effects of sexual abuse: A review and synthesis (pp. 3–14). In J. Briere (Ed.), *Treating victims of child sexual abuse.* San Francisco: Jossey-Bass; Follette, V. M. (1991). Marital therapy for sexual abuse survivors. In J. Briere (Ed.), *Treating victims of child sexual abuse.* San Francisco: Jossey-Bass; Follette, V. M., Polusny, M., Naugle, A., & Bechtle, A. (in press). Cumulative trauma effects: Impact of child sexual abuse, sexual assault, and spouse abuse. *Journal of Traumatic Stress.*

P. 133, *The inherently interpersonal:* Alexander, P. C., & Follette, V. M. (1987). Personal constructs in the group treatment of incest (pp. 211–229). In R. Neiymeyer & G. J. Neimeyer (Eds.), *Personal construct therapy casebook.* New York: Springer.

P. 133, *reducing the amount of distress:* Alexander, P. C., Neimeyer, R. A., Follette, V. M., Moore, M. K., & Harter S. (1989). A comparison of group treatments of women sexually abused as children. *Journal of Consulting and Clinical Psychology, 57*(4), 479–483; Follette, V. M., & Pistorello, J. *Group treatment of female sexual abuse survivors: An acceptance-based approach.* Unpublished paper.

P. 133, *married survivors did not benefit as much:* Follette, V. M., Alexander, P. C., & Follette, W. M. (1991). Individual predictors of outcome in group treatment for incest survivors. *Journal of Consulting and Clinical Psychology, 59*(1), 150–154.

P. 133, *survivors who were in a stable intimate relationship:* Burgess, A. W., & Holstrom, L. L. (1979). Adaptive strategies and recovery from rape. *American Journal of Psychiatry, 136,* 1278–1282.

P.133, *clients who deteriorated after group treatment:* Follette, V. M., & Pistorello, J. *Group treatment of female sexual abuse survivors: An acceptance-based approach.* Unpublished paper.

P. 133, *have the power to influence:* Herman, J. L. (1992). *Trauma and recovery,* p. 61. New York: HarperCollins.

P. 133, *woman's primary intimate relationship:* Follette, V. M. (1991). Marital therapy for sexual abuse survivors. In J. Briere (Ed.), *Treating victims of child sexual abuse.* San Francisco: Jossey-Bass.

P. 134, *ACT:* Hayes, S. C., McCurry, S., Afari, N., & Wilson, K. G. *Acceptance and Commitment Therapy (ACT): Treatment protocol.* (Unpublished); Hayes, S. C., & Wilson, K. G. (in press). Acceptance and Commitment Therapy: Altering the verbal support for experiential avoidance. *The Behavior Analyst;* Kohlenberg, R. J., Hayes, S. C., & Tsai, M. (1993). Radical behavioral psychotherapy: Two contemporary examples. *Clinical Psychology Review, 13*(6), 579–592; A thorough discussion of the theoretical underpinnings of ACT is beyond the scope of this chapter. However, the interested reader is referred to Hayes & Wilson (in press) and to Kohlenberg, Hayes, and Tsai (1993) for a radical behaviorist conceptualization of ACT.

P. 134, *At a technique level:* Hayes, S. C., McCurry, S. M., Afari, N., & Wilson, K. G. (1993). *Acceptance and commitment therapy: A manual for the treatment of emotional avoidance.* Reno: Context Press.

P. 135, *the survivor to be less autonomous and to be excessively other-directed:* Briere, J. N. (1992). *Child abuse trauma: Theory and treatment of the lasting effects.* Newbury Park, CA: Sage.

P. 136, *acceptance can be broken down into . . . and acceptance of others:* Hayes, S. C. (1994). Content, context, and the types of psychological acceptance. In S. C. Hayes, N. S. Jacobson, V. M. Follette, & M. J. Dougher (Eds.). *Acceptance and change: Content and context in psychotherapy.* Reno: Context Press; Pistorello, J., Follette, V. M., Wilson, K., & Hayes, S. C. (1994). *Acceptance in childhood sexual abuse survivors: A radical behaviorist perspective.* Paper presented at the annual meeting of the Association for Behavior Analysis, Atlanta.

P. 137, *Zen Buddhism:* Welwood, J. (1983). *Awakening the heart: East/West approaches to psychotherapy and the healing relationship.* Boston: New Science Library.

P. 140, *"Benevolent blame":* Follette, V. M. (1991). Marital therapy for sexual abuse survivors. In J. Briere (Ed.), *Treating victims of child sexual abuse.* San Francisco: Jossey-Bass.

P. 142, *have the partner read books:* Davis, L. (1991). *Allies in healing: When the person you love was sexually abused as a child.* New York: HarperCollins; Hansen, P. A. (1991). *Survivors and partners: Healing the relationships of sexual abuse survivors.* Longmont, CO: Heron Hill.

P. 143, *survivors may experience a range of sexual issues:* Maltz & Holman, *Incest and sexuality.*

P. 143, *some survivors fantasize:* Davis, *Allies in healing.*

P. 144, *find themselves with partners:* Alexander & Follette, *Personal constructs.*

P. 144, *low desire is a particularly prominent issue:* Maltz & Holman, *Incest and sexuality.*

P. 144, *periods of intense and frequent sexual contact:* Courtois, C. A. (1979). The incest experience and its aftermath. *Victimology: An International Journal, 4,* 337–347; Briere, *Child abuse trauma.*

P. 145, *Some therapists suggest . . . distracting the survivor:* Briere & Runtz, *The long-term effects of sexual abuse.*

P. 145, *"dialectic of trauma":* Herman, *Trauma and recovery.*

P. 145, *"neither the intrusive . . . the traumatic event":* Herman, *Trauma and recovery.*

P. 145, *"abuse dichotomy":* Briere, *Child abuse trauma.*

P. 149, *Thirty adult incest survivors . . . absence of derision or contempt:* Armsworth, M. S. (1989). Therapy of incest survivors: Abuse or support? *Child Abuse & Neglect, 13*(4), 549–562.

P. 150, *We should limit our input . . . she thinks best:* Follette, *Marital therapy.*

P. 150, *Childhood abuse . . . disruption of trust:* Courtois, C. A. (1988). *Healing the incest wound: Adult survivors in therapy.* New York: Norton; Briere, *Child abuse trauma;* Herman, *Trauma and recovery.*

P. 151, *difficulties with intimacy:* Armsworth, M. W. (1990). A qualitative analysis of adult incest survivors' responses to sexual involvement with therapists. *Child Abuse & Neglect, 14*(4), 541–554.

P. 151, *Herman suggests . . . "fluctuating need for closeness and distance":* Herman, *Trauma and recovery,* p. 63.

P. 151, *"damaged goods syndrome":* Sgroi, S. M. (1982). *Handbook of clinical intervention in child sexual abuse.* Lexington, KY: Heath.

P. 151, *disruption of the survivor's sense of self:* Courtois, *Healing the incest wound.*

P. 152, *As noted by Kohlenberg and Tsai:* Kohlenberg, R. J., & Tsai, M. (1991). *Functional analytic psychotherapy.* New York: Plenum Press.

P. 153, *"I" statements were reinforced:* Kohlenberg & Tsai, *Functional analytic psychotherapy.*

P. 154, *Baucom and Epstein:* Baucom, D. H., & Epstein, N. (1990). *Cognitive-behavioral marital therapy.* New York: Brunner/Mazel.

P. 154, *the work of Heiman:* Heiman, J. R. (1986). Treating sexually distressed marital relationships (pp. 361–384). In N. S. Jacobson & A. S. Gurman (Eds.), *Clinical handbook of marital therapy.* New York: Guilford Press.

P. 154, *special recommendations by Maltz and Holman:* Maltz & Holman, *Incest and sexuality.*

P. 155, *revictimization:* Briere, *Child abuse trauma.*

6

USING HYPNOSIS

Jose R. Maldonado and David Spiegel

Sexual abuse is a violation of both mind and body that deprives the child of a sense of basic trust and security. This early trauma impairs the child's future ability to develop healthy interpersonal relationships. The invasion of personal privacy, the violation of the body, and the lack of control that are inherent in episodes of sexual abuse can have devastating effects on anyone, especially a child. The long-term effects can range from behavioral problems and academic deterioration in a child, to dysfunction in the areas of sexuality and interpersonal relationships in later years. On occasion people who have experienced such abuse develop profound characterological dysfunction, ranging from borderline personality disorder (BPD), to psychopathology such as posttraumatic stress disorder (PTSD), or even dissociative identity disorder (DID; formerly known as multiple personality disorder, MPD).

As one of the therapeutic options for psychotherapists, we have found hypnosis to be a readily available and simple tool. Therapists may use hypnotic techniques as a way to help patients access repressed and dissociated memories while allowing them to maintain a sense of control. Eventually, we can teach this technique to our patients so they can use it as a means of achieving self-control and mastery.

In this chapter we review the relationship between childhood sexual trauma and trance phenomena. From this perspective, we discuss the rationale for using hypnosis in the treatment of this patient population. Following is a discussion on the application of hypnosis in the treatment of these patients. Finally, we consider the legal ramifications associated with the use of hypnosis in this setting.

RATIONALE FOR THE USE OF HYPNOSIS

There is ample evidence that patients undergoing intense trauma may use their own dissociative defenses to guard themselves against the impact of trauma. We know that later in life many of these same individuals use their already mastered hypnotic-like capacities to protect them from further traumatization. Some do this quite intentionally; others are completely unaware of the process.

One of our former patients was sexually abused as a child by a neighbor. She came to the United States as one of a family of European immigrants and had no social support. She felt helpless in many ways. She was just learning a new language, poorly mastered by her own parents. Her father was an alcoholic and "used to run around with many women." Both of these activities often kept him away from the home. Also, her mother had to work away from home to help support the household. All these circumstances meant that the patient spent a great deal of time unattended. She normally walked back and forth from school by herself. She lived in an old, three-story house in the city. One day, her third floor neighbor waited for her at the steps. This was not the first time she had found him sitting on the steps in front of her apartment as she came home. At times they would exchange a few words. But one particular afternoon he forced himself into her apartment and into her life.

Like many child victims of abuse, she was shocked. She wanted to tell her parents but was afraid of their reaction. The neighbor convinced her that nobody would believe her if she reported the abuse. Furthermore, she was afraid that if they did believe her, they would blame and punish her for it. So she never spoke a word. As in many unfortunate cases, the abuse took place repeatedly over a number of years. During all that time she had no source of help or escape other than her imagination. As a child, the patient learned, initially accidentally but later quite consciously, to enter a self-hypnotic trance and mentally transport herself to a beautiful and tranquil spot in the meadows. There she would entertain herself with scenes in which she played on the grass, ran after butterflies, and picked flowers along the nearby pond—all this while her body was being brutally violated. Later, when it was safe to return, she would "come back from the dream," run to the bathroom to wash herself, and then continue with her life "as if nothing ever happened."

As an adult, the patient continued this once protective but now pathological use of her dissociative defense. Not knowing what she was doing but believing that it would prevent further suffering, she induced a self-hypnotic, dissociative state whenever an emotionally charged experience elicited feelings that resembled those associated with the initial trauma. At the time she entered treatment, she had lost control of her defenses and was living a very painful existence. She had been admitted to an acute inpatient unit during one of her psychotic episodes. As indicated in her medical records, she had received almost every major diagnosis listed on Axis I of the DSM-III-R and about five of the eleven listed under Axis II. Some symptoms resembled a state of "hysterical psychosis."

It appeared as if she entered a self-hypnotic state every time her defenses were taxed. These psychotic symptoms were manifestations of a spontaneous dissociative state, not unlike the one she entered during episodes of sexual abuse. In her psychosis, she would fantasize about wanting to take care of people, especially children. In her worst times these thoughts would vary, ranging from claiming to be God, to horrible fear of demonic voices that haunted her for the perversity of her actions. She would not "switch" from one personality into another; rather, she would just dissociate into this "crazy" person who appeared to make no sense—but if listened to carefully was actually telling the story of the horrible life she endured years ago.

As in the case above, many of our patients continue to utilize hyp-notic-like phenomena when faced with the threat of a traumatic experience. Some who frequently utilized these dissociative defenses during childhood may have little conscious recollection, as in the cases of dissociative amnesia. More extreme disturbance is evidenced by those patients who develop a complicated dissociative system in which "somebody else" recalls and suffers the pain of the memories, as in dissociative identity disorder.

Furthermore, many of the dissociated memories continue to haunt these patients even though they don't remember them. While dissociated memories may be out of conscious awareness, they can continue to affect mood, behavior, and cognitive processes. Most of them are experienced as "an uneasy feeling" which the survivors get when in specific situations (such as being physically close to some-one). In fact "dissociated" information continues to exert a power-ful influence in current life events.

An example is the fifty-two-year-old married woman who presented for therapy because of feelings of depression and marital problems. When she began therapy the patient had no recollection of having being sexu-ally abused by her grandfather between the ages of two and six, or later by her father between the ages of seven and twelve. Even though she was able to "completely dissociate" the memories of the incest from con-sciousness, there were changes in her behavior that indicated she had not completely forgotten the abuse and that somehow this knowledge was able to influence her subsequent behavior.

She continued to "love" her father. Indeed, she was able to talk about how he taught her to appreciate opera, classical music, and ballet. She felt high regard for him but she remembers always "feeling funny when I was around him, especially when he hugged me." Sometimes she described this as "the silly feeling of fear of being in his presence, or being touched by him," even though she could not recall why. In addition, the patient could not tolerate the thought of her grandfather. Even mentioning his name "makes me sick to my stomach."

During the course of her therapy she was able to recall the abuse perpetrated by her grandfather, while initially there was no indication that her father had harmed her. On one occasion, the patient dissociated in her therapist's office while discussing a recurrent dream. She spontaneously regressed to the age of seven, and remained in that state. She was admitted to our hospital on the eighth day following the dissociation. At that point she was given a tentative diagnosis of dissociative identity disorder. Three days later we used hypnosis to elucidate the memories that had triggered the dissociation.

In hypnosis, we reprocessed memories pertaining to the known molestation by the grandfather. Despite having released and reprocessed the memories, she did not seem to respond as expected. Surprisingly, in the process of reframing the experiences concerning her grandfather, she discovered that she had also been sexually molested by her father. Her desire "not to know this information" was so great that she regressed to the age she had been just before the abuse by the father began. In this way she "could not have known" about the abuse.

Other patients reexperience the trauma in the form of dreams, nightmares, or flashbacks. There is controversy about the meaning and content of traumatic dreams. Many authors stress the replicative quality of these dreams. They claim that most of them are like "instant replays" of the original event. In our experience, most of the noncombat traumatic dreams may not be so obvious in content. Many of the victims of physical and sexual abuse report "repetitive disturbing dreams" which they cannot remember. On these occasions we know about the dreams because of the complaints of their bed partners or roommates. Not uncommonly, these "unremembered dreams" are a nightmare that repeats itself either in its totality or just the basic theme. For example, they remember being chased, followed, or killed, but they recall no details. The only common denominator in the dreams is that "they are very frightening" and they recur frequently.

An example of this type of repetitive dream is the case of another of our patients, a twenty-four-year-old married woman who came to therapy with complaints of recurrent depression. During the course of therapy she reported a repetitive theme in her nightmares. In them, she sees herself usually as a younger child playing in the house. A man arrives to attack her. She sees herself running through a convoluted maze of doors and hallways. But at the end he always catches up with her. Whenever she was able to get to a door there was nothing on the other side except a brick wall, and every window she could reach was locked by bars. Finally, her attacker grabs her, and stabs or shoots her. On many occasions she is able to "float out of my body and see my dead body lying down below while he still has the gun in his hand."

As in many other cases, this patient reported no history of sexual abuse at the beginning of therapy. It was later in therapy when she was able to make sense out of her nightmares that memories of sexual abuse by an uncle emerged.

Please refer to the section entitled Therapeutic Precautions for some words of warning regarding the "interpretation" of repetitive or traumatic dreams in the clinical setting.

BASIC CONCEPTS IN HYPNOSIS

It is not the intention of this chapter to review the technical aspects of hypnosis. But in order to facilitate the understanding of the techniques that follow, we provide here a brief explanation of the basic concepts. Those interested in learning more about the therapeutic applications of hypnosis may want to contact one of the many accredited institutions (such as the American Society of Clinical Hypnosis or the Society for Clinical and Experimental Hypnosis) for training seminar information, or read one of the many excellent textbooks written in the area.

Hypnosis can be defined as a psychophysiological state of aroused, attentive, and receptive focal concentration with a corresponding relative suspension of (or diminution in) peripheral awareness.

The phenomenon known as hypnosis can be conceptualized as having three main components: absorption, dissociation, and suggestibility.

Absorption refers to the tendency for altering our perceptions and surroundings while in a state of highly focused attention, such as when we watch an interesting movie or get deeply involved with what is happening in a novel. Highly hypnotizable individuals may become so engrossed in the imaginary action that they need time to re-orient themselves away from the action in the film and back into their own surroundings. The mechanism of dissociation allows us to carry on more than one complex task or action simultaneously (such as knitting while holding a conversation or watching television). It serves to compartmentalize various aspects of consciousness, memory, or identity. Suggestibility implies a heightened responsiveness to ideas or suggestions, including social cues. The belief that hypnotized individuals are deprived of their will is false. On the other hand, they are less likely to judge instructions critically and therefore are more likely to act on them.

The components of hypnotic phenomena are similar to many of the symptoms presented by patients who have been victims of sexual trauma at an early age, especially those trauma victims suffering from posttraumatic stress disorder. For example, flashbacks resemble hypnotic absorption. A simple environmental cue or an interpersonal event can trigger memories of the trauma. The trauma victim then becomes so absorbed in these memories that he or she loses touch with the present surroundings and even forgets that these events are in the past, so the person responds to them as if they are happening all over again. It is this capacity for absorption that allows highly hypnotizable individuals to discover and release early life memories while using hypnotic age regression techniques.

Hypnotized individuals may be able to separate or dissociate completely from an emotion or a somatic sensation while under trance. Some subjects are so suggestible that they can achieve this state to the extent of not recognizing a body part as being their own, or of not remembering a piece of information previously known to them, like someone's name or the existence of the number 6. Similarly, some trauma victims use their dissociative abilities to disconnect affect from their current experiences. By doing this, they can prevent feelings in the present from triggering past memories. But like many defense mechanisms, dissociation has it drawbacks. Such individuals separate feelings from their present actions, suffering a resultant loss of enjoyment and interest in their current lives.

Not only do patients sometimes dissociate feelings, but in many instances women who have been traumatized during childhood separate memories from bodily sensations. These patients later seek medical help for a given somatic complaint, usually pain, for which no organic etiology is discovered. On occasion, these bodily ailments are the only memories left of the abuse. As in the case of dreams, some of these physical complaints hold the key to forgotten memories of abuse. However, a clinician should not assume that symptoms with no physiological explanation are necessarily the result of earlier trauma.

Last, hypnotic suggestibility is similar to the hypersensitivity or responsivity to environmental cues observed in trauma patients. Highly hypnotizable individuals may "get dizzy" if someone suggests that they are riding a roller coaster. Similarly, sexually abused patients may act as if they were being attacked by their spouses during lovemaking or during the course of an argument. Trauma victims may also become excessively involved with cues when they watch a movie in which the actor portrays a scene of physical or sexual abuse. These patients tend to become agitated and fearful. Their responses may vary from covering their eyes in fear to running out of the movie theater in panic.

During the moment of trauma these patients experience a radical fragmentation and polarization. The victim alternates between the intense, vivid, and painful experience and a kind of artificial normality in which she attempts to avoid the full impact of the experience by dissociating. Years after the trauma, victims attempt to hold the memories and images associated with the traumatic event away from their awareness by using a mechanism similar to the one they invoked at the time of the trauma itself. The dissociative behavior exhibited by trauma victims may be linked to heightened hypnotic responsivity. Just as several authors have reported that Vietnam veterans who score high in PTSD symptomatology also have higher scores on hypnotizability scales, sexually abused women respond in a similar fashion on measures of dissociation.

Since the patients exposed to extreme trauma such as physical and sexual abuse are highly hypnotizable, and because of the striking resemblance between some of the symptoms suffered by victims of sexual trauma and the characteristics of hypnotic phenomena, it makes sense to consider the use of hypnosis in the treatment of these patients.

HYPNOSIS APPLIED IN THE COURSE OF PSYCHOTHERAPY

Several things should be considered in using hypnosis in the treatment of sexually abused women. First, hypnosis by itself is not therapy. Just to induce a hypnotic trance adds nothing to the treatment. What makes a difference when you use hypnosis is not the trance itself but the work you and your patient do while she is in trance. Hypnosis is as effective and useful as are the psychotherapeutic skills of the therapist using this technique.

Second, all hypnosis is really self-hypnosis. Therefore, the therapist who uses hypnosis is no more than a guide to patients. Our role is to help them use their own hypnotic capacity.

Third, there is nothing you can do with hypnosis that you cannot do without it. The advantage of using hypnosis is that it facilitates the client's recovery of affect and memories, her ability to dissociate memories from cognition, and the speed with which she achieves this.

Finally, because of the relationship between a history of childhood abuse and trance, these patients are usually highly hypnotizable.

Many victims of childhood sexual abuse, especially those suffering from PTSD, may unknowingly be using their own hypnotic capacities to keep secret the content of those memories; at the same time, however, they are creating different degrees of psychopathology. Many members of this particular population can be taught how to access and control their trance potential. Teaching these patients self-hypnosis is a way of turning a weakness into a strong tool for self-mastery and control. The controlled use of hypnosis, then, becomes a way to systematically access previously dissociated material.

As therapists, our intention is not simply to help the patient "remember the trauma." Even having an abreaction is not enough. In fact, every time a patient experiences a flashback she is experiencing an uncontrolled abreaction. We believe that the indiscriminate use of abreactive techniques may lead to further traumatization of the victim. Consequently, we believe that restructuring of the patient's cognitive schemes should be done before we facilitate a complete abreaction of the traumatic events. This should be followed by work on ego strengthening and the development of new and more mature defenses. It is in this therapeutic context that hypnosis can be effectively used to facilitate controlled retrieval of traumatic memories.

A hypnotic-like state is frequently spontaneously elicited during traumatic experiences. Because of research on state-dependent memory we know that we store memories along with their associated affect. Thus the experience of a situation with a similar affective charge may facilitate the retrieval of the initial memory. We can use this principle in two different ways during the course of psychotherapy.

First, as a client is engaged in therapy, the therapeutic process may elicit memories of a traumatic experience, activating the formerly repressed painful affect. Second, the reexperience of a dissociated state of mind (such as the therapeutic trance involving hypnosis) may trigger retrieval of memories and affects associated with the original trauma. The transition into the hypnotic trance can facilitate access to memories related to a dissociated state, as might have happened at the time of the trauma. Hypnosis is in itself a controlled form of dissociation, therefore facilitating the likelihood of retrieving strong emotional reactions and previously unavailable memories of the trauma.

Many trauma victims fear that if they allow traumatic memories to surface, they will open Pandora's Box and once again lose control over their minds, bodies, and lives. They have a difficult time separating themselves from their memories. Actually, many victims of childhood physical and sexual abuse continue to see themselves as they were at the time of the trauma: defenseless and vulnerable. Our task as therapists is to help patients retrieve the painful memories that haunt them, express them in ways that do not foster self-destructive feelings, and restructure the ways they think about themselves.

Hypnosis can prove invaluable during this process. Several hypnotic techniques allow patients to remember pieces of the traumatic experience at a pace they can tolerate. One such approach combines induced physical sensations of relaxation and the use of the "screen technique." The induction of the relaxing state can be achieved by teaching the patient to enter a safe and relaxed hypnotic state. Then she is encouraged to create, in her mind's eye, images associated with safety and control while imagining herself physically floating. Visions of floating in a hot tub, a river, a pool, or any other scene associated with physical relaxation can be used. Patients are instructed to maintain this sensation of floating, even when facing emotionally charged traumatic memories.

The second part of the technique consists of having the patient project the traumatic images or thoughts onto an imaginary screen. This helps them separate their cognitive memories from the physically painful sensations or somatic memories in order to minimize re-traumatization. This screen will allow the patient to manipulate the affect that invariably is mobilized during the retrieval of memories. She can control the intensity by making the images larger or smaller, or moving the screen closer or farther away. This technique lets her have an enhanced sense of control and a feeling of safety.

As she recalls the traumatic events, our function is to encourage the patient to remain physically calm while reassuring her that the memories are in the past and cannot harm her now. Then the patient is requested to divide the screen in half. After this, she should create a condensed image of the trauma and put it on the left side of the screen. We then encourage her to recall something she did in order to protect herself, and to project it onto the right side of the screen. On occasion, some patients may have difficulty remembering anything good about themselves. So we encourage them to recall what they did, and restructure their perception of powerlessness into a useful survival technique. Fighting back, screaming for help, or just lying still in order to avoid further abuse are some examples of common defensive acts. This process can allow their memories of the trauma to become more bearable because they can see the part of themselves that attempted to provide protection, maintain dignity, or protect others.

After this the patient has a more realistic view of the traumatic experience. Usually they have always seen themselves as depicted in the *sinister* (Latin for "left") side of the screen: defenseless, vulnerable, victimized. Now the remembered and restructured images on the right may help patients realize that while they were indeed victimized, they fought back in the only way they knew how.

Many of our trauma victims blame themselves for not having done more. It helps them to remember how small they were in comparison with the perpetrator, and to have a more realistic view of the situation. They can remember how they attempted to master the situation the best way they could. Some may remember exhibiting courage while defending themselves, another sibling, or a parent. Patients may then learn that the humiliation of the trauma, although one important aspect of the experience, is certainly not the only one. Thus the two images provide a reframed memory of the trauma.

A second technique by which the patient can recall dissociated memories is the use of "age regression." It may not provide the patient with the protective advantage of being able to project the memories away from herself, and usually is more intense. In general, highly hypnotizable individuals are able to use this technique to the extent of role-playing the events, as if "they are happening all over again." As with the screen technique, it allows for the recovery of long-forgotten memories. Either technique will allow access to repressed material, and more important, an insight into many questions these patients ask themselves over and over again, such as why they never told anyone, or why the abuse lasted as long as it did. Patients may be able to relate again to the fear that paralyzed them as children and did not allow them to escape. Others may remember the feeling they had that if they did not do as they were told something horrible would happen to them or their siblings. And some will remember the perpetrator having told them that their parents would not believe them if they were to tell the truth, or would punish them further if they knew.

One of the advantages of the use of hypnosis is that the affect elicited can be so powerful that most patients do not need to remember every single event of abuse or trauma. In fact, through the use of hypnosis the therapist may help the patient consolidate the memories in a constructive way, thus facilitating recovery. After a condensation of the traumatic experiences, patients are ready to accept the victimized self. Instead of continuing the self-blame and shame because of what happened to them, they can learn to acknowledge and even thank themselves for what they did in order to survive. This restructuring allows them to shift their perception of self, thus changing their self-image from that of a victim to one of a survivor. Hypnotic exercises can also be utilized in which the victim's memory, usually as a child, is comforted, cared for, and loved by the adult self, thus fostering the process of self-acceptance, learning, and growth.

Hypnosis has many uses in the treatment of women who have been sexually abused in childhood. It may help with the control of acute symptoms, including panic attacks and anxiety episodes. It can facilitate access to repressed memories. It can help the patient understand that the intrusive memories and other somatic symptoms represent the way the unconscious attempts to communicate and express painful and overwhelming memories. If they are able to find a controlled method by which to access these memories (such as self-hypnosis), they discover that the frequency of their symptoms often decreases. Hypnosis can also allow for the restructuring of their self-image and their perceptions of the traumatic episodes. It may serve to reverse the fragmentation of mind that was elicited by the trauma. And finally, by these mechanisms, it can provide them an enhanced sense of control over their memories and their lives.

THE CONDENSED "HYPNOTIC APPROACH"

The use of self-hypnosis as an adjuvant to psychotherapy in the treatment of PTSD can be summarized as having two major goals, which can be achieved by the use of six different techniques.

The goals are to bring into conscious awareness previously repressed memories and to develop a sense of congruence between past memories and current self-images. By making conscious previously repressed memories, the patient has the opportunity to understand, accept, and restructure them. If the client can develop a sense of congruence between the content of the "repressed" memories and the feelings associated with them and the current feelings and views of the self, she may no longer have the need for dissociation of memories. Concurrently, the presenting symptoms of anxiety, flashbacks, and intrusive thoughts diminish.

These goals are achieved by the use of six different techniques or treatment stages: confrontation, condensation, confession, consolation, concentration, and control.

1. The patient must confront the trauma. On many occasions important figures in the patient's life have told her to "forget it . . . , it is all in the past" or "there is nothing you can do about it, just let it go . . . ." Comments like these only add to a victim's feelings that there must be something wrong with her. This creates more guilt and the sense that these memories should be eliminated. It is the therapist's role to help the patient recognize the factors involved in the development of the symptoms for which she now seeks help.

2. The use of hypnosis can help the patient condense the traumatic memories. This can be achieved by defining a particularly frighten-

ing segment during the revision of traumatic memories that summarizes or condenses a series of conflicts with which the patient is now struggling. The intense focus of the hypnotic state can be used to facilitate recall of the experience and place boundaries around traumatic memories. Later hypnosis can help restructure these memories, and even allow the patient to "become aware of things you did at the moment (of trauma) in order to survive."

3. Confession of the feelings and/or experiences of which the patient is profoundly ashamed becomes part of the therapeutic process. Often these are things they may have told no one else before. It is paramount at this stage that the therapist convey a sense of "being present" for the patient while remaining as neutral as possible. It is important to encourage the patient to suspend judgment about the events she is able to recall. Many involve irrational self-blame or have been integrated from external sources, such as parents or religion.

4. After patients share these painful memories, the stage of consolation takes place. At this time we need to be emotionally available to the patient, commenting on the impact of the trauma, for example, saying "It must have been terribly frightening." This consolation must be carried on in a most professional manner. We should be aware that the bodily and emotional boundaries of these patients have been violated in the past and act cautiously. On occasions holding the patients hand or just leaning forward in the chair conveys a message of empathy.

5. One of the basic characteristics of hypnosis, concentration, becomes extremely useful in this context of therapy. This quality of the trance experience allows the patient to turn on the memories during the psychotherapeutic session, then shut them off once the work has been done. Patients who have been victims of sexual abuse have usually been overtaken by their assailants. Likewise most of them are afraid to allow themselves to remember for fear that the memories will take over, leaving them defenseless once more.

6. Finally, the patient needs to feel she is in control again. Remember that one of the effects of overwhelming trauma is that it renders its victims defenseless. It is this lack of physical and emotional control

that has triggered the need for dissociative defenses in an attempt to master their experiences. Using hypnosis, we can teach the patient to regain control over her memories. This should be done in an atmosphere of trust and safety. The patient is encouraged to remember as much as she feels she can safely remember. She should learn how to think about the trauma rather than attempt to negate the existence of these memories.

One reason we encourage the use of self-hypnosis is that it teaches patients they are in control of their experiences. It dispels their thinking that therapists magically "take the memories away." Rather, by modeling this sense of trust in their therapists, patients learn to trust themselves. They relearn to trust their own feelings and perceptions. Equally important, patients learn their own limitations and when to ask for help.

As consultants, we recently saw a young woman on the orthopedic/surgical ward of our hospital. She had been admitted with a compression fracture of her spine following a motor vehicle accident. During the first few days of the hospital stay, while lying helplessly in bed in traction, she developed recurrent flashbacks. Whenever she "dozed off" she would "see the accident being replayed over and over again." Shortly thereafter she became depressed, at which point we were consulted. Our interview revealed that in the past, her internist had prescribed fluoxetine (Prozac) for a few months due to "depression." She described that she had "already dealt in therapy a few years ago with the fact that I was sexually abused, once, when I was four."

Certainly she remembered that incident, but she could not see the connection to the current events, nor had she resolved the conflicts because of the lack of congruence between her perceptions of the world before and after the episode of sexual abuse. With the use of hypnosis we helped her "make the connection" in an unbiased way. The technique, called the "affect bridge," asks the patient to *concentrate* and allow herself to remember either the car accident or one of the flashbacks. Once she did, she signaled us whenever she was ready (giving her *control*), at which point we gave her the following instruction: "Allow your mind to take you to the very first time you ever felt this way before." Not surprisingly, she had a spontaneous age regression, remembering herself when she was four years old. She recalled being in the basement of her fourteen-year-old neighbor who molested her (*confrontation of the trauma*).

After key elements of this memory were retrieved (*condensation*) and the connection made, we interpreted them. It is likely that the sudden lack of control brought about by the accident, symbolized by the constant replay of being thrown forward against the dashboard, reminded the patient of the "forgotten" instance when she felt completely helpless in front of this "big man." We used the hypnotic experience to help the patient "see" what she did in order to save herself. She "could not come up with anything." But we helped her realize that by "freezing and not giving too much of a fight" she had indeed saved herself. She remembered how she felt that "if I scream again he will kill me, so I just froze there." She was reminded that it took a great deal of courage to overcome all her anxieties, fears, and pain and just to "numb myself in order not to suffer the pain." She was also reminded of how it is easy to look back and to know, as an adult, exactly what she should have done. But as a small four-year-old child, to whom everything is so big, the terror of the experience, the feeling of powerlessness, and the strength of the perpetrator are overpowering (*consolation*).

Slowly "everything became much clearer." She was able to understand that the accident "was bad in itself, but that the attached memories that it elicited were even more difficult to deal with, especially after trying so hard to forget." She was able to see the connection between her "episodes of depression and circumstances in my life when I believe I have no option, no control." After one session, the patient's flashbacks disappeared and she decided to go into therapy to deal with "so many unresolved issues."

HYPNOSIS AND GROUP THERAPY

In group psychotherapy, the trauma patient can experience the benefits of the stability and structure provided by the support group. Being in a group may also help to promote socialization. Finally, it aids victims in developing a new sense of trust and caring. In this context, hypnosis may be used to help the members of the group focus on the tasks at hand without being excessively overwhelmed by the memory of the trauma. As in the case of patients participating in individual psychotherapy, hypnotic exercises allow group members to reassess past situations, reframe traumatic experiences, and even practice future events while "maintaining a distance from painful memories."

Group therapy of sexually abused women may have two different approaches. It may either focus on the traumatic experience itself (a trauma-focused group) and the restructuring and resolution of the memories (as we have described throughout this chapter), or it may focus on the current psychosocial stressor and interpersonal relationships (a present-focused group) with no direct emphasis on the recovery of traumatic memories. Hypnosis may be useful in either approach.

In the context of the trauma-focused therapy, hypnosis can be used at the beginning of the group session to help the members of the group feel safe, while easing their access to traumatic memories. It can also be used at the end of the therapy to help the members consolidate the skills they have learned throughout the session as well as to project themselves into the future, giving them the opportunity to practice some of those skills. In a present-focused group, hypnosis can be used at the beginning of the session to examine a given maladaptive defense or interactive style, while toward the end of the session it can be used to consolidate the new and more adaptive mechanisms discussed during the session.

THERAPEUTIC PRECAUTIONS

The presence and strength of transference during the psychotherapy of trauma victims is enormous. The use of hypnosis does not prevent development of a transference reaction; hypnosis actually may facilitate its emergence earlier than in regular therapy because of the intensity with which the patient expresses material and recovers memories.

Reliving the traumatic experience along with the patient may allow for a special feeling of "being there with her" at the moment of trauma. This allows the therapist to provide guidance, support, protection, and comfort as the patient goes through the difficult path of reprocessing traumatic memories.

On the other hand, this kind of "traumatic transference" between the therapist and the victim of sexual assault is different as the feelings transferred are less related to early object relationships and more to the abuser or circumstances associated with the trauma. Instead of seeing this expressed anger at the therapist as a form of negative transference, we should explore the possibility that it may be a healthy attempt for the patient to experience anger toward the perpetrator. This provides more material to work through in the course of therapy. As therapists, we should attempt not to minimize or shut off these feelings. This will only confirm the patient's former perception that there was something wrong with her for having these feelings. Closing off these sensations will probably activate further dissociation of primitive defenses in the patient, including dissociation or acting out.

A more serious complication of the use of hypnosis with trauma victims is possible creation of false memories. Hypnosis, with its heightened sense of concentration, allows the patient to focus intensely on a given time or place, so it can enhance memory recall. Also the principle of state-dependent memory makes it plausible that the mere entrance into this trance state can facilitate retrieval of memories associated with a similar state of mind that may have occurred during the trauma and subsequent flashbacks. But not every memory recovered with the use of hypnosis is necessarily true. Hypnosis can facilitate improved recall of both true and confabulated material. Suggestibility is increased in hypnosis, and information can be implanted or imagined and reported as verdict. Because of this, therapists are warned about "believing" everything a patient is able to recall. Just as we use therapeutic judgment to analyze and interpret our patients' (nontraumatic) childhood memories, fantasies, and dreams, so should we treat hypnotically recovered material.

LEGAL IMPLICATIONS

Because hypnosis involves a suspension of critical judgment and therefore a state of heightened suggestibility or responsivity to social cues, it is important that the interview be conducted with a minimum of inserted information. To avoid the risk of contaminating the subject's memories, we recommend the use of open-ended questions, such as "What happens next?" rather than "How did he sexually abuse you?"

Therapists treating victims of sexual abuse must be aware that the use of hypnosis may compromise a witness's ability to testify in court. Indeed, several states like Arizona, California, New Jersey, and New York restrict the testimony of victims or witnesses who have used hypnosis to refresh their recollection. The courts' objection to the use of hypnosis is a recognition of both the real and exaggerated dangers of hypnosis. After much legal battle, some courts will now allow witnesses to testify after the use of hypnosis, provided that certain guidelines are followed. These relate primarily to the training and independence of the professional conducting the hypnotic interrogation and the electronic recording of the entire process.

Since it is almost impossible not to add some degree of contamination to the procedure, we recommend that at least the following steps be undertaken: first (with the patient's permission), consult with the victim's attorney. If an investigation is in progress or court proceedings are likely, you may also want to contact the district attorney's office or the police. Second, make a video (preferably) or audio recording of all contact with the victim. Make certain that you can hear clearly the victim's voice and your own, as well as the voice of anyone else participating in the process. Third, conduct the interview in a neutral tone. Guide the victim through the experience, but avoid using leading or suggestive questions. It is imperative to avoid introducing information during the interrogation. This is best achieved by asking open-ended, neutral questions based on the information already provided by the victim. For example, ask questions such as "Now, what is happening?" rather than "Did he knock you down?" or "Who raped you? Was it your father?"

To this date, there is no evidence to prove that the patient's pursuit of legal retribution toward the perpetrator(s) provides any therapeutic benefit. As therapists, we cannot be certain of which memories are real, which are completely confabulated, and which are a combination of both. Because of this uncertainty, we should not encourage our patients to take legal action. If, on the other hand, our patients insist in pursuing this avenue, it's our duty to warn them of our concerns but to be supportive of whatever final decision they make. Certainly we will do a service to our patients if we inform them of all the legal ramifications that the use of hypnosis, or any other form of memory enhancement, may have for their defense, including their ability to testify in court or to use the material recovered by such techniques.

The challenge in treating victims of childhood sexual abuse is to achieve a new sense of unity within the patient after the initial fragmentation caused by the traumatic experience. The trauma tends to cause sudden and radical discontinuities in consciousness, due to the nature of the assault itself. This leaves victims with a polarized view of themselves involving, on one hand, the old self prior to the trauma, and on the other, the helpless, defenseless, soiled victim.

The goal of therapy is to find a way to integrate these two aspects of the self. The purpose is not to deny that victimization did indeed happen once, but to do so while enabling the patient to come to some restructured self-image that recognizes the victimization but does not allow it to dominate the overall view of the self.

In effect, this approach can be seen as a form of grief work. Here the patient's task is to acknowledge, bear, and put into perspective painful life events, thereby making them acceptable to conscious awareness. The shift in concentration elicited in hypnosis, so useful in defending against the immediate impact of trauma as it is occurring, and so problematic in the aftermath of trauma, can be quite useful in mobilizing and putting into perspective traumatic memories and reducing the symptoms of PTSD.

The controlled experience of the hypnotic abreaction itself provides boundaries around the psychotherapeutic mourning process.

Instead of telling patients not to ruminate over the details of a traumatic experience, the therapist does the opposite. He or she teaches the patient how to think about the experience. The inferred message is that once this piece of therapeutic work has been accomplished, the patient can go on to work on other things. Patients are slowly separated from the victim role as they see themselves from a different perspective and assume the role of survivors, mastering rather than being mastered by their dissociative defenses.

NOTES

P. 165, *she had received . . . under Axis II:* American Psychiatric Association. (1987). *Diagnostic and statistical manual of mental disorders.* (3rd ed.) Washington, DC: American Psychiatric Press.

P. 165, *symptoms resembled a state of "hysterical psychosis":* Spiegel, D., & Fink, R. (1979). Hysterical psychosis and hypnotizability. *American Journal of Psychiatry, 136,* 777–781.

P. 166, *In fact "dissociated" . . . current life events:* Kilhstrom, J. F. (1984). Conscious, subconscious, unconscious: A cognitive perspective. In Bowers, K. S., & Meichenbaum, D. (Eds.), *The unconscious reconsidered* (pp. 149–211). New York: Wiley; Kilhstrom, J. F. (1990). Repression, dissociation and hypnosis. In J. L. Singer (Ed.), *Repression and dissociation* (pp. 180–208). Chicago: University of Chicago Press.

P. 167, *dissociative identity disorder:* American Psychiatric Association. (1994). *Diagnostic and statistical manual of mental disorders.* (4th ed.) Washington, DC: American Psychiatric Press.

P. 167, *They claim that most of them are like "instant replays" of the original event:* Hartmann, E. (1984). *The nightmare: The psychology and biology of terrifying dreams.* New York: Basic Books; Ross, R., Ball, W., Sullivan, K., & Caroff, S. (1976). Sleep disturbance as the hallmark of post traumatic stress disorder. *American Journal of Psychiatry, 146,* 697–707.

P. 169, *read one of the many excellent textbooks written in the area:* Crasilneck, H. B., & Hall, J. A. (1985). *Clinical hypnosis: Principles and applications.* New York: Grune & Stratton; D. C. Hammond, (Ed.). (1992). *Handbook of hypnotic suggestions & metaphors.* American Society of Clinical Hypnosis. New York: Norton & Co.; Spiegel, H., & Spiegel, D. (1978). *Trance & treatment: Clinical uses of hypnosis.* New York: Basic Books. Reprinted Washington, DC: American Psychiatric Press, 1978; Watkins, J. G. (1987). *Hypnotherapeutic Technique: The Practice of Clinical Hypnosis* (2 vols.). New York: Irvington Publishers.

P. 169, *Hypnosis can be defined . . . peripheral awareness:* Spiegel, D. (1990). Hypnosis, dissociation and trauma: Hidden and overt observers. In J. L. Singer (Ed.), *Repression and dissociation* (pp. 121–142). Chicago: University of Chicago Press.

P. 169, *The phenomenon known as hypnosis . . . and suggestibility:* Spiegel, D. (1988). Dissociation and hypnosis in posttraumatic stress disorder. *Journal of Traumatic Stress, 1,* 17–33.

P. 171, *Just as several authors . . . on hypnotizability scales:* Spiegel, D., Hunt, T., & Dondershine, H. E. (1988). Dissociation and hypnotizability in posttraumatic stress disorder. *American Journal of Psychiatry, 145,* 301–305; Stutman, R. K., & Bliss, E. L. (1985). Posttraumatic stress disorder, hypnotizability and imagery. *American Journal of Psychiatry, 142,* 741–743.

P. 171, *sexually abused women respond in a similar fashion on measures of dissociation:* Chu, D. A., & Dill, D. L. (1990). Dissociative symptoms in relation to childhood physical and sexual abuse. *American Journal of Psychiatry, 147,* 887–892; Herman J. L., Perry, J. C., & van der Kolk, B. A. (1989). Childhood trauma in borderline personality disorder. *American Journal of Psychiatry, 146,* 490–495.

P. 171, *Since the patients . . . highly hypnotizable:* Chu, D. A., & Dill, D. L. (1990). Dissociative symptoms in relation to childhood physical and sexual abuse. *American Journal of Psychiatry, 147,* 887–892; Hilgard, E. R. (1984). The hidden observer and multiple personality. *International Journal of Clinical and Experimental Hypnosis, 32,* 248–253; Nash, M. R., & Lynn, S. J. (1986). Child abuse and hypnotic ability. *Imagination, Cognition and Personality, 5,* 211–218; Putman, F. W. (1993). Dissociative disorders in children: Behavioral profiles and problems. *Child Abuse and Neglect, 17,* 39–45; Spiegel, D. (1988). Dissociation and hypnosis in posttraumatic stress disorder. *Journal of Traumatic Stress, 1,* 17–33; Spiegel, D. (1990). Hypnosis, dissociation and trauma: Hidden and overt observers. In J. L. Singer (Ed.), *Repression and dissociation* (pp. 121–142). Chicago: University of Chicago Press; Spiegel, D., Hunt, T., & Dondershine, H. E. (1988). Dissociation and hypnotizability in posttraumatic stress disorder. *American Journal of Psychiatry, 145,* 301–305.

P. 172, *they are creating different degrees of psychopathology:* Sanders, B., & Giolas, M. H. (1991). Dissociation and childhood trauma in psychologically disturbed adolescents. *American Journal of Psychiatry, 148,* 50–54; Spiegel, D. (1984). Multiple personality as a post-traumatic stress disorder. *The Psychiatric Clinics of North America, 7,* 101–110; Spiegel, D. (1989). Hypnosis in the treatment of victims of sexual abuse. *Psychiatric Clinics of North America, 12,* 295–305; Spiegel, D., Hunt, T., & Dondershine, H. E. (1988). Dissociation and hypnotizability in posttraumatic stress disorder. *American Journal of Psychiatry, 145,* 301–305; Terr, L. C. (1991). Childhood traumas: An outline and overview. *American Journal of Psychiatry, 148,* 10–20.

P. 172, *We believe that the . . . traumatization of the victim:* Spiegel, D. (1981). Vietnam grief work using hypnosis. *American Journal of Clinical Hypnosis, 24,* 33–40;

Kluft, R. P. (1992). The use of hypnosis with dissociative disorders. *Psychiatric Medicine, 10*(4), 31–46; Kluft, R. P. (1993). The physician as perpetrator of the abuse. *Primary Care: Clinics in Office Practice, 20*, 459–480.

P. 172, *Because of research on state-dependent memory:* Bower, G. H. (1981). Mood and memory. *American Psychology, 36*, 129–148.

P. 173, *Hypnosis is in itself . . . memories of the trauma:* Spiegel, D. (1981). Vietnam grief work using hypnosis. *American Journal of Clinical Hypnosis, 24*, 33–40.

P. 173, *"screen technique":* Spiegel, D. (1989). Hypnosis in the treatment of victims of sexual abuse. *Psychiatric Clinics of North America, 12*, 295–305.

P. 176, *The use of self-hypnosis . . . six different techniques:* Maldonado, J. R., & Spiegel, D. (1994). Treatment of post traumatic stress disorder. In S. J. Lynn & R. Rhue (Eds.), *Dissociation: Clinical, theoretical and research perspectives.* New York: Guilford Press; Spiegel, D. (1992). The use of hypnosis in the treatment of PTSD. *Psychiatric Medicine, 10*, 21–30.

P. 180, *Group therapy of sexually abused women may have two different approaches:* Classen, C., & Spiegel, D. (In press). Group treatment for women sexually abused in childhood. *American Journal of Clinical Hypnosis.*

P. 180, *The use of hypnosis . . . recovers memories:* Maldonado, J. R., & Spiegel, D. (1994). Treatment of post traumatic stress disorder. In S. J. Lynn & R. Rhue (Eds.), *Dissociation: Clinical, theoretical and research perspectives.* New York: Guilford Press.

P. 181, *On the other hand . . . associated with the trauma:* Spiegel, D. (1992). The use of hypnosis in the treatment of PTSD. *Psychiatric Medicine, 10*, 21–30.

P. 182, *Arizona:* State ex rel Collins v Superior Court, 132 Ariz 180, 644 P2d1266 (1982), supplemental opinion filed May 4, 1982.

P. 182, *California:* People v Guerra, (1984). C-41916 Sup Ct Orange County, CA; People v Hughes 59 NY Law J, July 7, 1983, p 4.

P. 182, *New Jersey:* People v Hurd, Sup. Ct., NJ, Somerset Co, April 2, 1980.

P. 182, *New York:* People v Shirley, 31 Cal3d 18, 641 P2d775 (1982); modified 918a (1982).

P. 182, *The courts' objection . . . exaggerated dangers of hypnosis:* Spiegel, D. (1987). The Shirley decision: The cure is worse than the disease. In R. Rieber (Ed.), *Advances in forensic psychology and psychiatry* (Vol. 2). New Jersey: Ablex.

P. 182, *After much legal battle, some courts:* California Legislature, AB 2669 Chapter 7, *Hypnosis of witnesses,* added to chapter 7, division 6 of the evidence Code, Enacted January 1, 1985.

P. 182, *These relate primarily . . . of the entire process:* Spiegel, D., & Spiegel, H. (1986). Forensic uses of hypnosis. In I. B. Weiner & A. K. Hess (Eds.), *Handbook of forensic psychology.* New York: Wiley.

7

TRANSFERENCE AND COUNTERTRANSFERENCE

Diana M. Elliott and John Briere

As human beings, we spend considerable time and energy processing past experiences. It is probably a biological imperative that we integrate these experiences into meaningful models of reality so that we can apply their lessons to challenges in our current environment. In many cases, access to past experiences facilitates our functioning in the world by providing meaningful information that can be called upon as needed. On other occasions, however, our past experience can color or distort our perceptions, leading to less than adaptive responses to environmental stimuli.

This interaction between past experience and current awareness is present in most interpersonal relationships. In no dyad is the interplay more relevant than in psychotherapy, especially when experiences as profound as childhood sexual abuse are being addressed. Because sexual abuse is often a traumatic event with many long-term effects, abuse-related intrusions and distortions are common for adult survivors during psychotherapy. Similarly, aspects of the survivor's abuse history and current presentation can evoke complex reactions in the therapist—some of which are benign or helpful, and some of which can impede or even destroy therapy if allowed expression.

This chapter outlines a general model of these past and present, intra- and interpersonal forces in what is referred to as *transference* and *countertransference*. The model is presented here in the context of abuse-focused psychotherapy. It is psychodynamic and relational in nature, and assumes that such processes are not only inevitable but intrinsic to therapy.

Obviously not all cognitive or emotional responses in therapy are strictly transferential or countertransferential; the critical issues are whether the response represents a distortion of reality, and whether it is based on unresolved life experiences. During psychotherapy, the survivor can be expected to have some relatively undistorted reactions to her therapist's statements, behaviors, and overall stimulus value, as well as to project onto the therapist abuse-related assumptions and affects. Because the survivor's perception of therapy reflects this combination of more or less accurate perceptions and distortions based on early experience, she may react to "new" therapeutic events with a combination of situationally appropriate responses and more obviously transferential dynamics arising from "old" (abuse-related) issues and perceptions.

Similarly, the therapist can respond to client behaviors, experiences, and personality styles either in terms of their inherent meaning or as a result of their activation of emotional reactions associated with his or her own negative childhood or adult experiences. If the therapist's history includes unresolved maltreatment (sexual or otherwise), unhelpful or even hurtful therapist projections onto the client are possible.

There are at least four interactive possibilities that can occur between therapist and client in abuse-focused psychotherapy. These are presented in Figure 7.1.

Although this figure suggests that client or therapist response is either contemporaneous or projected from past history, obviously both often occur together. In fact, it is usually not *whether* transference or countertransference is present, but rather the extent to which it dominates contemporaneous awareness and influences client or therapist behavior, and the extent to which such processes are a help or a hindrance. The interplay between transferential and contemporaneous responses is not always readily apparent. For example, although a survivor's anger at her seemingly withholding therapist could represent her projection of childhood abandonment issues onto a relatively benign individual, it is also possible that her

Figure 7.1
Interactive Possibilities Between Therapist and Client

	Client Response	Therapist Response
Based on immediate stimuli	Responses to therapist motivated by therapist's current behaviors or characteristics CONTEMPORANEOUS RESPONSE	Responses to client motivated by client's current behaviors or characteristics CONTEMPORANEOUS RESPONSE
Based on projected experience	Responses to therapist based on client's history TRANSFERENTIAL RESPONSE	Responses to client based on therapist's history COUNTER-TRANSFERENTIAL RESPONSE

anger is primarily contemporaneous—the therapist indeed may be withholding and the client may be expressing appropriate "here and now" concerns.

Many of the concepts regarding transference and countertransference are more clearly understood in the context of clinical data. Thus, throughout this chapter, certain concepts will be illustrated through a case example, that of Gayle.

GAYLE

Gayle is a bright, attractive, thirty-five-year-old engineer who had worked for the same company since obtaining her master's degree twelve years earlier. At intake, she reported no significant difficulties at work other than her anxiety in the interpersonal area. Her life consisted of a fifty-hour work week, Thursday evening with her lover, Saturday morning at the market, Sunday afternoon at her parents' home, and the remainder of time inside her home with her two cats.

Gayle had never been married, but had had several affairs with married men who were at best controlling, at worst physically and sexually abusive toward her. She sought counseling after being confronted by a co-worker about the bruises seen on her arms. Her goals for treatment were to end the relationship with her current lover, reduce the level of anxiety she felt around people, and "perhaps I could find a friend."

During the intake, when asked generically about her childhood, Gayle reported that it was "average." She was the oldest of five sisters "raised by two hardworking stable parents." When asked more specific questions, however, she acknowledged a history of sexual abuse from ages five to eleven perpetrated by her maternal grandfather during the six summers she spent in his home. Although she became "hysterical" before leaving for her grandparents' home each summer, she was typically called an "ungrateful brat" and told that her mother needed a break from her. During the school year, she was perpetually criticized by both parents, and occasionally physically abused by her father.

Her affect during intake varied between depressed, anxious, and dissociated. For the most part, she recounted events in a flat tone, made little eye contact, and held her body in rigid positions. Occasionally when upset, however, she made rocking autistic-like motions and hit herself with her fists. She voiced considerable skepticism regarding the process of therapy, indicating that she had "tried it four times before." (Case notes were obtained from three of the four therapists, with treatment lasting between one and six months on each occasion.) "I either felt crowded in by them, didn't know what they wanted from me, or felt like they were more screwed up than me." Therapy with the current therapist lasted just over five years. During the middle three years she was seen twice weekly, the remainder of the time, she was seen one time per week.

CLIENT RESPONSE

The two main types of client response are abuse-related transferential responses and contemporaneous responses. These are discussed in the following sections.

Abuse-related Transferential Responses

For survivors of sexual abuse, transference typically manifests itself in one of four abuse-related responses. They are discussed below and include the following:

- Cognitive-perceptual distortions that have generalized from abuse-era learning about self, others, and the environment
- Responses associated with early attachment disruption that are elicited by the relational aspects of the therapy
- Specific abuse-related affects and sensory experiences that are re-stimulated by therapist characteristics or behaviors
- Reenactment of childhood behaviors arising from unresolved traumatic experiences, triggered by current interpersonal events or aspects of the therapeutic relationship

Transferential responses lead to a variety of feelings and behaviors within and outside the therapy session. When they involve especially inappropriate or extreme behaviors and occur outside the therapy session, they are typically referred to as "acting out" and seen as a pathological response. An alternative view, held by the current authors, is that these extra-therapeutic reactions are either logical responses to restimulated abuse-related traumatic material, or transferential reenactments of childhood behaviors activated by some aspect of the therapeutic relationship reminiscent of the original abuse.

Client transference should not be considered necessarily neurotic or inherently undesirable. The first component of transference—cognitive distortions—can produce misunderstandings and contextually inappropriate behavior if not addressed adequately. However, the other three components, which involve more direct reexperiencing of abuse-related phenomena, can provide the survivor with an opportunity to "do it again," that is, revisit painful childhood experience with adult awareness and efficacy in the presence of a benevolent and helpful other. Even in the case of cognitive distortions, good therapy allows the survivor to examine archaic models of understanding as they emerge in the context of a new, more positive relationship. Viewed in this way, transference provides the survivor with the opportunity to learn critically important intrapsychic and interpersonal skills and perspectives that otherwise might not be acquired.

Cognitive-Perceptual Distortions. Alterations in the survivor's perception of the therapist and the therapeutic relationship (among other people and relationships) can arise from her childhood reactions to abuse-specific events and her early attempts to make sense of the abuse. These thought patterns were initially logical, developing out of the child victim's perception of herself as helpless and inadequate, others as powerful and malignant, and her environment as inherently dangerous. In adulthood, these perceptions often result in low self-esteem, passivity, expectations of betrayal and continued victimization, and hypervigilance to danger.

Such distortions impact many aspects of everyday relationships, including the therapeutic one. They are best seen as an interaction between unanalyzed perspectives arising from the conditions under which the abuse took place and the tendency for the therapeutic environment to "pull" for abuse-related assumptions. The following illustrates some of the origins of Gayle's low self-esteem and the consequences of her self-beliefs in her relationship with the therapist.

During the first two years of treatment, Gayle never made a single phone call to her therapist. She was never late, never missed a session, and always paid on time. She was a "good patient" in the hope of being seen as special by her therapist. "I was the black sheep in my family . . . I hated feeling unwanted . . . I need you to like me. I think about everything I do and say to make sure that I don't displease you."

Despite her partial awareness of the process, the underlying assumption of the need for acquiescence affected her behavior in session. It was present in her avoidance of expressed anger, her reluctance to disagree with the therapist, and her unwillingness to express thoughts before rehearsing them. Although these issues were frequently addressed, she was well into her third year of treatment before her hypervigilance significantly abated.

Not only does sexual abuse teach the survivor that others can be dangerous, it alters her perceptions of and response to power, intimacy, and relationship—all of which are operative during psychotherapy. One effect of this process is the survivor's tendency to project or transfer abuse-based understanding of powerful others onto the therapist. The clinician can become more of a representation of what the client expects or fears (such as betrayal, rejection, or exploitation) than a real person. This representation motivates reactive and defensive behaviors during treatment that are less relevant to the actual therapeutic situation than to events long past.

Several distortions can occur in the survivor's perception of the therapist. Four of the most common are:

- Parent
- Perpetrator
- Rescuer
- Lover

When the therapist is seen as *Parent*, he or she can be cast either as one who requires obedience and appeasement or as a caretaker who cannot be counted on for protection or safety. The survivor may assume that her worth is predicated on her ability to satisfy the expectations of power figures (especially but not exclusively male ones). The client's resultant desire to placate can result in blanket acceptance of the therapist's statements about and recommendations for the client. By uncritically accepting this "good client" behavior, the therapist unknowingly reinforces a related survivor assumption—that independence and self-efficacy in relationships with powerful others are impossible. Alternatively, the (typically female) therapist may be the recipient of angry projections and behaviors from the client in response to her restimulated expectations of abandonment or unwillingness to protect.

Some abuse survivors come to see the therapist as a potential *Perpetrator* rather than as an ally. Sexual abuse is implicitly an object lesson in lack of control over one's own well-being. For survivors, power can be seen as inherently malevolent. Thus, those in power are perceived as intrinsically dangerous. This projection is more likely to occur with male therapists, although those abused by women may project danger onto female clinicians. The survivor's resultant fear and acquiescence can be reinforced in the therapeutic relationship by virtue of the power invested in the therapist and the assumption that the client is to be acted on.

When the therapist is unable or unwilling to weaken the connection between attributed power and the survivor's assumptions of resultant danger (psychological or otherwise), the survivor will continue to project abuser-like characteristics on the therapist. In response to these projections, the survivor may feel either frightened or angry. Both reactions can motivate behaviors that were adaptive in, or reactive to, the original abusive relationship such as acquiescence, placation, or grooming of the therapist; avoidance or escape from treatment; or aggression or retaliation to perceived abuse. Also present may be frequent assumptions that the therapist whose sex matches that of the original abuser has sexual interest in the client and that the therapist has the ongoing potential of becoming a sexual assailant.

Another client response to her power projections onto the therapist might seem antithetic to the previous pattern, in that it initially motivates adoration or idealization rather than obvious fear or anger. The client may fantasize the therapist to be a *Rescuer,* the one who was longed for when the survivor was being abused as a child. In this dynamic, the therapist is placed in the role of an all-knowing, all-powerful being, and the survivor views her own role as recipient of the therapist's wisdom and healing powers. This projection often leads the client to assume a passive role in and out of session, similar to that found in the *Perpetrator* projection. Because the client believes she has found someone whose power will bestow a cure, she can become less motivated to do things for herself, seeking instead to provide the right conditions, demands, or prompts for the therapist's beneficence. Ultimately, however, as with the *Perpetrator* pattern, this transferential pattern results in survivor anger or fear. Inevitably, the human therapist will violate the idealized role by failing to provide a cure or by not maintaining complete empathy at all times, thereby running the risk of becoming devalued as a betrayer or abandoner.

Another cognitive distortion associated with sexual abuse casts the therapist into the role of *Lover*. This distortion reflects the sexual or romantic associations with power, developed when the exploitation and boundary violations of abuse were combined with positive attention, sexual feelings, or perpetrator statements of love. This projection usually occurs with therapists whose sex matches the sexual orientation of the client. However, many clinicians have been surprised to discover this response in clients who "shouldn't" be attracted to someone of the therapist's sex. The survivor can come to assume that positive responses from powerful others (especially those of the perpetrator's sex) are inherently sexual or romantic, and that the acquisition of such power figures is a basis for happiness.

Faced with this goal, the survivor may logically call on the lessons learned during sexual abuse: that her sexual stimulus value is a powerful motivator and that boundaries are negotiable and made to be transgressed. There can be a desire to be the therapist's "one and only," in a way that she assumes only sexual intimacy can confer. The client might consequently pursue special times with the therapist, request the latest possible evening session, or seek late-night phone contact. This need can become quite elaborate and a powerful source of sexual fantasies, especially when the original sexual abuse was chronic and pseudoparticipatory. In its milder forms, this sexualized response can result in coy behavior or attempts to appear attractive to the therapist. When the "eroticized" transference is stronger, there may be overtly seductive behavior, attempts to titillate the therapist with "sexy" clothing or blatantly sexual propositions.

Responses Associated with Early Attachment Disruption. Many sexual abuse survivors were also psychologically neglected early in life. Both sexual abuse and child neglect have been associated with attachment failure. The failure or disruption of the child-caretaker attachment bond can easily lead to significant interpersonal difficulties later in life, especially difficulties associated with underdeveloped self capacities and unmet needs for parental nurturance and love. Individuals with significant attachment problems are likely to project self issues and unresolved attachment needs onto the therapist and the client-therapist relationship. Especially relevant to the current discussion is the tendency for the more severely injured survivor to experience (1) compelling needs for reliability, safety, close connection, and other analogues of caretaker love during treatment (especially in the presence of a female therapist), and (2) abuse-relevant negative affects when she perceives abandonment, unavailability, or deficiencies in these areas during therapy.

Survivor expectations of nurturance during psychotherapy undoubtedly reflect the tendency for unresolved attachment needs to be restimulated in any relationship with a potential parental figure. When this dynamic exists, the therapist can expect some level of survivor "entitlement" during treatment as the client projects onto therapy her childhood-appropriate rights to consistent parental support and loving attention.

Unfortunately for the survivor, the episodic (once or twice a week) nature of psychotherapy and the necessary constraints of the psychotherapeutic relationship can easily restimulate feelings of abandonment and betrayal—reactions that first occurred during the survivor's childhood deprivation of caregiver love and support. Just as the abandoned or unloved child responded to abuse and neglect with anger, fear, and sadness, the adult survivor may respond to appropriate therapist distance or minor therapist errors in empathy with archaic rage, despondence, or terror, as illustrated in the following case.

The first time Gayle's therapist took an extended vacation was during the third year of her treatment. Gayle was told four months ahead of time that her therapist would be out of town for two weeks. As the time approached, Gayle voiced some sadness and anticipation that the time would be difficult for her. During the first session after her therapist's return, Gayle began to cry. Although the therapist felt quite attuned to Gayle and the pain she felt in the therapist's absence, Gayle soon became rageful. After the session, she left a message on the answering machine, screaming "I hate you! I hate you! I hate you!" She canceled the next session. When she returned, Gayle began to discuss her fear and anger at the pain of the abandonment she felt in the therapist's absence.

The seemingly primitive character of some restimulated attachment issues can be startling to the unprepared therapist as the survivor's "neediness" grows and parent-child attachment dynamics intensify. It is just this reexperiencing of unmet attachment needs, however, that allows the adult survivor to address childhood deprivation long after the fact, thereby providing an opportunity for the resolution of early trauma that otherwise would be unavailable for treatment. This reworking of attachment issues requires considerable patience and stability on the part of the therapist, and calls on the therapist's ability to resist any countertransferential need to parent or to join the survivor in boundary violations.

Specific Abuse-related Affects and Sensory Experience. Although many survivor responses in therapy reflect the projection of cognitive distortions and attachment-related needs onto the client-therapist relationship, some of the client's reactions during treatment reflect more direct posttraumatic restimulation. These can occur either as (1) dissociated abuse-era affects or (2) therapy-triggered abuse-specific flashbacks. An example of the former is illustrated in the next case.

Gayle was talking about what seemed to be fairly benign work-related issues. The therapist made an observation that Gayle interpreted as critical of her behavior. Almost instantaneously, she withdrew from the therapist into a autistic-like state. The next few minutes of silence were interrupted by the therapist's request for Gayle to try to articulate her internal experience. The question itself seemed to push Gayle further into her own world. She spent the remaining thirty-five minutes of the session in silence with her back turned away from her therapist and her legs curled into her body. She was unresponsive to the few subsequent attempts on the part of the therapist to access her. One minute before the session was to end, she quietly stood up and left the room without a word.

During the next session, Gayle discussed her response. "I felt like you were making fun of me. I knew you weren't, but this intense anger came over me like I could kill you. And then I just shut down. I was livid and my thoughts raced, but it was like I was paralyzed. This used to happen at my grandparents' house, especially after my grandfather had come into my room. When it happened then, and again with you, it didn't feel like I had any control over it. I fall into this angry little-kid place and can't get out of it until after I wake up from sleep or greatly completely change my environment."

This sort of dissociated affect typically occurs when the survivor's history is restimulated during therapy by an abuse-relevant stimulus (such as perceived rejection, abandonment, or maltreatment) that is reminiscent of a specific instance of severe childhood abuse or attachment disruption. Because of its similarity to unresolved child abuse issues, this stimulus can induce powerful, dissociated feelings of rage, terror, anxiety, self-loathing, and/or grief. These emotional reactions can appear to "come out of nowhere," in that neither the client nor the therapist is aware of their precipitants, and the dissociated character of the response can blur its connection to a specific therapeutic incident.

Alternatively, the client might respond to the therapist in the context of an actual flashback. In this instance, the therapist might observe sudden terror or dissociated behavior as was seen with Gayle.

Gayle opened a session by mentioning a dream in which she had been raped, providing no details about the actual assault, as was typical for her. (When asked about her sexual abuse, for example, she would use global descriptors like "we had sex," and become quite distressed or dissociated when invited to be more specific.) After briefly mentioning the dream, Gayle commented on how cold it was in the office. The therapist noted that the air conditioning was being worked on and asked the client if she wanted a throw blanket that was over the back of the couch. The client was handed the blanket and she resettled with the blanket around her.

The therapist picked up the conversation and asked Gayle if she could describe what happened in the dream. The client pulled her legs up into herself, began to rock and weep, eventually crying "Don't make me, don't make me." It appeared to the therapist that Gayle was reacting to the previous question. Despite attempts by the therapist to help the client ground herself, Gayle was unable to respond to the therapist until just before the session was to end. Gayle stated that when the therapist leaned forward to give her the throw blanket, she "flashed back" to her grandfather coming toward her with a large towel just after she had climbed out of the bathtub. She pulled the towel over her, curled into a ball in the corner of the bathroom, and cried "Don't make me, don't make me."

The presence of dissociated affects or abuse-specific flashbacks during therapy typically signals the presence of major unresolved childhood trauma, as opposed to the more "garden variety" difficulties of less psychologically injured clients. Such intrusions into the therapy session are not always included in the typical discussion of transference, partially because trauma-focused therapy only recently has been considered, and partially because transference is often described in terms of less acutely intrusive phenomena.

Nevertheless, posttraumatic transference, involving dissociative states and intrusive experiences, is an important aspect of work with sexual abuse survivors, both in terms of its disruption of "here and now" awareness in treatment, and its stimulation of intense affects that may not have obvious meaning in the context of contemporaneous therapeutic events.

Reenactment of Childhood Behaviors.   A common problem described by survivors of chronic or intrafamilial sexual abuse is the repetition of dysfunctional patterns in their interpersonal relationships. Research suggests that as a group, sexual abuse survivors have less flexibility in their choice and mode of intimate relationships, and have greater trouble altering hurtful interpersonal patterns than their nonabused peers. This lack of flexibility is thought to be due, at least in part, to the archaic basis of such repetitive patterns (such as childhood abuse) as opposed to arising solely from current dynamics or environmental contingencies. As a result, the survivor can find herself repeating behaviors and patterns relevant to her earliest relationships with untrustworthy individuals, often independent of the actual characteristics of her current relationships.

The basis for the client's repetition of interpersonal patterns is typically not within her conscious awareness. As noted earlier, the survivor may operate from unanalyzed cognitive models that reflect abuse-based assumptions regarding herself and others. When cognitive distortions of current events lead her to believe she is being abandoned, betrayed, or in some way violated, she is apt to engage in abuse-era behaviors.

Since she is, to some extent, responding to an abuse-related projection with an abuse-relevant response, her activity in the contemporaneous relationship is a reenactment of her childhood trauma. Because such reenactments are internally primed and potentially released by a wide variety of misinterpreted stimuli in the survivor's interpersonal environment, the likelihood of repetitive, seemingly inappropriate and dysfunctional behaviors can be high. As noted earlier and illustrated below, the therapeutic relationship can be an especially powerful trigger for such responses.

Gayle remembered that when she was at her grandparents' home, she often cried, wanting her mother to help her. When she called her mother, no solace was provided. "I hated needing her. . . . I hate needing anyone. Eventually, I got so that the only way I would let her help me was if there was some huge problem that wasn't my fault." Gayle made it clear that she did not want to need or depend on her therapist. However, during the thick of processing her trauma, Gayle would have particularly difficult times on weekends. She felt more dependent on, but also more afraid of, her therapist.

On two separate occasions, Gayle's therapist was surprised by calls from emergency services personnel who, in each instance, were responding to a crisis involving Gayle (the first was her involvement in an automobile accident, and the second was her driving to the desert and becoming lost). The emergency calls were surprising because Gayle was normally a tightly controlled person—an unlikely candidate for any behavior that would precipitate an emergency. After considerable therapy, Gayle was able to describe the depths of despondence she would feel on some weekends and her subsequent dissociated involvement in risky behaviors that were likely to result in crisis situations. "I wanted you to help me, take care of me, but I kept thinking you wouldn't do anything unless it was an emergency. . . . Then I'd find myself in an emergency."

Repetitive treatment-related dysfunctional behaviors can represent a client's attempt to communicate or resolve traumatic materials; they can also arise from misperceptions of current interpersonal events based on childhood learning. The client who is unable to verbally express or consciously examine painful material sometimes addresses it behaviorally through the transference. What could be viewed as "acting out" in such instances might better be considered a behavioral flashback—an expression of previously avoided trauma that behaviorally intrudes into the treatment in much the same manner as a visual flashback. As such, behavioral flashbacks represent an unconscious response to unresolved trauma, triggered in some way by the therapeutic process, and unconsciously designed to cause the exploration and desensitization of heretofore unverbalized injury.

In the third year of treatment, Gayle began missing sessions. She was actively processing the trauma and frequently expressed raw emotion connected to her abuse. Missed sessions appeared to follow sessions in which she expressed considerable sadness. After a missed session, Gayle acknowledged her absence but was unable to articulate any reason for the cancellation. The therapist wondered aloud if it might have been related to overwhelming feelings of pain and the need for a vacation of sorts. According to Gayle, "It could be. That makes sense. But I actually feel kind of proud of myself for how hard I'm working."

Gayle had another difficult session soon thereafter. She opened the following session saying, "I almost canceled today. But then I tried to figure out why. I think it's about being embarrassed or ashamed or something like that. I couldn't bear the thought of you seeing me today. . . . I couldn't be in your presence. It isn't because of what happened in the last session. . . . it's more about what I'm expecting to happen now. . . . It feels like you will laugh at me."

With further exploration, Gayle was able to discuss how her parents made fun of her when she cried, pointed out contortions in her facial features, and encouraged her siblings to do the same. Because of her growing shame when this happened, she quickly learned how not to cry. Since early adolescence, she had never cried in the presence of another individual. Her current work in therapy brought this conflict to the fore, where it manifested itself behaviorally in the avoidance of sessions.

Contemporaneous Responses

As previously stated, there are times when the client's response to the therapist is based primarily on the characteristics and behaviors of the therapist. Sexual abuse survivors in particular are acutely attuned to subtle changes in the therapist's state, mood, or level of attention. What presents now as hypervigilance to therapist nuance was originally a survival skill developed to detect imminent danger of abuse or abandonment. While it could be cast into the role of a "defense" or a "symptom," this ability often accurately (or at least in part) informs the survivor about the true aspects of the therapist. Many therapists have expressed wonderment (or chagrin!) regarding their survivor client's ability to detect subtle evidence of therapist boredom, anxiety, anger, sexual response, or distraction. The survivor's substantial "other-directedness" can so attune her to the therapist's process that she might appear almost prescient.

Gayle rarely asked questions about the personal life of her therapist. But she had a remarkable capacity to intuit aspects of the therapist's life that, to most people, would not be remotely apparent. On one occasion, the therapist had spent a day in the hospital following a relatively minor car accident. The client had neither been informed about the accident nor the hospitalization. No session or phone call had been missed due to the accident. In the next session, for the first time, the client asked twice about the health of the therapist, and ended the session stating "Take good care of yourself. You're all I have."

One could hypothesize that Gayle raised concerns about the therapist's health in an attempt to avoid her own issues. More likely, however, Gayle had detected some bodily stiffness or discomfort that only an astute (and motivated) observer would have noticed. The client was responding to reality, as should the therapist by treating the comment as an undistorted statement. While there was no obvious need to acknowledge the accident, the comment should not be treated as a form of projection or transference. Treating client responses to contemporaneous events as transference runs the risk of duplicating childhood abuse experiences of denial, contradiction, and misrepresentation.

During one session, the therapist was particularly tired after returning home early that morning on an overnight flight. Gayle commented that the therapist seemed preoccupied and became angry that she didn't have the kind of access to the therapist that she should have had. She was accurate in her observation and the therapist acknowledged it. Gayle initially acted surprised by the therapist's response, which included an apology for the reduced availability. She was silent for several minutes and then began to quietly cry. "I've never been in a relationship where someone would own their stuff or apologize if they'd done something wrong."

Although the survivor may be accurately aware of real fluctuations in the therapist's state, her responses might be based only partially in contemporaneous reality. It is not uncommon, for example, for a client who senses actual therapist irritability or attention lapses to respond in a relatively extreme manner with abuse-related rage, abandonment concerns, sudden passivity, or even a dissociative episode. In such an instance, the client's perceptions are contemporaneous, but her responses are transferential.

There were several extremely traumatized survivor-clients in the caseload of Gayle's therapist, one of whom had to be hospitalized in a crisis just hours before Gayle's session. Although her therapist worked hard to concentrate on Gayle and not to worry about this other client, Gayle immediately noticed the therapist's incomplete attunement to her. Gayle angrily accused the therapist of "not caring" and "probably thinking about your weekend instead of me," and stormed out of session, kicking the wastebasket as she left.

Working with Survivor Transference

A basic axiom of abuse-focused treatment and other contemporary dynamic approaches is that transference should not be treated as pathological or as an impediment to therapy, but as a normal process to be expected and, ultimately, to be utilized. All transference is, by definition, congruent with the client's history.

To the extent that abuse-related transference is present, the therapist has the opportunity to facilitate the resolution of issues that, but for the capacity of humans to reenact unintegrated traumatic experience, might otherwise be too ancient to access. Working within the context of transference also allows the survivor to update abuse-related assumptions and perceptions "online" within a nonabusive adult relationship. Finally, because transference is a powerful restimulator of abuse-era affects, cognitions, and sensory experiences (such as flashbacks), abuse-focused therapy can be a place where traumatic memories are desensitized and new behaviors (for example, greater affect regulation skills) are acquired.

This focus means that the transference is used to inform both client and therapist. As a team, both seek to observe and correct the client's distortions, make connections between her current behavior and her childhood experiences, and provide an environment that, in and of itself, counterconditions those reflexive projections arising from abuse early in life. The therapist's use of careful reflections and gentle questions stimulates exploration, encourages understanding, and facilitates the client's discovery of important personal truths.

Initially, the client might respond negatively to the therapist, assuming that the reflections are subtle judgments and that questions require a "correct" answer. She may feel as though she is being interrogated or manipulated, and thus resist the process. Over time, the client comes to trust the therapist's actual interest in and lack of judgmental responses to her unfolding. Such a process is far from linear, however, as successful interventions set the stage for additional transferential responses that, in turn, restimulate other problems that must be addressed.

The approach outlined above uses relatively nondirective interventions, as opposed to, for example, the heavy use of the classic therapeutic interpretation. Although the therapist, through observation of the transferential patterns, offers gentle, tentative hypotheses about possible connections between current problems and childhood experiences, the client should not be "told" what is true. Among other things, the therapist could be wrong—an error that easily clouds the uncovering process and confuses the survivor, especially if she suffers from significant difficulties in the self domain.

The therapist should avoid definitive statements regarding the client's phenomenologic experience. If the therapist offers such interpretations to the survivor as inherently accurate representations of truth, there is the risk of negatively affecting the quality of the client-therapist relationship. By definition, interpretations are not part of the client's current understanding. Given the survivor's frequent difficulties with trust, strongly asserted interpretations can be perceived as false, disconfirming, or controlling. Alternatively, the therapist's interpretations might be accepted by the client as complete truth via the *Rescuer* projection. In the latter case, the implicit "flip side" of the *Rescuer* model is reinforced—that the survivor can only *receive* insight, not develop it personally. The role of follower and supplicant is well known to many survivors and is easily assumed. The net effect, unfortunately, may be excessive survivor dependency and associated low self-esteem.

An important assumption of abuse-focused therapy, one that is especially relevant to work with survivor transference, is the importance of reality-based interactions between client and therapist to the extent that the survivor can tolerate them. Although the therapist does not deride or reject the transference, the client's fantasies of the therapist are best not to be reinforced. The focus of therapy is clarification and awareness, thereby developing the client's increasing ability to view herself and others without distortion. Although the therapist works within the context of transferentially restimulated attachment dynamics and abuse-era affects, the goal is to help the survivor understand, process, and outgrow the need for such phenomena rather than reinforce them through direct participation. As noted in the following section, the therapist must consistently seek a place in treatment defined as "reality," an admittedly elusive location given the subjectivity of psychotherapy. Nevertheless, by reliably attempting to uncover what is "really" happening in a given session, the therapist models the value of moving beyond distortion and reenactment.

THERAPIST RESPONSE

Like the client, the therapist brings to the therapy hour both positive and negative life experiences. Therapy is inevitably influenced by the clinician's childhood experiences and current personality characteristics. Ideally, the influence will be in the positive direction—the therapist's stable sense of self, clinical experience, and acquired interpersonal skills will increase his or her capacity to be helpful to the client.

For some therapists, a combination of adequate (or better) childhood experiences and high interpersonal functioning allow relatively unencumbered participation in the therapy process. Such individuals might not have significant countertransferential responses to their clients, although they run the risk of not entirely understanding the demons with which many survivors struggle.

For therapists whose life experiences have not been as positive and have yet to be processed and integrated, personal psychotherapy may be a necessary prerequisite to effective therapeutic functioning. The introspection required by personal psychotherapy is apt to increase the therapist's conscious awareness of his or her own issues and their impact on thoughts, feelings, and behaviors in interactions with clients. To this end, therapist training programs often stress the value of one's own psychotherapy and, in fact, some have a didactic therapy requirement for graduation. The therapist's own therapy is especially appropriate in the context of abuse-focused psychotherapy. The intensity and extremity of the client's sexual abuse–related transference, as noted earlier, means that any possibility of therapist countertransference increases—especially if the therapist has unresolved issues, regardless of their origin.

The concept of the "wounded healer" has been discussed by many authors who suggest that negative experiences in childhood enable therapists to identify with the problems of their clients and relate to them in an empathic manner. The potentially positive contribution of survivorhood to the therapist's work with other survivors has been discussed. The therapist who has worked through and come to terms with his or her own abuse history may be optimally suited to providing sensitive, nondiscounting services to other survivors. Such individuals can ultimately become the best of therapists—people who know what it is to feel significant pain but whose own awareness and resolution of these difficulties protects and informs the treatment process.

Therapist responses to clients are apt to include both conscious and unconscious aspects. When the therapist has conscious, less-projected reactions to the client's life, pain, or transference, it is referred to here as a contemporaneous response. When the therapist's response is primarily an unconscious reaction (either to his or her own life history or to the client's transference), or when it is not based primarily in the client's issues, it is likely to be countertransference.

Contemporaneous Responses

Several types of contemporaneous responses are experienced by trauma-focused therapists. Common sources of these responses are:

- The client's immediate state or presentation
- The sexual content disclosed by the client
- The nature of trauma work

The Client's State or Presentation. As in other intimate relationships, both client and therapist can be expected to have a wide range of feelings based on the personal stimulus value of the other person. Although therapist responses in this domain may not represent childhood-specific projections, it is nevertheless the clinician's responsibility to "keep tabs" on his or her contemporaneous feelings toward the client. Therapist feelings typically vary in intensity, may or may not be appropriate to be expressed to the survivor at any given moment in therapy, and can be an important source of information about the client's current experience.

Gayle was a bright, articulate woman. She had a delightful sense of humor, and when not dissociated or excessively hypervigilant, she used both her intelligence and her humor to confront her abuse courageously. Throughout treatment, the therapist was aware of a deep respect for and enjoyment of the client. Also present at any given time were other feelings and reactions to Gayle.

When, for example, she repeatedly left telephone messages that sounded despondent and desperate, but then coolly refused any contact with the therapist when the call was returned, the therapist often felt some level of intrusion, anger, hurt, and helplessness. Alternatively, when she recounted distressing aspects of her abuse, the therapist felt sadness over her pain, anger toward the injustice in the world, and/or protectiveness and tenderness toward the client.

Therapists who successfully work with adult survivors are usually caring individuals, most of whom at some level are able to identify with the problems of their client and attune themselves to the client's phenomenology. As a result, client recounting of painful experiences frequently stimulates a set of parallel (but hopefully less intense) feelings in the therapist, including compassion, concern, and caring. Alternatively, however, when the client's work has either stagnated or plateaued, the therapist can find him- or herself feeling bored or impatient. This parallel processing of client experience often allows the therapist to be aware of a client affect or response before it is expressed—or sometimes even perceived—by the client. In this way the clinician can gain valuable information about the client's current state and struggles, and the necessary work remaining for the client.

The Sexual Content. Therapy for sexual abuse trauma usually includes the survivor's detailed recounting of the sexual acts performed against her. Because the original abuse involved sexualization of power and submission, and the sometimes forced exchange of sexual acts for a version of love and attention, it is not unusual for the survivor to reexperience sexual stimuli during her recounting of such abuse to the therapist. The survivor's physical and verbal expression of sexual content, whether in terms of the original abuse or later nonabusive sexual interactions, can tap into the same empathic attunement in the therapist that was available for the survivor's descriptions of pain or sadness.

The survivor's sexual reactions during the psychotherapy session—along with the possibility that she might reenact sexual power dynamics through sexualization of the therapist—can produce some level of therapist sexual arousal or attraction to the client. An understandable response for many therapists is to feel uncomfortable, embarrassed, or ashamed at such reactions, and to push these feelings "underground." Ignoring them, however, or attempting to dismiss them is in the best interest of neither the client nor the therapist.

During the fourth year of Gayle's treatment, she became romantically involved with a caring, sensitive architect. This was her first romantic involvement since terminating the relationship with the abusive lover that precipitated treatment. As their sexual relationship developed, Gayle's capacity to articulate specific sexual content markedly increased.

She verbalized the striking contrast between the sexual contact with her lover and the abusive contact with her grandfather. She described interactions with her lover as if it were her first sexual contact, with romantic, highly passionate, and erotic components. There was no apparent motivation on her part to eroticize the contact with the therapist. As well, there was an absence of any "as if" or "storytelling" qualities when she spoke of their sexual contact. It was the details of her feelings and the specific physical contact with her lover that solidified for Gayle the reality that she had changed—that she no longer lived in the world as a sexually abused child. These same details stimulated subtle erotic feelings in the therapist.

Arousal to such content can be egosyntonic for therapists who recognize the sexual stimuli for what it is and who accept having normal internal responses to such stimuli. It is as inappropriate for the therapist to divert the content away from sexual matters in order to increase his or her own sense of comfort as it would be to encourage such content because of a conscious or unconscious attraction to the client.

There is some disagreement in the psychotherapy field regarding whether the therapist should verbally express to the client any contemporaneous sexual feelings he or she might have during therapy. Some suggest that the therapist's sexual response to the client can be discussed carefully when appropriate, just as feelings of sadness or irritability should be analyzed in the session. Such writers suggest that "projective identification" and other reciprocating client-therapist dynamics mean that the therapist's sexual responses often reflect client dynamics and thus require conscious examination in the session.

We take a more conservative view on this issue. In our experience, sexual response to one's client is a function of a number of therapist variables. Less experienced therapists seem to report more sexual responses in treatment than do the more experienced. By virtue of sex-role socialization, males tend to sexualize intimacy more than females. Additionally, sexual response is mediated by the general level of comfort and impulse control the therapist possesses regarding sexual issues in general. The complexity of such issues, as well as the potential for therapist issues to intrude at a behavioral level, require considerable attention before anything as explosive as therapist sexual response can be broached in treatment.

Because sexuality is such a complex issue, the therapist may not be fully cognizant of its origins in the session, including the possibility that the therapist is inappropriately sexualizing the client by virtue of social training or unresolved abuse issues. Additionally, although the survivor needs to process sexual issues within abuse-focused treatment, she is likely to feel very unsafe in any therapeutic interaction that involves the therapist's own expressed sexuality. For these reasons, we strongly suggest that the therapist avoid any reference to his or her sexual responses should they come up in a session. The stimulus value of therapist sexuality is likely to be so powerful and threatening for the survivor, by virtue of her experience of sexual danger in at least one previous power-laden relationship, that the clinician is counseled to seek out consultation with a colleague whenever significant sexual response to a client is experienced.

Such consultation does not imply that the clinician has done anything wrong or improper by having an internal sexual response, but rather acknowledges that the intrusion of such issues into treatment can easily disrupt or destroy the frail trust the survivor feels for the therapist. The clinician should utilize consultation to probe the basis for the sexual response, to seek perspective, and to discuss ways to ensure the avoidance of any therapist sexual communication or unconscious sexual behavior during the session. To the extent that this clarification process is helpful, the client has the opportunity to process some of her most frightening and threatening concerns in the context of a safe therapeutic container, where the possibility of "seduction" (abuse) by the therapist rests solely in the survivor's fearful projection.

The Nature of Trauma Work. Researchers are beginning to examine the impact of repeatedly listening to traumatic, painful, or sadistic acts on the psyche of the therapist. Therapists working with individuals diagnosed with PTSD sometimes develop secondary posttraumatic stress that evidences itself in intrusive experiences, hypervigilance, and numbing of affect. To the extent that the therapist's secondary posttraumatic symptoms intrude into the psychotherapy session, the clinician can frighten the client or become less effective as a facilitator of healing.

Gayle was raped by a stranger during the course of treatment. As she processed her revictimization in therapy, the therapist, too, had strong reactions to the attack and the pain it caused Gayle. The day the attack was reported to the therapist, the therapist had intrusive images of the attack while working with other clients. That night, the therapist had a nightmare in which the client was physically attacked and the therapist was forced to watch, unable to prevent the assault. For several days following, the therapist was aware of a mixture of sadness and anger, as well as being less "centered" when working with Gayle and other survivors.

It is in this domain that the issue of therapist "burnout" is often raised. Because the therapist can develop a "PTSD by proxy," associated therapist dynamics can intrude on the session. The therapist can become especially preoccupied with the client's safety and may unconsciously fail to reinforce (or actually discourage) client risk-taking associated with growing autonomy. Alternatively, the therapist might avoid attending to traumatic material the client needs to address as a way of avoiding further secondary traumatization.

Although such responses could be considered countertransferential to the extent that they involve responses to multiple clients based on experience with one, they also represent contemporaneous responses to an extremely taxing and sometimes overwhelming occupation. As is the case with contemporaneous sexual responses, posttraumatic stress in therapists requires careful consultation with colleagues so that internal responses do not become negative or destructive therapist behaviors. Especially severe secondary traumatization can require a temporary break from treating trauma survivors or the initiation (or re-initiation) of one's own therapy.

Countertransference

When the therapist's responses are not primarily based in contemporaneous reactions to the client or client issues, it is generally assumed that the therapist is experiencing countertransference—the reciprocal concept of transference. The therapist who has not resolved salient issues associated with current life traumas, conflicts, child abuse, or family dysfunction runs the risk of impeding effective therapeutic process and negatively affecting the client. Countertransference has several faces, none of which are helpful to the client or the therapeutic process if acted upon. They include the following:

- Overidentification
- Underidentification
- Classic projection
- Boundary violation

Overidentification. Any empathic therapist who works with child abuse victims can become absorbed in the pain that pervades their lives. In fact, it is a common developmental task of abuse therapists, early in their careers, to find some sort of working balance between empathy for the survivor's often extreme distress and adaptive strategies that protect the therapist from being overwhelmed.

For some clinicians, however, unresolved personal issues can produce an absorption in the client's ongoing pain that results in lost perspective, sometimes to the extent that the clinician falls into the role of a distressed peer or even co-client. The overidentified therapist may then attempt to protect (or as discussed in the next section, distract) the survivor as a way of reducing the therapist's restimulated abuse-related distress. In the process, the therapist loses track of the survivor's actual needs or best interests.

There are at least two significant dangers in therapist overidentification: (1) the therapist can display heightened affective responses to the client's abuse-related issues, thereby both decreasing therapeutic effectiveness and paying a personal psychic price; or (2) the therapist may engage in caretaking behaviors that infantilize or overprotect the client and reduce her self-efficacy.

Related to the first danger, overidentification can occur when the therapist's empathic response to a client is unconsciously intensified by his or her own unresolved trauma or experiences of childhood maltreatment. Therapists who identify too strongly can become overinvolved in certain therapeutic agendas, to the detriment of the client's need to address other issues as well. For example, if the therapist experiences rage toward perpetrators, he or she may encourage or direct the client to express anger at her abuser, perhaps despite the survivor's need to either (1) develop a greater sense of safety and self-control before engaging in such a threatening activity, or (2) express a range of other important feelings, such as sadness, longing, or love for the offender.

Alternatively, the therapist's reexperiencing of trauma in the context of the survivor's distress can lead to inappropriate disclosures or personal processing of therapist issues during the session, instead of more client-directed activities.

Gayle spoke of one of her previous therapists: "I was talking about my grandfather and feeling pretty sad, and then my therapist began to cry. At first I thought it was sweet, but then she seemed sadder than me. Later she told me that she had been abused and that she could really relate to how I must feel. I guess that would have been okay to know, but it felt too weird. I didn't know if she was relating to me or just feeling her own pain. I felt like now I was supposed to help take care of her. I was afraid I might make her sad when I talked about my abuse.

An alternative manifestation of overinvolvement is an overinvestment in soothing the client, rescuing her from difficult situations, or becoming too involved in her day-to-day life. Whatever the form, it may result in unnecessary caretaking activities that infantilize the client, decreasing her capacity to develop an internal sense of an autonomous, efficacious self.

Gayle spoke of a second therapist who had taken Gayle to her home. On more than one occasion, she had eaten dinner with the therapist's family, watched television with her children, and helped put her children to bed. Gayle described her own feeling of confusion—enjoying seeing a "healthy family" but resenting the attention her therapist was giving the children. Information from the therapist indicated that she based her treatment of Gayle on the assumption that survivors needed to be "reparented." She provided infant toys, held clients in her lap, read them children's stories, and so on. The result for Gayle (and probably other clients) was confusion and intense attachment restimulation that promoted further regression rather than growth.

Many survivors were raised in environments where caregivers were not able to relate to them as independent agents with needs and experiences different from those of the caregiver. The survivor's healing is, to some extent, reliant on the therapist's ability to keep client issues separate from therapist issues, and thus provide a safe environment for the work. This involves not only the obvious physical and sexual boundaries, but also the psychological boundaries associated with not infantilizing the client, making decisions that the client could make, or assuming a familiarity with her that infringes on the client's privacy.

Finally, therapist overidentification can result in blurred boundaries between the giving and receiving of therapy. Many survivors have been taught by childhood to be other-directed—focused on others to the detriment of their own need fulfillment. As a result, the survivor can become involved in taking care of the therapist, based on the latter's conscious or unconscious communications regarding his or her own pain. To the extent that this role reversal occurs, therapy is undermined.

Underidentification. Therapists can feel emotionally overwhelmed by the amount of injury and distress to which they are exposed on a daily basis. This sense of being inundated by pain can be exacerbated by the therapist's own restimulated distress or trauma. As noted previously, some clinicians in this position will overidentify with the presumed source of the pain, that is, the client. Others, however, respond by emotionally distancing themselves from that source. The result is underidentification, although this term is a misnomer to the extent that the therapist is, in fact, being restimulated by identifying with the survivor prior to defending against her.

The primary manifestations of underidentification are (1) cognitive attempts to minimize the pain and consequences of child abuse, and (2) decreased therapeutic attunement. In each instance, the underlying, typically unconscious strategy is the same: reduce empathy and thereby reduce therapist restimulated pain.

With minimization, therapist resistance to believing the survivor's child abuse history—and the psychic implications of that history—serves a psychological need, although it is rarely acknowledged as such. The clinician may over-rely on simplistic assumptions regarding the incidence or impacts of sexual abuse, primarily in terms of denying the existence or primacy of abuse in a given client's history. Although client abuse reports require the same level of clinical evaluation as do any other statements during therapy, some clinicians become especially critical and questioning when abuse comes up as an issue during treatment.

Gayle described her first therapist as a man who, although pleasant enough when she spoke of her long-term depressive symptoms, became cold and intellectualized when Gayle raised the possible role of her childhood sexual abuse experiences in her current distress. "He was like a nice father-figure at first, but then he got distant when the abuse came up. I don't think he believed I really had been abused. He told me that it was unlikely that my abuse was important. One time, he gave me a lecture that went on for most of the session."

In any given instance, the therapist could be expressing real (contemporaneous) concerns about the validity of a specific historical statement. It is likely, however, that some therapists who steadfastly reject abuse reports as fictitious are motivated by the need either (1) to avoid restimulation of their own abuse-related issues, or (2) to circumvent the intrusion of their own sexual responses to the idea or images of abuse. By denying the reality, relevance, or importance of a survivor's childhood history, the underidentified clinician may seek to apply the same rule to his or her own childhood pain or current sexual conflicts.

In contrast to complete rejection of the reality of abuse, a second form of underinvolvement manifests as reduced attunement to the client when abuse issues are being processed in therapy. When this presents as a chronic pattern, the clinician tends to respond with relative indifference or professional coolness to the pain of survivors. Although professional objectivity is an important tool in the day-to-day management of what otherwise might be overwhelming work-related distress, its overdevelopment usually signals a more personal defense, often against one's own restimulated pain.

Some therapists, although generally able to interact with compassion during clinical work, can enter a somewhat dissociated disattunement when certain upsetting issues come up. Although the clinician may be attempting to disengage from survivor stimuli that resonate with unresolved personal issues as a means of self-protection, the survivor is likely to see the process as therapist disinterest or abandonment.

Gayle celebrated the first birthday of her only child during the week that her therapist miscarried for the second time. Gayle frequently brought in pictures of her child that led to fruitful discussion about her fears of being a mother, her own attachment issues, and related matters. During the first session subsequent to the therapist's miscarriage, Gayle brought in pictures of her own child's birthday party. The therapist was less interactive in the session and the discussion stagnated. The next time she brought pictures, Gayle asked for the first time, "Is it okay that I bring in pictures to show you?"

The therapist's temporary disengagement from Gayle required reparation in later sessions. This included both clarification of the client's right to make use of the therapy hour in the best way she saw fit as well as the therapist's "owning" the disattunement with Gayle. Because the therapist was able to quickly observe and address the issue, there was no permanent setback in the therapeutic process.

Classic Projection. Unlike overidentification, which is an intensification of true aspects of client pain, projection is based more directly in the therapist's own unresolved distress and conflicts and can be essentially unrelated to client affect or behavior. It develops when unresolved issues, either from the therapist's current life events or childhood history, are confused with perceptions of the client.

During an early session, Gayle was talking about a family reunion and her need to make a decision about her attendance. She seemed to be hesitating and editing information she gave the therapist. The therapist commented on the process to Gayle who responded, "When I was seeing Presley (a previous psychologist), he'd get really angry every time I'd talk about visiting my family, particularly if my father or my grandfather were going to be there. Sometimes I would get frightened; I wasn't sure if he was angry at me or them, or what he was angry at. I guess I was waiting to see how you'd respond." Case notes from the previous therapist indicated that he was frustrated with the client because "she refuses to stand up to her perpetrators." In his treatment goals, the therapist indicated that Gayle needed to express her obvious anger at her father and grandfather for their physical and sexual abuse of her.

Review of the style and content of these notes suggested a less than objective approach.

It seems likely that Gayle's previous therapist was responding to something other than Gayle's issues and goals in treatment. At that time, she was ambivalent in her feelings toward her family, aware that she would increase her isolation in the world if she reduced contact, and evaluating the relative worth of continued interactions with family members. The therapist's anger appeared out of context for the issues presented by the client, who was appropriately processing her feelings. Additionally, it caused fear in the client and resulted in her editing future information she gave to the therapist.

On a milder level, the therapist could project impatience or boredom onto the client when, in fact, the therapist is the one having difficulties with the pace or process of therapy. The therapist who has an excessive need for control, perhaps based on childhood needs for safety and predictability, might perceive the client as highly manipulative. The clinician who has unresolved sexual issues might respond to innocuous client behaviors as evidence that the client is being seductive. Similarly, the fearful therapist might project danger onto the client or the client's environment when there is none.

At one point in Gayle's treatment, the therapist's own life and the lives of significant others had been threatened in the context of another child abuse case. The therapist, who was not ordinarily a fearful person, became vigilant to the real danger associated with the perpetrator in this case. The day after the therapist had been followed when leaving the office, Gayle jokingly spoke of a stranger who had approached her coming into the therapist's office building. While Gayle was rather proud of the way she handled the situation, the therapist became hypervigilant about real or fantasized dangers for the client and spoke to her in an irritated, if not angry, tone of voice. Fortunately for both client and therapist, the therapist recognized the projection within a relatively short amount of time and shifted to more appropriate responses.

It is not true, of course, that the therapist's expression of anger (or other emotions) is necessarily inappropriate in all instances. However, it is not helpful when personal issues lead the therapist to selectively respond to those aspects of the client's situation most reminiscent of the therapist's own experience. The therapist with untreated physical abuse trauma, for example, might project onto a prostitute in treatment intense anger upon hearing of her being badly beaten by a customer. The survivor's primary issue at that moment, however, may be more immediate fear of displeasing or angering her pimp. The critical issue here is not the therapist's appropriate empathy for the client, but rather, the point at which the therapist's own response significantly impacts perceptions of, or responses to, the client's process.

Projection can be especially problematic because the survivor inherently relies on the therapist for objective data and uncontaminated responses. The therapist must be able to assess the client's state accurately in order to provide relevant therapeutic interventions. To the extent that the therapist's past or present life events impair his or her ability to do these things, the client's progress in treatment will suffer. Thus, the therapist who has worked through childhood issues may be able to use that history and the recovery process to be informed about the client's issues. Alternatively, the clinician who has not addressed critical personal issues may confuse personal history and needs with client needs and, as a result, will be less able to provide accurate assessment and treatment.

Boundary Violation. Intrinsic to childhood sexual victimization is violation of psychological and bodily space. This transgression can impair the development of boundary awareness and impact the victim's ability to perceive and relate to others independent of herself. Thus, a crucial aspect of successful treatment is the provision of an environment where the survivor can learn to establish and maintain appropriate boundaries in adult relationships. Any therapist behavior that intrudes on the client or violates her rights to self-definition can have the doubly negative effects of (1) destroying the trust from which the most important work occurs and (2) directly discouraging the development of such self–other demarcation.

Countertransferential boundary violations occur when the therapist's issues prevent him or her from being able to discriminate appropriate from inappropriate—and helpful from intrusive—behavior during treatment, or when the therapist fails to resist the drive to reenact boundary violations on the client. Such boundary violations include:

- Any type of sexual behavior with clients
- Inappropriate personal disclosures
- Excessively intrusive questions or statements
- Habitual interruptions
- Violations of personal space
- Conscious or unconscious use of the client to gratify the therapist's needs

When such violations occur, they may not be recognized as such by the therapist, or may be seen as out of his or her control. Boundary confusion typically arises from one of two phenomena: (1) the therapist's incomplete awareness of client-therapist boundaries due to his or her own inadequate boundary learning, or (2) as a form or reenactment of the therapist's childhood boundary violations. Neither of these dynamics is indicative of adequate psychological health in the psychotherapist. (Some therapist boundary violations, such as explicit sexual contact, are not necessarily based on boundary confusion nor are they strictly countertransferential in nature; instead, they represent intentional victimization/exploitation of the client. They are better thought of as solely malicious or criminal rather than as arising from unresolved therapist issues.)

Depending on the extent of violation involved, boundary confusion can range from nontherapeutic to tragically destructive. At minimum, such behaviors restimulate and reinforce abuse-related issues and trauma in the survivor, and potentially prevent or destroy the development of trust in the therapeutic relationship. Research suggests that at the most extreme end of the violation continuum, sexual abuse survivors who are sexually revictimized by their therapists suffer greater distress than do survivors who are not revictimized during treatment. Less obvious victims of therapist boundary violations (for example, those who are repeatedly exposed to intrusive questions, inappropriate statements, or lack of respect for client defenses) suffer as well, either by a resurgence in post-abuse trauma or in terms of being deprived of a safe therapeutic environment.

Intervention in Therapist Countertransference

Because of the critical importance of therapist objectivity and trustworthiness in work with sexual abuse survivors, countertransference must be addressed whenever it intrudes into treatment. Not only does countertransference impact the therapy and potentially derail effective treatment, but it also signals therapist distress and the need for external assistance or intervention.

To this end, regular consultation is recommended as an important component of abuse-focused psychotherapy. Such support allows therapists to share the burden of daily exposure to others' pain, as well as to explore ways in which their own personal issues might distort their perception and practice, producing negative therapeutic outcomes. In many instances, inappropriate identification or projection can be remediated by the consistent availability of an objective consultant who is alert to countertransferential issues in general, and the clinician's vulnerabilities specifically. Although minor over- or underidentification and projection can respond to clinical vigilance alone, higher levels of these problems and almost any form of boundary confusion typically require outside intervention.

Abuse-related boundary confusion involving any sexual behavior or other major client exploitation is of sufficient gravity to require immediate and incisive intervention. In the case of sexual violation, the individual must remove him- or herself from the practice of psychotherapy, refer clients to another therapist, and notify the appropriate professional and legal authorities. Less obvious boundary confusion may require less extreme actions; nevertheless, the therapist should seek objective consultation from another professional to determine the extent of the difficulty and the most appropriate intervention(s).

This chapter has touched on a number of issues associated with an inevitable human phenomenon: the contribution of life history to the quality and form of intense interpersonal interactions. As one of the most human and most intense of these, psychotherapy can be thought of as a mutually projected endeavor where two humans (one called "client" and one called "therapist") come together in the service of assisting only one of them. To the extent that the responses of the client to the therapist are distorted by the client's history, or the therapist is less able to assist the client for similar historical reasons, issues of transference and countertransference must be raised and addressed.

Since perception is the basis for most behavior, and because perception is composed of both objective and subjective components, transference- and countertransference-interactions are to be expected. By accepting these as normal, and by paying attention to the rich associations triggered by the therapeutic interaction, the clinician can provide both an environment where the client's psychic pain and negative learning can be reworked, and at the same time avoid processes that reenact—rather than resolve—childhood injury.

NOTES

P. 187, *Because sexual abuse is often a traumatic event:* Briere, J., & Elliott, D. M. (1994). Immediate and long-term impacts of child sexual abuse. *The Future of Children, 4,* 54–69; Kendall-Tackett, K. A., Williams, L. M., & Finkelhor, D. (1993). Impact of sexual abuse on children: A review and synthesis of recent empirical studies." *Psychological Bulletin, 113,* 164–180.

P. 187, *The model is presented here in the context of abuse-focused psychotherapy:* Briere, J. *Child abuse trauma: Theory and treatment of the lasting effects.* Newbury Park, CA: Sage.

P. 189, *certain concepts will be illustrated through a case example:* Gayle is not a "real" person, in the sense of representing a single client-survivor. She does reflect a composite of clients disguised in the interest of confidentiality.

P. 192, *Alterations in the survivor's perception:* Briere, J. (1989). *Therapy for adults molested as children: Beyond survival.* New York: Springer; Jehu, D. (1988). *Beyond sexual abuse: Therapy with women who were childhood victims.* Chichester, UK: Wiley.

P. 196, *Both sexual abuse and child neglect:* Alexander, P. (1992). Application of attachment theory to the study of sexual abuse. *Journal of Consulting and Clinical Psychology, 60,* 185–195; Erickson, M. F., Egeland, B., Pianta, R. (1989). *The effects of maltreatment on the development of young children.* In D. Cicchett and V. Carlson (Eds.), *Research and theory: Child maltreatment.* London: Cambridge.

P. 196, *The failure or disruption of the child-caretaker attachment bond:* Bowlby, J. (1973). *Separation: Anxiety and anger.* London: Hogarth.

P. 200, *Research suggests that as a group, sexual abuse survivors:* Elliott, D. M. (1994). Impaired object relations in professional women molested as children. *Psychotherapy, 31,* 79–86.

P. 203, *The survivor's substantial "other-directedness":* Briere, J. (1989). *Therapy for adults molested as children: Beyond survival.* New York: Springer.

P. 205, *abuse-focused therapy can be a place where traumatic memories are desensitized:* Briere, J. (in press). Special issues in psychotherapy with adults: Dealing with the trauma and the self. In J. Briere, L. Berliner, J. Bulkey, C. Jenney, & T. Reid (Eds.), *The APSAC handbook of child maltreatment.* Newbury Park, CA: Sage.

P. 206, *An important assumption of abuse-focused therapy:* Briere, J. *Child abuse trauma: Theory and treatment of the lasting effects.* Newbury Park, CA: Sage.

P. 208, *especially if the therapist has unresolved issues:* Elliott, D. M., & Guy, J. D. (1993). Mental health versus non-mental health professionals: Childhood trauma and adult functioning. *Professional Psychology: Theory and Practice, 24,* 83–90. Therapists are more likely than other professionals to have experienced a traumatic event in their childhood and report more dysfunctional dynamics in their family of origin than did women from other professions. Interestingly, despite an increased likelihood of a history of child abuse, therapists experienced significantly less anxiety, depression, dissociation, sleep disturbance, and impairment in interpersonal relationships than did women in other professions.

P. 208, *The concept of the "wounded healer":* Golberg, C. (1986). *On being a psychotherapist: The journey of the healer.* New York: Gardner; Guy, J. D. (1987). *The personal life of the psychotherapist.* New York: Wiley; Scott, C., & Hawk, J. (Eds.). (1986). *Heal thyself: The health of heath care professionals.* New York: Brunner/Mazel.

P. 208, *The potentially positive contribution of survivorhood:* Briere, J. *Child abuse trauma: Theory and treatment of the lasting effects.* Newbury Park, CA: Sage.

P. 211, *Some suggest that the therapist's sexual response to the client can be discussed:* Davies, J. M., & Frauley, M. G. (1994). *Treating the adult survivor of childhood sexual abuse: A psychoanalytic perspective.* New York: Basic Books.

P. 212, *Researchers are beginning to examine the impact of repeatedly listening to traumatic:* Jones, J. M., & Dunning, C. M. (1993, October). Protecting the protectors: Proactive training for child protective workers. Paper presented at the Annual Meeting of the International Society for Traumatic Stress Studies, San Antonio, Texas; McCann, L., & Pearlman, L. A. (1990). *Psychological trauma and the adult survivor.* New York: Brunner/Mazel; Munroe, J. (1993, October). *Preventing traumatized therapists: Coping with survivor engagement patterns.* Paper presented at the Annual Meeting of the International Society for Traumatic Stress Studies, San Antonio, Texas.

P. 213, *"PTSD by proxy":* Briere, J. (1989). *Therapy for adults molested as children: Beyond survival.* New York: Springer.

P. 221, *This transgression can impair the development of boundary awareness:* Elliott, D. M. (1994). Impaired object relations in professional women molested as children. *Psychotherapy, 31,* 79–86.

P. 222, *Research suggests that . . . sexual abuse survivors who are sexually revictimized by their therapists:* Magana, D. (1990). *The impact of client-therapist sexual intimacy and child sexual abuse on psychosexual and psychological functioning.* (Unpublished dissertation, University of California at Los Angeles).

P. 223, *Abuse-related boundary confusion involving any sexual behavior:* Pope, K. S. (1994). *Sexual involvement with therapists: Patient assessment, subsequent therapy, forensics.* Washington, DC: American Psychological Association.

ABOUT THE AUTHORS

Brian R. Abbott, Ph.D., holds a doctorate in clinical psychology and a master's degree in social work. He serves as the executive director of the Giarretto Institute, which operates the first Child Sexual Abuse Treatment Program (CSATP) and professional training center established worldwide. Since 1971, the institute has treated more than 20,000 individuals. The efforts of its professional training program have resulted in the creation of more than 150 CSATPs in the United States and other countries and, according to a recent federally funded study, "is the most widely replicated child sexual abuse treatment model nationwide." Abbott is a noted clinician, trainer, and researcher in the field of child sexual abuse. While at the Giarretto Institute, Abbott has developed model treatment programs for adolescent sexual offenders and abuse reactive children. He has made numerous presentations at local, state, and national conferences and symposiums as well as in the print and electronic media. Abbott has published articles and materials related to his clinical and research work with victims and perpetrators of sexual abuse.

John Briere, Ph.D., is associate professor of psychiatry at the University of Southern California School of Medicine and a clinical psychologist at the Department of Emergency Psychiatric Services of the LAC-USC Medical Center. He is author of numerous articles, book chapters, and books, primarily in the areas of child abuse, psychological trauma, and interpersonal violence. He is on the editorial boards of several scholarly journals and is a member of the board of directors of the American Professional Society on the Abuse of Children (APSAC) and the International Society for Traumatic Stress Studies (ISTSS).

Catherine Classen, Ph.D., is a clinical psychologist and research associate in the Department of Psychiatry and Behavioral Sciences at Stanford University School of Medicine. She is clinical director of a study evaluating group approaches for treating women molested in childhood. Her primary research and clinical interest is the impact of trauma on the adult survivor.

Christine A. Courtois, Ph.D., is a psychologist in private practice in Washington, D.C., and clinical director, Center for Abuse Recovery and Empowerment, the Psychiatric Institute of Washington, Washington, D.C. She conducts workshops nationwide on the treatment of incest and other forms of sexual assault. She is the author of *Healing the Incest Wound: Adult Survivors in Therapy* (1988) and *Adult Survivors of Child Sexual Abuse*, a workshop model (1993); she has co-edited an issue of *The Counseling Psychologist* (1988) on the topic of victimization and its aftermath. She is currently under contract with W. W. Norton for a new book with the working title of *Incest and Dissociation*. Dr. Courtois is a member of the program committee, Eastern Regional Conference on Abuse and Multiple Personality Disorder, was appointed to the American Psychological Association Working Group on the Investigation of Childhood Memories and the President's Task Force on Family Violence, and is a Fellow, APA Divisions 17 and 29.

Diana M. Elliott, Ph.D., is director of training and research at the Sexual Abuse Crisis Center at Harbor-UCLA Medical Center where she is on staff as a clinical psychologist. She is assistant clinical professor of psychiatry in the School of Medicine at the University of California, Los Angeles. Her primary research and clinical interest is the impact and treatment of interpersonal trauma in child and adult victims.

Victoria M. Follette, Ph.D., is associate professor of psychology and director of clinical training at the University of Nevada, Reno. She received her B.S. (1983) and M.S. (1985) degrees from the University of Washington and her Ph.D. (1989) from Memphis State University. Her research and clinical interests include the assessment and treatment of survivors of child sexual abuse and domestic violence, as well as psychotherapy outcome research on contextual treatments. Additionally, she is the executive director of the American Association of Applied and Preventive Psychology.

Mary R. Harvey, Ph.D., is a clinical and community psychologist and lecturer in psychiatry at Harvard Medical School. She is the founding director of the Cambridge Hospital Victims of Violence Program and is the author or co-author of numerous publications concerning the nature of psychological trauma and sexual victimization. Dr. Harvey is the co-author with Dr. Mary P. Koss of *The Rape Victim: Clinical and Community Interventions* (Sage Publications, 1992).

Patricia A. Harney, Ph.D., received her doctorate in clinical psychology from the University of Kansas and completed her clinical internship in the Department of Psychiatry at Cambridge Hospital. She is currently a post-doctoral clinical psychology fellow at the Cambridge Hospital Victims of Violence Program and the Department of Psychiatry at Harvard Medical School. Dr. Harney's clinical and research interests are in the area of sexual and physical violence.

Jose R. Maldonado, M.D., is assistant professor of psychiatry and behavioral sciences and director of the Medical Psychotherapy Clinic, Stanford University School of Medicine.

Jacqueline Pistorello, B.A., was educated in Brazil and at the University of Nevada, Reno, where she obtained her B.A. degree (1989) and is now pursuing her Ph.D. in clinical psychology. She has worked with Dr. Victoria M. Follette in implementing a contextual psychotherapy approach in the treatment of adult survivors of childhood sexual abuse, and she currently practices as an Acceptance and Commitment Therapy (ACT) clinician under the supervision of Steven C. Hayes. A continued interest in the treatment of trauma survivors and acceptance-based treatments has culminated in the materials presented in this chapter.

David Spiegel, M.D., is professor of psychiatry and behavioral sciences and director of the Psychosocial Treatment Laboratory, Stanford University School of Medicine. He is the author of the recently published book, *Living Beyond Limits*.

Joan A. Turkus, M.D., practices general and forensic psychiatry in McLean, Virginia. She is the medical director of the Center for Abuse Recovery and Empowerment at the Psychiatric Institute of Washington, D.C. She has extensive clinical experience in the diagnosis and treatment of posttraumatic-dissociative disorders and is frequently called upon for supervision, consultation, and teaching on a local and national basis. She has published several chapters on the treatment of these disorders and is the co-editor of an upcoming book titled *Dissociative Identity Disorder: Continuum of Care*, to be published in 1995.

INDEX

A

Abandonment issues, 122–123, 196–197

Abbott, B. R., *xxvii*, 95–127

Abreactive techniques, 172

Absorption, hypnotic, 169–170

Abuse dichotomy pattern, 145–146

Acceptance: defined, 136; and dichotomizing, 145–146; and hypnosis, 176; of one's history, 136–137; of others, 138–139; of self, 137–138, 151–152

Acceptance and Commitment Therapy (ACT), 134–139

Acting out: in adolescence, *xviii*; in survivors, *xxii–xxiii*; and transference, 191, 202

Addiction: to medication, 45; to trauma, 38–39. *See also* Alcoholism; Substance abuse

Adolescence, impact of sexual abuse during, *xviii*

Affect: and confusion, 153; dissociation of, 170, 196–200; expression of, in group therapy, 105–106; gaining tolerance for, 79–80; integration of memory with, 78–79, 89–91, 92; and memory retrieval, 172–173, 175, 178–179; in transference, 191, 197–200

Affect bridge, 178–179

Affective disorders, *xxii*, 64

Age of victim: average, 11; effects of, on response, *xvi–xix*, 11; and repressed memory, *xxiii*

Alcoholism: and crisis management, 54–56; in families, 37; in presentation, 66

Allies in Healing (Davis), 142

Alter ego technique, 116

American Psychiatric Association, 13, 27

American Society of Clinical Hypnosis, 169

Amnesia, traumatic: age factors in, *xix*; changing attitudes toward, 5–8; in childhood, *xvi, xviii*; and dissociation, 12–13, 19, 166–167; gaining authority over, 76–78, 89–91, 177–179; incidence of, 5; reasons for, 10–12; as symptom, 18. *See also* Memory; Remembering; Repressed memory

Anger, 18; assessment instruments for, 26; towards therapist, 181, 188–189, 194, 196–197, 198

Anti-anxiety agents, 45, 47–48, 49, 57

Antidepressants, 45, 48, 51, 52, 53, 56

Antipsychotic agents, 45–46

Anxiety: assessment instruments for, 26; disorders, *xxii*; with flashbacks, 111–112; in group therapy, 102; medication for, 45, 47–48, 49, 57; as symptom of sexual abuse, 18, 36; tolerance for, 79–80

Approach-avoid presentation, 17

Art therapy, 51, 58–59, 73

Assertiveness, 152–153

Assessment, 1–8; in crisis management, 47; direct inquiry approach to, 4–5, 22; ecological model for, 72–76; guidelines for, 15–26, 28–30, 41–42; including family members in, 24–25; instruments for, 26–29; interview techniques for, 19–26; and memory issues, 8–14; self-, in group therapy, 123

Attachment disruption, and transference, 191, 196–197, 198

Attractiveness issues, 152

Aversion, 19

Avoidance: Acceptance and Commitment Therapy approach for, 134–139; in adolescence, *xviii*; assess-